VIENNA 2019

ENCOUNTERING THE OTHER:
WITHIN US, BETWEEN US AND IN THE WORLD

PROCEEDINGS OF THE TWENTY-FIRST CONGRESS
OF THE INTERNATIONAL ASSOCIATION
FOR ANALYTICAL PSYCHOLOGY

Vienna 2019
Encountering the Other:
Within us, between us and in the world

Proceedings of the Twenty-First Congress
of the International Association
for Analytical Psychology

Edited by Emilija Kiehl

DAIMON
VERLAG

The articles in this publication were compiled and edited to provide as true as possible a record of the Proceedings of the Twenty-First Congress of the IAAP held in Vienna in August 2019.
This print edition contains the plenary sessions.
A separate e-book contains both the plenary and breakout sessions.

Cover photo: © Universität Wien/Franz Pflügl.

Copyright © 2020 by Daimon Verlag and the authors,
Am Klosterplatz, CH-8840 Einsiedeln, Switzerland.

ISBN 978-3-85630-780-6

All rights reserved. This book, or parts thereof, may not be reproduced in any form without written permission from the publisher.

Contents

Note from the Editors
    Emilija Kiehl 2
    Jacqueline Egli 3

Welcome Address
    Marianne Müller 5

Opening Address
    Toshio Kawai 7

Monday, 26 August 2019

Deifying the Soul – from Ibn Arabi to C.G. Jung
    Navid Kermani 13

Apocalyptic Themes in Times of Trouble: When Young Men are Deeply Alienated
    Robert Tyminski 33

Tuesday, 27 August 2019

Panel: Encountering the other within: Dream research in Analytical Psychology and the relationship of ego and other parts of the psyche
    Christian Roesler 51
    Yasuhiro Tanaka 69
    Tamar Kron 78

Integration versus conflict between schools of dream theory and dreamwork: integrating the psychological core qualities of dreams with the contemporary knowledge of the dreaming brain
    Ole Vedfelt 86

Wednesday, 28 August 2019

Freud and Jung on Freud and Jung
    Ernst Falzeder 115

Opening the closed heart: affect-focused clinical work with the victims of early trauma
    Donald E. Kalsched 137

Thursday, 29 August 2019

The other between fear and desire – countertransference fantasy as a bridge between me and the other
    Daniela Eulert-Fuchs   155

Self, Other and Individuation: resolving narcissism through the lunar and solar paths of the Rosarium
    Marcus West   170

Friday, 30 August 2019

Panel: Encountering the Other – Jungian Analysts and Traditional Healers in South Africa

Part I: The History
    Peter Ammann   197

Part 2: The Context
    Fred Borchardt   200

Part 3: The Traditional Health Practitioner's Stance and the World View
    Nomfundo Lily-Rose Mlisa   203

Part 4: Conclusion
    Renee Ramsden   207

From horror to ethical responsibility: Carl Gustav Jung and Stephen King encounter the dark half within us, between us and in the world
    Chiara Tozzi   211

Farewell Address
    Marianne Müller   225

Thank you, Marianne
    Toshio Kawai   232

Additional content in the e-book version   234

Author Index (e-book)   246

The e-book version which includes all the breakout sessions can be downloaded here: https://www.daimon.ch/_iaap-Vienna-2019_/

List of IAAP Committees

Officers:
Marianne Müller, President
Toshio Kawai, President Elect
Misser Berg, Vice President
George Hogenson, Vice President
Martin Schmidt, Honorary Secretary

Executive Committee:
Pilar Amezaga (SUAPA)
Alvaro Ancona de Faria (SBrPA)
Gražina Gudaite (LAAP)
Christine Hejinian (CGIJSF)
Emilija Kiehl (BJAA)
Margaret Klenck (JPA)
Batya Brosh Palmoni (IIJP)
Regina Renn (DGAP)
Brigit Soubrouillard (SFPA)

Standing Committees:

Ethics Committee:
Penny Pickles, Chair
Paula Boechat, Honorary Secretary
Andrea Cone-Farran
Ulrich Stuck
Elena Volodina
Mark Winborn

Congress Program Committee:
George Hogenson, (CSJA), Vice President, Chair
Misser Berg (DSAP), Vice President
Gerhard Burda (ÖGAP)
Eduardo Carvallo (SCJA)
Toshio Kawai (AJAJ, AGAP), President Elect
Marianne Müller (SGAP), President
Martin Schmidt (SAP), Honorary Secretary
Jacqueline West (NMSJA)
Luisa Zoppi (AIPA)

Local Organising Committee:
Petra Denk (ÖGAP), Co-Chair
Åsa Liljenroth-Denk (ÖGAP), Co-Chair
Eleonore Armster (ÖGAP)
Gerhard Burda (ÖGAP)
Reinhard Skolek (ÖGAP)
Regins Skolek (ÖGAP)
Anton Tölk (ÖGAP)

IAAP Secretary: Selma Gubser

Note from the Editors

London, May 2020

This IAAP Congress brought together the most significant number of participants from all over the world, offering an abundance of contemporary Jungian thinking on the theoretical, clinical, and psychosocial aspects of our work. It was an event we will remember for a long time to come.

Following the Proceedings from the previous two Congresses, Copenhagen (2013) and Kyoto (2016), I had the privilege and great pleasure of also editing the plenaries from this Congress. Once again, our colleagues' creative, profoundly insightful, and often fascinating accounts of their ventures into the inner workings of the psyche rekindled my inspiration and love for the work we do.

There is, however, a marked difference in the experience and the conditions under which I was working on these Proceedings. Throughout the entire period, London has been in the "lockdown", and the world we shared and so enjoyed in Vienna had vanished in the dark cloud of the coronavirus pandemic. Our community has not been spared the grief for loved ones, including dear colleagues, the loss of income and loss of employment. Most of us now work online, and many have been admirably swift in their response to the world crisis by offering online psychological help for those most affected by the pandemic.

As I write this note, it is still uncertain whether or not, and to which degree, it will be possible to return to what was hitherto considered "normality". The pandemic has exposed our physical, psychological, social and other vulnerabilities and brought up some unsettling questions about the sustainability – political, ecological, ethical and otherwise, of the world we have created. The justifiability of the bio-socio-economical "laws" we have imposed on the planet and its creatures to satisfy our many appetites is under long-awaited scrutiny too.

Jungian contribution in humanity's search for answers to these critical questions could be a potentially evolutive rethinking of our world – beyond the perpetual battles that reign in the realm of the Ego and towards the wisdom that can be found in the realm of the Self.

I am grateful to all the presenters at the Congress and delighted to share the wealth I found in their presentations with the readers of this volume.

My heartfelt thanks to my colleague, Jacqueline Egli, for her diligent and creative work on the breakout presentations. Robert Hinshaw and Robert Imhoff of Daimon Verlag, thank you for our, as always, warm and rewarding collaboration on yet another IAAP Congress Proceedings.

Emilija Kiehl

*

After a wonderful experience in Vienna, my first IAAP Congress, meeting new faces and attending many sessions (I focused on attending sessions that sounded particularly 'other' to me), it was with great trepidation and honour that I accepted to edit the Breakout and Poster Sessions, these remarkably rich and varied papers. It was a daunting prospect, as I was unsure how I would fit in reading – and in some cases re-reading – approximately 160 papers with the necessary attention and precision required alongside a rather busy practice. Each one of them brought new insights, touched me or tickled my curiosity; some papers were very moving, others from areas I had never explored, and, in all honesty, a few disturbed me enough to arouse the prejudices hidden in the backroom of my psyche. All grist to the mill and great food for thought! It was like being at a banquet of very rich pickings indeed, which is now laid out herewith for your enjoyment!

Apart from the Breakout and Poster Sessions, we received summaries and papers describing the work presented in a Pre-Congress Workshop, a Master Class of Supervision and Dominique Lepori kindly provided a summary of her experience of the Social Dreaming Matrix.

I would like to thank each one of the participants – not only for having provided me and everyone present in Vienna with the opportunity to share in their line of thinking and then allowing for the publication of their work in the Proceedings – but for having worked with me, put up with my niggly queries and demands, showing patience and respect when clearly my 'green-ness' as a relatively new member of the IAAP was evidenced. I enjoyed our exchanges, mostly in English, but also in French and German – a reminder of the strong connection I feel to Continental Europe which I hope to continue to nurture into the future. Furthermore, 'travelling' through the papers to all continents has allowed me to expand my Eurocentric views. My thanks also go to Emilija Kiehl who encouraged me to take this task on. This work introduced me to many of you, allowed me to start feeling included more fully as a member of the IAAP and I look forward to a time beyond the pandemic when we will hopefully meet face-to-face again.

Jacqueline Egli

Welcome Address

Marianne Müller
President IAAP

Dear Colleagues

As President of the IAAP, I warmly welcome you to the XXI Congress of the International Association for Analytical Psychology, here in Vienna, one of the most beautiful, historically and culturally most significant and outstanding cities of Europe.

I would like to express my sincere thanks to the colleagues from the Austrian Society for Analytical Psychology, for inviting us to hold our triennial international Congress here, in Vienna. They have chosen for us truly beautiful venues, such as the City Hall for the reception last night, and the main building of the University of Vienna, where today we open the scientific program.

Now we are here, where Freud and Jung met over one hundred and twelve years ago. It was a most creative encounter and the beginning of an extraordinarily comprehensive work which, today, we are still part of. The theme we have chosen for the Congress, "Encountering the Other: Within us, between us and in the world", of course, fits well with what happened to these two great personalities. The Program Committee has succeeded in putting together a rich and clearly outlined program from the many proposals that were submitted. While working on the design of the program, we became more and more aware of how topical the congress theme is. It invites us to reflect intensively on the various aspects and questions related to the "Other", whatever or whoever that may be. I very much hope that this will encourage us to use the time and the space provided by this event to experience encounters with others, here and now, including with colleagues from different linguistic, cultural, ethnic and political backgrounds and perhaps different approaches to Analytical Psychology.

The number of participants who have registered for this Congress has exceeded all our expectations. We have never been so many. I am sure that this is partly due to the great attractiveness of this city, its history and central location in Europe, and of course, we do hope that the topic and the program in particular have persuaded you to attend the Congress. The impressive number of participants testifies that our community is expanding. It is a pleasure to be a witness to this development and to the growing interest in Analytical Psychology as well as to have the opportunity for exchanges with colleagues from all over the world.

A significant number of you have played an essential part in making this Congress a reality, particularly all those who will contribute to the program with their presentations. I would like to thank you all for your great work, and, above all, of course, the Program Committee, chaired by George Hogenson, and the Organizing Committee here in Vienna, under the leadership of Asa Lilijenroth-Denk and Petra Denk.

I wish us all a stimulating and enriching Congress. I am confident that this is how we will remember it.

I now hand over to Toshio Kawai, President-elect of the IAAP, for his Opening Address.

Opening Address

Toshio Kawai
President-Elect IAAP

Dear colleagues, dear guests, dear friends,

It is a great honour and pleasure for me to welcome you all to the XXI IAAP Congress here in Vienna.

Vienna is historically and culturally one of the most important and most attractive cities in Europe and in the world. We already felt this yesterday at the reception in the beautiful City Hall. Probably because of the captivating charm of this city, we expect to have more than one thousand participants, which is a record number for an IAAP Congress. Vienna also has a geographical advantage with regards to travel. While most of the participants had to take a long and expensive flight to Japan for the Kyoto Congress three years ago, some of you were able to get to Vienna by train or by car whether you were travelling from the West, East or Central European countries.

However, it is certainly not only because of the particular cultural and geographical features of Vienna, but also because of the attractive programme, that we have so many registrations for this Congress. In this context, I would like to thank the Programme Committee chaired by George Hogenson and the Local Organizing Committee led by Petra Denk and Åsa Liljenroth-Denk for their hard and diligent work on this event. I also cannot help but mention the strong leadership and attentive support of our IAAP president, Marianne Müller, who shares the German language and lives in a neighbouring country.

As Chair of the Programme Committee of the previous Congress in Kyoto, I am very pleased to note that those initiatives, which were started in Kyoto, have been adopted here in Vienna. Following the requests for more focus on the clinical aspects of our work, we started supervision master classes in Kyoto and in the pre-Congress program yesterday we had those master classes here in Vienna, too. Another Kyoto initiative which has been adopted here in Vienna was a change in the poster presentation, with an added brief oral presentation, to make it more attractive and more in line with the academic standards.

It is interesting to observe the contrasts and links between the previous Congress in Kyoto and this one in Vienna: While Kyoto was an exotic and unfamiliar city for the majority of participants, one could say that it was an experience of "the Other", the Congress theme was

"Anima Mundi" – an all-embracing and subsuming concept. In sharp contrast, this Congress takes place in the heart of Europe, in a familiar city for most of you, and its theme is "Encountering the Other". This seems to suggest that we need both inclusiveness and differentiation in order to encounter the other.

But what does "the other" mean? There are various aspects to the other. Firstly, we can understand it in the cultural and political contexts. Currently, refugees and immigrants stand in the centre of political discussions all over the world, including here in Europe and in Vienna. Understanding other cultures, especially African ones, has been at the heart of discussions in Analytical Psychology.

Let me speak from my personal experience: I came to Zurich when I was four years old. It was my first contact with the other, another culture, and I found everything strange and foreign. Because of this feeling of alienation, I had an intense longing to return to Japan, which came true three years. later. But then I noticed that the Japan I was longing for existed only in my fantasy, and I encountered the other again there. Twenty years later, I came back to Zurich to study and to undergo a Jungian training. Again, I found many things strange but, overall, I enjoyed the training and clinical work. When I went back to Japan after finishing the training, I had to change a lot in order to apply what I had learned and practiced in Switzerland to my clinical work and training in Japan.

I speak here of my own experiences of the other, of the East-West conflict, in my context. But here in Vienna, the notions of East and West do not necessarily mean East Asia and Europe. In its history, Vienna was twice surrounded by the Ottoman army and so, in this context, the Eastern Other might rather refer to the Islamic world in contrast to the Christian world. This is one of the reasons why we invited the German novelist, Navid Kermani, whose parents came from Iran, to be the keynote speaker at our Congress. I am very much looking forward to his presentation "Deifying the soul from Ibn Arabi to C. G. Jung". I am familiar with Ibn Arabi only from the Eranos contributions by Henri Corbin and Toshihiko Izutsu. I am curious to hear what Ibn Arabi can contribute to Analytical Psychology, as the Other to C. G. Jung.

Vienna was once the capital of the Austro-Hungarian Empire so then the eastern "other" also meant Eastern Europe. This Congress has many presenters and participants from Central and Eastern Europe and this is a valuable opportunity for getting to know more about Analytical Psychology in that part of Europe.

The multi-faceted meaning of the "eastern other" shows how the Other can be different according to personal and historical contexts. Furthermore, this seems to suggest that we have to respect the otherness of other persons and other contexts. Even if one is eagerly engaged in the integration of the other into one's own context, this can exclude that otherness in other contexts, and hence contradict the idea of integration and inclusion of the other. More inclusiveness and diversity have to be respected. This is one of the reasons why the IAAP has set up the "Diversity Working Party" which will report on its activities and will offer a forum for discussion at this Congress. The programme offers various ways of approaching the other from different cultural and political contexts.

Secondly, one obvious Other for Analytical Psychology is the psychoanalysis of Sigmund Freud. Whilst Analytical Psychology started in Zurich and is strongly connected with that place, Vienna is the birthplace of psychoanalysis. This Congress offers us an excellent opportunity to reflect on the relationship between Analytical Psychology and psychoanalysis. The programme has presentations on this subject such as Ernst Falzeder's paper "Freud and Jung about Freud and Jung" as a plenary on Wednesday.

Thirdly, Analytical Psychology is more and more involved in the psychological and social work outside the classical setting of analysis. These include outreach work in crisis interventions, in hospitals and in social institutions, which can be regarded as Other to Analytical Psychology. Very often our clients in outreach work are unable to pay the fee by themselves and may not have a differentiated consciousness for psychotherapy, for example they may be lacking the capacity for verbalization. However, such work provides very compelling evidence of the effectiveness of psychotherapy with the use of images such as in sandplay therapy. Having been personally involved in the psychological care for the victims of a devastating earthquake, and working with somatic patients, I am very much aware of the importance of this field for the future of Analytical Psychology. In our programme, we have a pre-Congress workshop and some presentations which belong in this other category of psychological work.

Finally, the academic and scientific world may be regarded as being the Other to Analytical Psychology since Jung left his professorial position at Zurich University. However, it is very important to revise our theory, to keep up to date with the latest developments in science and also to contribute to the academic and scientific world. This can evoke more interest in Analytical Psychology amongst the younger generations. This is why the IAAP has not only organised the 5th joint conference with the IAJS in Frankfurt but has also held joint conferences with other universities such as in Vilnius and Basel last year. There was also the Academic Pre-Congress for the 4th European Congress of Analytical Psychology in Avignon entitled: "Analytical Psychology meets academic research".

In our programme for this Congress, we have a Pre-Congress Workshop concerning research in Analytical Psychology, and a number of presentations on research. In the next administration, I would like to continue in this direction, including organising further joint conferences with universities and joint researches projects with academics.

The limited time allowed me to mention here only four fields of the Other, in relation to Analytica Psychology. However, other Others are also included in our programme. As I have pointed out, a focus on one Other should not exclude, but should respect, other involvements with Others. Moreover, I hope that this Congress gives us an opportunity to reflect upon the idea of Other and to explore other encounters with the Other that are not taken up in this Congress.

Last year, I attended the Latin American Congress of Jungian Psychology; the gathering at CNASJA (The Council of North American Societies of Jungian Analysts), and the European Congress of Analytical Psychology. From the viewpoint of the IAAP, knowing about regional developments, needs and problems is crucial. But what was even more important, was the direct contact with colleagues whom, until then, I knew only in cyberspace. The theme of this Congress is "Encountering the Other: Within us, between us and in the world". It will be very nice, and it is part of our Congress theme, to encounter the other here between us, among colleagues from all over the world.

So, I wish us all a rich and stimulating encounter with the other in the Congress presentations, between the presentations and after the presentations.

Monday, 26 August 2019

Deifying the Soul – from Ibn Arabi to C.G. Jung[1]

Navid Kermani
Cologne, Germany

Dear analysts, ladies and gentlemen[2],
   When Muhyi d-Din Ibn Arabi arrived in Mecca in July or August of the year 1202, he was thirty-seven years old and already one of the great mystical leaders of Islam. He was so self-assured as to consider himself one of the four cornerstones 'on which the structure of the universe and of mankind rests', and he was so respected that no one contradicted him. He had been little more than a child when Averroes, the most famous philosopher in the world at that time, received him, and Averroes had turned pale, had trembled, had literally broke out in a sweat at the boldness of his young visitor's replies, at the self-assurance of his demeanour. While still a young man, Ibn Arabi had acquired all the accessible knowledge of the time, had learned a good deal of Islamic literature by heart, including the *Quran*, and, most importantly, had spent days, weeks, months in contemplation. After having been initiated in a dream by Sufism's three great spiritual teachers all together, Moses, Jesus, and Muhammad – something which had never happened before – Ibn Arabi had left his home in Andalusia, where the Reconquista was in full swing, to preach in various cities of the Maghreb. He had studied with all the major mystics of the Islamic West, and taken leave of them as their master. He had received such clear and spectacular visions as no one else since the Prophet Muhammad himself, so that the professional dream interpreters predicted he would reveal 'the highest mysteries, the particular properties of the stars and the letters, which will be given to no one else in his lifetime'. On his way to Mecca, the 'mother of all cities', he had stopped in Hebron, where Abraham and the other patriarchs are buried; he had prayed in Jerusalem, the city of David and the later prophets; he had meditated in Medina, where the last resting place of Muhammad lies, thus physically retracing the Prophet's celestial journey, which he had already experienced in inner contemplation. At night, having arrived at last at his destination, Ibn Arabi circled the 'heart of the world', the Kaaba:

---

1 Speech to the conference of the International Association for Analytical Psychology (IAAP), Vienna, August 2019.
2 English translation by Tony Crawford.

I felt a deep peace, a very delicate feeling, of which I was nonetheless perfectly conscious. I left the immediate area of the stone, which is paved with tiles, because the crowding there was too great, and continued circling further away, on the sand. Suddenly some verses entered my mind, which I recited so loudly that another person could have heard them if he were standing directly behind me:

> Would that I were aware whether they knew what heart they possessed!
> And would that my heart knew what mountain-pass they threaded!
> Dost thou deem them safe or dost thou deem them dead?
> Lovers lose their way in love and become entangled.

I had hardly recited these verses when I felt the touch of a hand softer than silk on my shoulder. I turned around and beheld a young woman, one of the princesses of Byzantium. Never had I seen a more beautiful face, never heard a gentler voice, never felt a more tender heart, never shared deeper thoughts, never listened to subtler parables. She surpassed all people of our time in wit and culture, in beauty and wisdom.

Ibn Arabi's preface to the *Interpreter of Desires*, *Tarjumān al-Ashwāq*

The meeting at the Kaaba with the sensually and intellectually attractive Nizam bint Makin ad-Din is the turning point in Ibn Arabi's life, and in his work. Thirteen years later he dedicated to her the *Interpreter of Desires, Tarjumān al-Ashwāq*, a volume of love poetry which was quite unusual even for him, explicitly erotic, and which is one of the most famous cycles of lyric poetry in Arabic literature today. In the preface to his poems, Ibn Arabi wrote about their addressee, 'Whenever I mention a name, I am always alluding to her, and whatever house I mention, I always mean her house.' On hearing names invoked, every Muslim thinks of the names of God; at the mention of a house, the house of God, the Kaaba. Ibn Arabi perceived in the young woman nothing less than the reality of God Himself. Thus, it is far from coincidence that, soon after his encounter with Nizam, Ibn Arabi began writing the many volumes of his *Meccan Revelations, Al-Futūḥāt al-Makkīya*, the most important and certainly the most influential work of Islamic mystical literature, if not all religious literature in the scope of Islamic culture. The *Revelations* contain the summa of Sufi knowledge, and at the same time expose a fundamentally new, sensational approach to divine truth, which in Islam is supposed to be objectless, hence absolutely abstract, but in Sufism becomes perfectly concrete and perceptible anywhere, to anyone. Nizam – who in reality was not Byzantine, but Persian, the daughter of two highly educated and aristocratic pilgrims from Isfahan – Nizam bint Makin ad-Din was Ibn Arabi's Beatrice.

We are no longer accustomed to taking seriously the mystical references that Dante Alighieri attributed to his meeting with Beatrice. But there is no reason to doubt that, in his consuming love, he also had a deep religious experience. To Dante, Beatrice reflected the incarnation of God in Jesus Christ; moreover, her beauty was to him a medium through which God himself appeared. As Nizam was to Ibn Arabi, Beatrice was to Dante earthly love and divine revelation at once, wellspring of inspiration and at the same time an object of longing, his muse and at the same time his addressee. When we consider that translations of Islamic journeys to Heaven, and perhaps even excerpts of the account Ibn Arabi had written of his dream vision, were very probably available to Dante when he began the *Divine Comedy*, the correspondence raises questions about the relation between East and West, questions which ought to be posed anew today in view of the growing, often antagonistic dichotomy. But the differences between the two poets are still more interesting than their similarities. For Dante was, yes, first and foremost a poet, not a Christian scholar, while Ibn Arabi, although, like many Islamic scholars, he often expressed himself in verse, was considered a religious authority, an outstanding scholar of the *Quran*, and the *Shaykh al-Akbar*, the undisputed 'Greatest Master' of Sufism. The title alone of his magnum opus points to its eminently religious orientation, since neither the place it names nor the genre it announces is meant metaphorically: the basis of the text consists of religious visions which were perceived by the author, and by most of his readers, as 'revelations', and which occurred nowhere else but in Mecca. In Christianity, Ibn Arabi would have to be compared with Meister Eckhart or Jacob Böhme rather than Dante or Hölderlin, except that mysticism has never been the mainstream of Latin Christianity, whereas Sufism was the broadest religious movement in Islam even into the twentieth century. It permeated not only high culture – literature, music, architecture and art – but also ran deep in popular piety. The Sufi teachers were usually closer to the so-called simple people than the dogmaticians and legal scholars who became the focus of Western research on Islam, and even in our time, thousands of people pray every day at the tomb of Ibn Arabi in Damascus; during the war, the crowds are said to have been even bigger, even though the shrine would have been a logical target of attacks by the 'Islamic State'.

The difference between Dante and Ibn Arabi, then, concerns their status within their respective religions – that is, their reception. The close structural similarity of all mystical traditions, and especially

Christian and Islamic mysticism, has often been described: the progression of religious experience and its expressions, the universal character of the messages of salvation, the motif of the holy fool. But, once again, the differences interest me more than the similarities, and most of all, the relation to the material world. None of the well-known Christian mystics had a Nizam, a Beatrice. Erotic though the mystics' texts often appear – especially those of women, such as Teresa of Avila and Hildegard of Bingen – the relation of earthy love to divine love is one of analogy, not identity. And in Christian mysticism, physical union is not the locus, but the image of mystical annihilation; neither Teresa nor Hildegard can be assumed to have had a real lover who served as her medium of divine revelation. Nizam on the other hand is a real, historical person, and, in the same way as Ibn Arabi's love for her was intrinsic to his religious experience, other Islamic mystics too had altogether earthy lovers, some of them women, some men, who to them embodied God in the truest sense of the word. 'For one who loves religiously is mind without body, and one who loves naturally is body without mind,' say the *Meccan Revelations*, 'but spiritual love includes both the body *and* the mind.' Ibn Arabi even goes so far as to write that ignorance of sexuality is nothing less than a religious deficiency.

> When I first trod this path, I was in all God's creation one of the greatest loathers of women and of sexual intercourse. I remained in this condition for some eighteen years. This contempt left me when I learned of the saying handed down from the Prophet that God had made women worthy of His Prophet's love.
>
> Ibn Arabi, *Meccan Revelations*

Since Ibn Arabi entered the mystical path in 1184 and arrived in Mecca 18 years later, it is evident that he realized the importance of physical love only during the pilgrimage. It is unlikely, however, that he had a sexual relationship with the young Nizam; after all, she was the religious, highly educated daughter of two aristocratic and devout pilgrims from Isfahan, and Ibn Arabi was a regular visitor at their guesthouse. Besides the fact that Ibn Arabi himself later denied ever having been Nizam's lover, it is difficult for practical reasons to imagine a secret rendezvous between the two during the pilgrimage. Moreover, it is known that, during this first sojourn in Mecca, Ibn Arabi married another woman, Fatima bint Yunus Amir al-Haramayn. As her name implies, she belonged to one of the most venerable Arabian families – her father was the superintendent of the holy sites in Mecca and Medina, the *ḥaramayn* – who presumably would not have permitted even the suspicion of an extramarital relationship. And yet not Fatima, but Nizam became the quintessential beloved in Ibn Arabi's work. The reason is surely related to the fact that, in premodern literature, love was associated with symptoms that we today would assign to infatuation: rapid heartbeat, loss of appetite, foolish and embarrassing behavior; whereas marriage was a pragmatic partnership and seldom the stuff of poetry. Not until the modern period did marriage for love become an ideal. This explains why Ibn Arabi was able to see the divine beauty in Nizam, and yet marry Fatima, whom he mentions in his writings invariably as loving, but rather as a companion on the mystic path.

In the preface which Ibn Arabi added to the *Interpreter of Longing* after it had been in circulation for several years, he writes that his love for Nizam was a purely spiritual one and, accordingly, the physical images must not be taken literally. Rather, Nizam embodies 'a sublime and divine, essential and sacred wisdom [in the sense of the Greek *sophia*], which was visibly manifested to the author of this poem, and indeed with such sweetness that he was overcome with ecstasy and happiness, with tenderness and joy.' This has often been interpreted as self-serving claim on Ibn Arabi's part in response to accusations that he had written pornographic poems. But that wouldn't mean his explanation was necessarily false. In his *Revelations*, Ibn Arabi explains how God reveals himself first and foremost in sexuality, 'the most perfect union that exists in love'; yet over the course of the mystic path, knowledge is increasingly realized in the imagination, and thus transcends material experience. It would be in keeping with his teaching for Ibn Arabi to have had a love relationship with Nizam without ever touching her, not because he would have rejected physical love – that remains a step on the mystical path, discussed in detail in his theoretical writings – but because he, at the highest stage of his spiritual development, no longer needed it.

It is certainly not a mistake at this point – and I thank my good friend the philosopher Almut Shulamit Bruckstein for the suggestion – to remember Jewish conceptions of the bride as infinitely heightening the sexual desire of her earthly lover by messianically elevating its fulfillment. The consummation of love would be at the same time *tikkun olam* – the healing of the world. The bride – an expression which attests to the greatest familiarity – who is able to delay the actual union until the moment of *tikkun olam*, a moment which would be at the same time the healing of the soul – the bride is Nizam, who is called Shulamite in the Song of Solomon, the fairest among women, whose breasts are as clusters of the vine, and the smell of whose nose is like apples, and the roof of whose mouth is like the best wine, causing the lips of sleepers to speak: 'A garden inclosed[!] is my sister, my spouse; a spring shut up[!], a fountain sealed[!]' (Song of Solomon, 4:12).

Today the Song of Solomon is modernized in audiobooks, celebrated at church conferences, interpreted in radio worship services; its open eroticism is closer to the spirit of our times than, say, the ban on contraception. It is often overlooked, however, that Solomon speaks of desire, not fulfilment: 'There is no sexual relation,' to use the words of Lacan, whose thinking is not as mysterious as it is said to be once we know the mystical tradition from which he stems: 'Love makes up for the absence of the sexual relation.'

Even the fact that Ibn Arabi calls Nizam a Byzantine, a Christian in other words, indicates the religious significance he attached to the meeting at the Kaaba. For in Islamic mysticism, God's appearance in a human being is inevitably connected with the example of Jesus Christ; all theophany is attributed to the 'Christian sophia' or wisdom, *al-ḥikma al-'isawīya*. Nizam herself underscores the precedence of mystical knowledge – that is, experienced truth – over rational consideration in her accusatory words to Ibn Arabi:

> My lord, how can you declaim: 'Would that I were aware whether they knew what heart they possessed'? I am surprised to hear such a thing from you, the greatest mystic of our time. Is not everything we possess also something which we know? Can there be such a thing as possession without knowledge? What I wish is the deeper consciousness that is made known through not-being, and the path which consists of truthful speech. How can someone like you permit such thoughts?

As the young Nizam reprimands the great Ibn Arabi for the first line, she goes on to censure every line of his poem. For the questions that trouble him are still questions posed by his intellect. But mystical insights follow the laws of love, not logic. Only when it is indifferent to him whether he is dead or safe, because the one leads to the other, nothingness and perfection converge, only then will the mystic approach God. Through his meeting with a young girl, Ibn Arabi learns that he must leave behind the knowledge he has learned if he wants to understand the divine truth. When he shyly asks her name, she answers with another riddle: 'Solace of the Eyes' (*qurrat al-'ayn*). She is alluding to a saying of the Prophet that 'the solace of the eyes is granted in prayer,' but at the same time she is referring to her own beauty, of which she is apparently aware. Then the young woman takes her leave, leaving the greatest mystic of his time, and perhaps of all time, to gape after her like a child. Thirteen years later, Ibn Arabi writes in the *Interpreter of Longing*:

> Threefold is my beloved and yet one as the entities of God are only one

Nizam was a woman, and to Ibn Arabi she was connected with Christianity, which teaches the Trinity of God. These two facts have a deeper significance: although Ibn Arabi was born in patriarchal conditions, women were influential in his work – his teachers, his beloved Nizam, both his wives, his daughter, his students, most of whom were women. Against the orthodox mainstream, he emphatically declared women to be equal in religion, and empowered to interpret the Quran, to lead the congregation in prayer, and to receive illumination from God. At the same time, Ibn Arabi found instruction and inspiration in Jesus Christ as in no other prophet. And these two facts are connected: for in his compassion, his beauty and his ability to raise the dead – that is, to give life – Jesus represents the female principle of God, which Ibn Arabi has emphasized as no other Islamic mystic. In the *Interpreter of Longing*, he writes about Nizam:

> When she kills with her glances, her speech restores to life, as though she, in giving life thereby, were Jesus.
> The smooth surface of her legs is the Tora in brightness, and I follow it and tread in its footsteps as though I were Moses.
> She is a bishopess, one of the daughters of Rome, unadorned: thou seest in her a radiant Goodness.
> Wild is she, none can make her his friend; she has gotten in her solitary chamber a mausoleum for remembrance.
> She has baffled everyone who is learned in our religion, every student of the Psalms of David, every Jewish doctor, every Christian priest.

Dear analysts, as scholars if not followers of the teachings of C. G. Jung, your ears will be ringing by this point: here is the female principle that Jung called anima and considered fundamental to every psychic impulse; here too is the incarnation of God as a paradigm which is rooted in the human psyche as a relationship between the Self and the ego. In Ibn Arabi, anima is joined with the symbol of Christ: God appeared to him at the Kaaba, not in the generic form of a human being, but in the form of a woman and a Christian. The interweaving of woman and Incarnation is by no means alien to Christianity, as early representations attest in which the Redeemer bears disturbingly feminine features, and C. G. Jung in particular has pointed out Christ's androgyny, calling it 'the utmost concession the Church has made to the problem of opposites' (Jung 1944, para. 22). The idea that religious insight, like aesthetic insight for that matter, being non-discursive cannot be directly named, and hence can only be expressed in veiled terms, in images, in parables, as paradox or by means of negation, is found in all the world's religious traditions, and especially the mystical traditions; it is best known perhaps in Taoist formulas such as 'The Way that can be followed is not the true Way.' The Sufi literature is full of paradoxical expressions, such as black light or the colour of water, and Ibn Arabi himself calls God the 'totality of mutually contradictory names.' Consequently, in the *Interpreter of Longing* he praises the beautiful, godlike Nizam over and over again as the unity of opposites:

> The whiteness of her forehead is the sun's, the blackness of the hair on her brow is the night's: most wondrous of forms is she – a sun and a night together!
> Through her we are in daylight during the night and in a night of hair at noon.

'The union of opposites is not rationally possible,' Ibn Arabi himself commented the image of the light-dark Nizam, and quoted the early Islamic mystic Abū Sa'īd al-Kharrāz, who said, when asked how he had recognized God:

> 'By His uniting two opposites, for "He is the First and the Last, and the Outward and the Inward"', and that always simultaneously and equally, not alternately or under different aspects, as the scholastic would have it, employing his conceptual faculties and dividing Truth into categories.

Because the One and Eternal is necessarily revealed in the manifold, temporal, and also contradictory nature of human experience, writes Ibn Arabi in the *Meccan Revelations*, they err who recognize God only in a certain form, in their own truth, in a limited time, or only in one faith. The divine truth must be embraced in the different religions, indeed in all phenomena, in sexuality, in civilization, even in everyday experiences, in the most ordinary objects, and even in heresy, as another poem in the *Interpreter*, perhaps the most famous one, has it:

> My heart has become capable of every form: it is a pasture for gazelles and a convent for Christian monks,
> And a temple for idols and the pilgrim's Ka'ba and the tables of the Tora and the book of the Koran.
> I follow the religion of Love; whatever way Love's camels take, that is my religion and my faith.

It is astounding that C.G. Jung did not know Ibn Arabi when he asked whether one might also choose to believe 'that God has expressed himself in many languages and appeared in divers forms and that all these statements are *true*.' But it is not so astounding after all, for Jung formulates an insight which is at the bottom of all religions, even Christianity, although Christianity makes a more definite claim to exclusivity than any other religion. I quote from his book on *Psychology and Alchemy*:

> The objection raised, more particularly by Christians, that it is impossible for contradictory statements to be true, must permit

itself to be politely asked: Does one equal three? How can three be one? Can a mother be a virgin? And so on. Has it not yet been observed that all religious statements contain logical contradictions and assertions that are impossible in principle, that this is in fact the very essence of religious assertion? As witness to this we have Tertullian's avowal: 'And the Son of God is dead, which is worthy of belief because it is absurd. And when buried He rose again, which is certain because it is impossible.' If Christianity demands faith in such contradictions it does not seem to me that it can very well condemn those who assert a few paradoxes more. Oddly enough the paradox is one of our most valuable spiritual possessions, while uniformity of meaning is a sign of weakness. Hence a religion becomes inwardly impoverished when it loses or waters down its paradoxes; but their multiplication enriches because only the paradox comes anywhere near to comprehending the fullness of life. Non-ambiguity and non-contradiction are one-sided and thus unsuited to express the incomprehensible.

(Jung 1944, para. 18)

Here I will once again pass over the conclusions to be drawn from religious scholarship in regard to present-day debates: that the struggle against ambiguity impoverishes not only religions, but likewise societies, cultures, literatures and identities. Nonetheless, I would like to remind those who publicly represent Islam, or pass judgment on it, that one of the greatest, perhaps the greatest scholar in the history of Islamic philosophy finds, in conformance with tradition and supported by many *Quran* verses, that God reveals Himself precisely in diversity and contradiction. Is it not written in a *ḥadīth qudsī*, an extraquranic word of God in Islam, 'I agree with the view that My believer has of Me'? And did not the Prophet say that the paths to God are as numerous as the breaths of a lifetime? To Ibn Arabi, the rational incongruity of experiences of God and images of God is, in its totality, God, whose reality surpasses human understanding:

> This explains why we are required in our all-embracing religion to believe in the truth of all religions. They do not cancel one another out – that would be the opinion of the ignorant.

By setting the very diversity of beliefs in relation to the unity of God, Ibn Arabi not only resolves the irreconcilability of monotheism and polytheism, recognizing even those religions which orthodox Islam considers pagan, but he goes so far as to teach that every single person's faith is a unique arrangement of an unlimited number of possible states of consciousness which, in their totality, refer to God: 'Every seeker of God is ruled by the property of one of God's names. This name is revealed to him and makes the divine self-revelation a personal, individual faith'. In Ibn Arabi's religious conception, the paradigm of this self-revelation, and of the ultimate paradox, is Jesus Christ: God, the abstract, all-embracing One, is perceptible and effable only in His reification and particularity, and hence diversity – God, man, and their union. This trinity persists even in Hegel's phenomenology and in Marxism as dialectic, which must also be driven by a world spirit, or, in secularized terms, by the cunning of reason. The 'brothers' in the chorus of Beethoven's Ninth Symphony, who incorporate the common genealogy of all humanity, and hence the monotheistic heritage of the Enlightenment, become 'comrades' in Socialist rhetoric, united by their membership in the Party, that is, by an act of will. Moreover, trinity is also the fundamental structure, not only of human development, but of all development on earth: man, woman, and their love which makes them creators. Not only two cells, but also their drive to unite. Ibn Arabi writes: 'Nothing arises from one alone. Therefore, the first real number is two. And nothing arises from two unless there is a third to unite them and relate them to each other'.

As God incarnates Himself in Jesus, Jesus must in turn unite all opposites: be a man with feminine features, a child with all the insignia of the Lord, attractively beautiful and at the same time repellingly severe – in his perfection a paradigm for all people, who are made in God's image. He is Mary's son, but at the same time, in his godhead, her Creator; thus St. Bernard worships the Mother of God in the last canto of the *Divine Comedy* as the 'daughter of your son', and in many old pictures Mary is painted as younger than her son. As early as the Revelation of John, Jesus Christ is a *complexio oppositorum*, as for example in the paradoxical image of the wrathful lamb. C. G. Jung interpreted Christ in this same comprehensive sense, which few Christians today bear in mind, as the most highly developed and differentiated symbol of the Self besides the figure of Buddha. The symbol places the individual human consciousness in a meaningful relation to the outside world without denying the world's enigmatic, arbitrary character: the believer hears the divine word, 'Behold, it was very good'; he accepts as truth, although it contradicts his experience, that the world is arranged without even the slightest flaw. At the pinnacle of faith, the believer denounces God, as Job does, and yet adheres to Him. The only higher paradox is reserved to God Himself, Who becomes a suffering human.

You would have to be blind, C. G. Jung remarks in his *Answer to Job*, one of the most profound religious studies of the twentieth century – you would have to be blind not to see the glaring light that Mount Golgotha casts on God's character. For a father to sacrifice his own son – a terrifying idea to every one of us, one which disturbs us deeply in the story of Abraham as well – contradicts the notion of God as the *summum bonum*. As man experiences the world in its terror *and* its beauty, without the one cancelling out the other, as grace in ecstasy, as punishment in distress, the dreadfulness of Christ in the Apocalypse complements His love in the Sermon on the Mount. In other words: in its paradoxical image of God, the *Bible* is consistent with reality. And in any case, the holy scriptures are perceived as divine not because they conjure up supernatural phenomena, things outside reality: on the contrary, it is because they capture sensory experience in its totality. The *Bible* is divine – one might say in another paradox – the *Bible* is divine in the extreme inasmuch as it is human. For the drama of Job and the consummation of Jesus take place not just in history, whether real history or salvation history: they take place in every one of us.

Permit me, dear analysts, ladies and gentlemen, to cite at this juncture another good friend, the philosopher Carl Hegemann, who for many years was head of dramaturgy at the Volksbühne theatre in Berlin. In his book on identity and self-destruction, Hegemann defines drama in the theatre as the consequence of contradictory conditions to which human beings are necessary subjected. The following sentences, although written in regard to consciousness, could just as well refer theologically to Job, who rebels against the God in Whom he believes:

> Consciousness experiences itself as distinct from the world only when that world has a determining influence on it, and when it does not submit to that influence, but resists it or rebels against it. When it fights oppression without questioning the necessity of the oppression. In the moment when that happens, self-awareness arises as the pain of pressure or friction against the other which resists the self. This feeling of external resistance is fundamental to the subject and cannot be done away with – even though we work all the time, necessarily, at eliminating that resistance, in the theatre just as we do in the world. We must accept what opposes us, for without it, we would not exist as beings conscious of ourselves.
>
> (Hegemann 2017, p. 226)

If the Gospel had been something completely new and unheard of, it would hardly have spread so rapidly. In fact, it was consistent with the psychic conditions of ancient man; it made the transcendent and hidden God, already known in Judaism, visible in the human form of Christ. In doing so, Christianity went beyond the pagan religions, in which God merely manifests Himself in animal or human forms, and likewise went beyond Judaism, which has a concept of the deification of man in such figures as the Son of Man, but knows no humanization of God. Only the Incarnation makes it possible to say that Christ dwells in the person who believes in Him. This, as C. G. Jung notes, is psychologically the same relation that exists in the Indian conception between Atman and the individual consciousness: on one hand the Self as the totality of the psyche, which encompasses the unconscious, including its collective, prenatal and mythic connections; on the other the ego, which merely represents the individual consciousness and its transitory content. And it is by no means probable, Jung continues, that this connection between the universal foundation of being and the individual, which is anchored in the structure of the psyche, is broken with the advent of Christianity. Christ himself assures his disciples that he is always with them, indeed in them; and as if that were not enough, he promises to send them a paraclete, that is, an advocate, in his place. And Jesus reminds the Jews, who accuse him of making himself into a god, of Psalm 82:6, in which God has said to them, 'Ye are gods.'

For that reason, Jesus in Islamic mysticism stands not so much for the unique occurrence of God's incarnation as a man, but the reverse: for man's – every person's – potential to unfold the divinity that is in our nature. Jesus is the model of a holy man who is so completely filled with God that he cries out in ecstasy, as the mystic al-Hallaj did, 'I am God!' But Jesus is not only the unique model of the saints: in the formula 'die and live anew', the Incarnation is the model of all knowledge. Ibn Arabi extends the idea of a continuing revelation, one which does not end with the death on the Cross, by relating it to every single moment of life; he sees Creation renewed with every breath. After all, the word for 'breath' is contained in the Arabic word *rūh*, which stands for 'spirit', as it is in the Sanskrit word *Ātman*, and thus every person has a holy spirit which connects them with God. Every person inhales and exhales, with every breath, 'the breath of the Merciful', *an-nafas ar-raḥmāni*. Ibn Arabi writes:

> Man does not realize that with every breath he ceases to exist, and then exists again. And when I say 'then', I do not mean a temporal delay, but a purely logical sequence. In the 're-creation in every breath', the moment of annihilation coincides with the moment of creation of a likeness.

For according to both biblical and quranic teaching, God reveals Himself not only in the prophets; He is visible in all creatures and natural phenomena. In this context, Ibn Arabi reminds us that the Prophet Muhammad had the habit of standing outdoors with his head bare as soon as it rained, and that the Prophet said the rain came fresh from his Lord. 'Is there anything more full of light, more sublime and clear?' asks Ibn Arabi. 'Thus the noblest of men enchanted the rain with its nearness to his Lord; the rain was as the celestial messenger who brought him the divine inspiration.'

One might object that seeing God in every soul, in a drop of rain, or in the sexual act implies dragging him down to the level of humans and material things. In the mystic's view, however, the opposite is the case: people and things are absorbed in God the moment the believer, to use Hölderlin's famous expression from *Hyperion*, is 'one with all that lives'. The unity of being, *waḥdat al-wujūd*, which underlies all existence, is a key concept of Ibn Arabi's teaching. Or, to put it in C. G. Jung's words: 'I have been accused of deifying the soul. Not I but God Himself deified it' (Jung 1944, para. 14).

Certainly, C. G. Jung was not trying to prove the existence of God. Much less was he interested in setting one religion above another. Rather, he was exposing the religious structure of the psyche, which exists independently of specific faiths, and regardless of whether the individual person believes. The atheist too is confronted, by the very fact of birth and death, with situations that transcend his earthly existence. Even if he explains man's fate rationally in terms of 'chance' or 'nothingness', he relates to it. 'The competence of psychology as an empirical science only goes so far as to establish ... whether for instance the imprint found in the psyche can or cannot reasonably be termed a "God-image"', writes Jung in *Psychology and Alchemy*. That does not imply any assertion, 'positive or negative ... about the possible existence of God, any more than the archetype of the "hero" posits the actual existence of a hero' (ibid., para. 15).

Nonetheless, our relation to the world and to those around us changes when we see them in their relation to God. According to Jung, the religious attitude does not prove the existence of God, but from a psychotherapeutic perspective, it helps people to affirm life, and contributed to the recovery of many of his patients. Ibn Arabi recounts in the *Meccan Revelations* how, as a young, already respected scholar, he once carried a basketful of rotting, horribly stinking fish across the market. His companions thought he was carrying the basket as a penance, or in an effort to purify his soul by performing an unpleasant and embarrassing service that was not in keeping with his social status. 'No,' Ibn Arabi said, 'that was not my intention. I simply saw that God, for all His greatness, had not found it beneath Him to create these things. How then could it be beneath me to carry them?'

Christianity has institutionalized the idea that divine indwelling is continuously renewed in the miracle of Pentecost: it is the Church which the Holy Spirit indwells; two or three must be gathered together in Christ's name, and there He is in the midst of them. The institution of the Church largely removes God's indwelling from the personal experience of faith, and perhaps it could not be otherwise: in taking shape, the Church had to emphasize the uniqueness of God's revelation in Jesus Christ in order to claim a monopoly on the work of redemption; otherwise Jesus' message probably would have dissolved into a multitude of sects. The notion that the divine spirit can work in each person immediately has been preserved in

Gnosticism, in the Asian and pagan religious traditions of course, in Jewish mysticism, and, with a pronounced Christian connotation, in Sufism. And, as we know, ideas from Islam have certainly contributed to the development of a mysticism within Christianity as well: Meister Eckhart drew on Arabic philosophy; Mechthild of Magdeburg would hardly have developed an eroticism of prayer if the Sufis' erotic love of God, and the motif of romantic love itself, had not spread through Europe from Andalusia with the troubadours in the 11th century. And then, in the late hymns to Christ of Friedrich Hölderlin, who was also heavily influenced by Christian mysticism, Jesus reappears as a demigod, alongside the gods turned human of classical antiquity, but also alongside the poet Empedocles:

> I alone
> Was God, and I said it in bold pride.

Thus, the Incarnation, the central occurrence of Christianity, is unique, and the Cross expresses the singularity of the salvation history; but at the same time, the strength and the legitimation of Christianity lie in the very universality of its central motif: the incarnation of God, in its progression from the virgin birth to the death on the cross, is better able than any theory to encompass a universal human experience in all its contradictions. It is the experience of every child which has been pressed out of its mother's womb. As a new-born child we do not yet divide our present world from the previous one. We have no I as long as we have no Thou. We do not yet experience ourself as a boy or a girl. We experience our parents, and especially our mother, as an indefinite, omnipotent, and yet beneficent power. We cry when we are hungry, when we feel pain, and when we are afraid because we are alone. We soon smile when we are picked up and cuddled. We are afraid when we are scolded or punished. We learn the names first. We grow up and become in our turn the mother, the father, that we once thought to be God. We grow old, we decay and become, in death if not before, as helpless, and as lonely, as a new-born child. In Christianity, God has a very human biography. C. G. Jung reminds us that it is mainly in the West that religion stands in opposition to science. In most other cultures, it is conceived as a wisdom which interprets the empirical world and is consistent with it. In fact, he writes, from a psychological perspective, the assumption of invisible gods or demons who directly intervene in life is a much more persuasive portrayal of the unconscious than a passive explanation of it as the absence of the conscious mind. Jung writes:

> Theory has to disregard the emotional values of the experience. Dogma, on the other hand, is extremely eloquent in just this respect. One scientific theory is soon superseded by another.

> Dogma lasts for untold centuries. The suffering God-Man may be at least five thousand years old and the Trinity is probably even older.... Dogma expresses the psyche more completely than a scientific theory, for the latter gives expression to and formulates the conscious mind alone. Furthermore, a theory can do nothing except formulate a living thing in abstract terms. Dogma, on the contrary, aptly expresses the living process of the unconscious in the form of the drama of sin, repentance, sacrifice, and redemption.
>
> (Jung 1938/40, para. 81-82)

Christianity has given such expression to the human incarnation of God, which is inversely accessible to every individual consciousness as the experience of God, and even to the atheist as the experience of a non-ego element of the Self, as the oceanic feeling that even Freud accords to the human consciousness in ecstasy – the Christian cross has given an anthropological experience of suffering, love and transcendence such a valid, engaging, irresistible and persuasive expression that it persists even today against all rational plausibility, and the God-Man himself is associated even in Islam with Jesus. Yet Ibn Arabi associates his beloved Nizam, in whom a higher reality is revealed, not only with Christianity. She is also a highly attractive young woman, as the *Interpreter of Longing* attests:

> She takes with a hand soft and delicate, like pure silk, anointed with *nadd* and shredded musk.
> When she looks, she gazes with the deep eye of a young gazelle: to her eye belongs the blackness of antimony.
> Her eyes are adorned with languishment and killing magic, her sides are girt with amazement and incomparable beauty.
> A slender one, she loves not that which I love and she does not fulfil her threats with sincerity.
> She let down her plaited lock as a black serpent, that she might frighten with it those who were following her.
> By God, I fear not death; my only fear is that I shall die and shall not see her to-morrow.

To Ibn Arabi, who had more women teachers than men, the beatific vision, which is necessarily communicated to humans through concrete earthly experiences – of nature, love, dream visions and, most strongly, sexuality – reaches its highest perfection in women. For women incorporate both aspects of the divine, the passive and the creative, conception and childbirth, patiens and agens, anima and animus. Men on the other hand are born, but do not give birth. That means that Ibn Arabi explicitly attributes the passive, female, receptive aspect to God as well, and conceives His relation to humanity as a mutual one in which we depend on Him, but He is equally dependent on our love. 'Do not blame me if I call God a bride', Ibn Arabi writes, conscious that his teaching must be provocative in the context of Islam, insisting, in contravention of the Arabic usage, that God combines both genders or, conversely, is genderless.

Dear analysts, ladies and gentlemen, as you know, the rift between C.G. Jung and his teacher, Sigmund Freud, involved not least the question of libido. To the Swiss pastor's son – and I do believe that the different religious and cultural backgrounds played a part in their disagreement – erotic desire is a remarkably blank spot in comparison with Freud, and although the Arab mystic Ibn Arabi speaks eloquently in support of Jung's sacralization of the psyche, he also confirms Freud, who called sexuality the 'shibboleth' of his school, that is, its badge or watchword. It is certainly no coincidence that Freud uses a Hebrew word here, not only because he was a Jew, like almost all his students, Jung excepted.

In this connection, I thank Almut Bruckstein, whom I have already mentioned, for another remarkable idea: she sees the motif of the divine beloved carried forward in the form of Freud's analytical session. Shulamite or Nizam would then be the figure of the analyst himself, who sits outside the patient's field of vision – the invisible object at which desire is directed. Sexual desire enters into the analytical process. And where Ibn Arabi in the *Interpreter of Longing* retains the image of union, not in spite of, but because of the intensity of his love, Freud is right after all in a certain sense. His thinking is Jewish: the messianic theme is a postponement of fulfillment. And, to follow Almut Bruckstein's train of thought further, he places it in the middle of the psychoanalytical space: the patient's couch is the lover's bed in the Song of Solomon, the bed of Ibn Arabi who aphysically desires Nizam; it is the place where desire was sublimated in language, because the fulfilment is yet to come. 'It seems to me no contradiction at all that I love God in His creatures, for that unites the two opposite realities,' say the *Meccan Revelations*:

> Where God reveals Himself, the observer [the observer!] sees himself in his partner. He sees himself in the woman, and his love and her attraction are heightened all the more as his own self takes shape in her. We have already explained to you that this is the shape of the truth through which God becomes present. Thus the lover sees nothing but true being, but with an ardent, indomitable longing and with the enjoyment of physical ecstasy. He merges with the beloved in the most sublime rapture. Not only their bodies, but their being meets in complete harmony. He vanishes in her. There is nothing of him which is not her. He is flooded with love from top to bottom; his whole being is joined with her. He finally dissolves so

completely in her as would not be possible in a love for something that was not himself. He becomes one with the beloved, saying, 'I am she whom I desire, and the one who desires me is myself.' At the highest point, he cries out, 'I am God!'

Sigmund Freud adhered to a decidedly patriarchal concept of God the Father, and his resistance against religious beliefs was nourished by his general rejection of dependency and passivity, which he associated, stereotypically, with femininity. His lapse in degrading the female leaves him behind even the religions which he considered obsolete. Judaism too has a feminine image of God, from the 'Wisdom' of biblical texts to the 'Shekinah' of the Kabbalah, which is described as a woman, as bride and daughter of the male power. Christianity initially took up the female dimension of God in the early representations of Jesus as a beautiful shepherd with remarkably feminine features. In Islamic mysticism as well, Jesus is associated not only with compassion, but at the same time with beauty. Only the joining of compassion with beauty allowed being to arise out of nothing, say the *Meccan Revelations*; God's mercy alone would not have provoked the desire for a correlative. God longed to be perceived in His beauty; He not only loves, but wants to be loved: that is why He created the world. Thus the Creation, to Ibn Arabi, is an expression of God's creative femininity. This is where the figure of Mary appears in Sufi Islam, psychologically representing the Jungian anima as mother and at the same time bride of Christ, while Jesus himself combines masculine and feminine traits. Mary represents God's femininity, while Jesus incorporates God in His entirety with His contradictions. But it is also in Mary that Christianity retained the feminine traits long after the androgyny of the early representations of Christ – such as the Ravenna mosaics I have written about in *Wonder Beyond Belief* – had been supplanted by a purely male *Salvator mundi*.

According to C. G. Jung, the insight that male and female are united in the original divine being is older than history, and God's wanting to become human through a human mother was known long before Christianity in the royal theology of ancient Egypt. One of the most surprising aspects of Jung's 1952 *Answer to Job* is the vindication of the Madonna, a figure Freud ignores completely. But Jung's fellow Protestants must also have been shocked to see him call the dogma of the Assumption, which Pius XII had promulgated shortly before, in 1950, 'the most important religious event since the Reformation': Jung understood the bodily reception of the Virgin into Heaven, which the dogma proclaims, as an image of Mary the bride united with the Son and as Sophia united with the godhead in the celestial bridechamber. That may seem preposterous to the unpsychological mind, Jung admits, but the papal argument makes sense to the psychologist, based as it is on a 'tradition of religious assertions reaching back for more than a thousand years': 'Equality requires to be metaphysically anchored in the figure of a "divine" woman, the bride of Christ.' Hence the dogma is indeed timely, and relegates Jung's own background, that is, Protestantism, to 'the odium of being nothing but a *man's religion* which allows no metaphysical representation of woman.'

Again, I will pass over the consequences for social policy, which would be worth considering not only for Protestantism, but likewise for the men's club of Catholicism, and how much the more so for Islam, which accords women equal rights in almost no respect. But I am also passing over the difficulties with C. G. Jung, and still more with Ibn Arabi, that must irritate a feminism which sees masculinity and femininity as social constructs rather than realities that work in opposite ways in each of us, whether man or woman. I prefer, in closing, to quote once more from the *Interpreter of Desires*, in which 'the greatest shaykh' of Islam so eloquently desires a Christian as a God-woman:

> Who will show me her of the dyed fingers? Who will show me her of the honeyed tongue?
> She is one of the girls with swelling breasts who guard their honour, tender, virgin and beautiful,
> Full moons over branches: they fear no waning.
> In a garden of my body's country is a dove perched on a *bān* bough,
> Dying of desire, melting with passion, because that which befell me hath befallen her;
> Mourning for a mate, blaming Time, who shot her unerringly, as he shot me.
> Parted from a neighbour and far from a home! Alas, in my time of severance, for my time of union!
> Who will bring me her who is pleased with my torment? I am helpless because of that with which she is pleased.

Dear analysts, ladies and gentlemen, before you begin your scholarly discussions, permit me one postscript. In my talk, I have repeatedly alluded to social and political implications without expanding on them. But I would like to venture once into the present, although not into politics. Instead I would like to lead you into my own field, literature. You have probably wondered by now how I have so many friends – I haven't; it's just that there are not so many authors in Germany in our time who concern themselves with spiritual matters. We can't lose sight of one another, in the gigantic space between Heaven and Earth, if only because the crowd has thinned out so in literature.

When I read contemporary books, good books, important books, books I can only be envious of because mine never turn out as brilliant, I often can't help having the impression that they are missing something essential. I mean: I miss something essential; but of course every reader speaks only for himself. I have the impression that literature, and especially German-language literature, whose metaphysical references once constituted part of its fame and greatness, whether Gryphius or Goethe, whether Jean Paul or Hölderlin, whether Kafka or Thomas Mann – I have the impression that most of our novels today fix their gaze firmly on the ground, on our social existence. That they are contemporary and nothing else. That's my feeling, subjective I admit – but when have feelings ever been fair? – when I read a contemporary German novel that everyone else says is brilliant, or when I don't read it because according to the reviews it's only about the here and now – and the here and now is so tiny!

After all, transcendence, in the context of art and culture, doesn't necessarily mean God – or His absence, which even the earliest poets deplored. To an artist, transcendence means first of all belonging to a tradition that is so old we can't remember its beginnings. Transcendence means going beyond the world of our immediate experience. That can also mean consciously renouncing a tradition. But we ought to know the tradition first, back to its roots in myth.

> We always start with the naïve assumption that we are masters in our own house. Hence we must first accustom ourselves to the thought that, in our most intimate psychic life as well, we live in a kind of house which at least has doors and windows to the world, but that, although the objects or contents of this world act upon us, they do not belong to us.
>
> (Jung 1928, para. 329)

Naturally there are historic novels – which I seldom read; on history I'd choose a monograph – and novels that are set in far-off lands – I'd choose a book of reportage – yet most of those novels are merely set in the past or in the remote country; they are not descended from it. Many novels that are praised as worldly today are written no differently from all the others: they do not incorporate foreign philosophy, themes, language into their own structure, as Kafka integrated Jewish thought or Goethe Middle Eastern literature. And the books that are being written, discussed and praised in the German-speaking countries today rarely claim a tradition more than twenty, thirty years old; sometimes they trace their lineage as far back as the sixties, the beginnings of pop (which by now is something of a forefather to much of contemporary culture, which is ironic in itself). People still read the moderns, or at most the literature of the eighteenth, nineteenth centuries, but they hardly engage with it, and when there are references, the author cannot expect them to be recognized by the critics; more likely by those of his readers who have a classical education, whom he recognizes, in their letters or at readings, by other quirks – their clothes, their letter paper. And religion has no place at all, unless it is mentioned as a political problem.

But if a book has neither a past nor another world – a distant past I mean, one that goes farther back than an individual memory, and I mean another world in the general sense that there is more than human beings can see here on Earth – if a book neither claims a tradition nor looks up to the heavens, if the immediate circumstances are all that matters, then something is missing, the essential thing, I would say, although I am surely in the minority among readers, not least as a believer. To use the Sufis' beautiful image: what is missing is that the present glows black, from within, from darkness, because in all the diversity and particularity we do not see the influence of the common origin. This is precisely the lack that I feel, in spite of all my admiration and in spite of my envy when someone writes better than I; this is the solitude that I feel as a reader today. And that makes it all the more beautiful to be with you, dear analysts, scholars, if not followers, of Carl Gustav Jung. 'We carry our past with us, to wit, the primitive and inferior man with his desires and emotions, and it is only with an enormous effort that we can detach ourselves from this burden', he writes in *Psychology and Religion*:

> If it comes to a neurosis, we invariably have to deal with a considerably intensified shadow. And if such a person wants to be cured it is necessary to find a way in which his conscious personality and his shadow can live together.
>
> (Jung 1938/40, para. 132)

Literature too is a way of living together with the shadow that falls on us from the past or from the other world.

I thank you for your attention and wish you a rewarding conference.

References

Hegemann, C. (2017). *Identität und Selbst-Zerstörung: Grundlagen einer historischen Kritik moderner Lebensbedingungen bei Fichte und Marx (1978) plus Das Drama der Subjektkonstitution (2012)*. Berlin: Alexander Verlag.

Jung, C.G. (1928). 'The relations between the ego and the unconscious'. *CW* 7.

– (1938/40). 'Psychology and Religion (The Terry Lectures)'. *CW* 11.

– (1944). *Psychology and Alchemy*. *CW* 12.

Ibn Arabi. (1911). *Tarjuman al-Ashwaq*. Trans. Reynold, A. Nicholson. London: Royal Asiatic Society. [available at: archive.org/details/TarjumanIbnAlArabiNicholson/page/n59].

Apocalyptic Themes in Times of Trouble: When Young Men are Deeply Alienated

Robert Tyminski
CGJISF, San Francisco

Introduction

A young man says to me, 'I really like destroying things.' Why, I wonder.

Today, I'll use a case to discuss some possibilities. This case is not at all uncommon, either in my practice or in teaching and supervision when I hear of problematic clinical situations. I'll call my patient 'Herman', which, as a German name, means warrior or soldier. This case does not only reflect aspects of a hero's journey, although there are elements of the hero archetype, as well as traces of the trickster, demon, monster, and clown. I will show some images that characterize archetypal dimensions of apocalypse, which are prevalent in many video games that primarily boys and men play.

Before telling you about Herman, a quick word about terms that you will read in this paper. *Apocalypse* is a strong word with ancient meanings. It now refers mostly to doomsday and end-of-time scenarios, and is used in the media to describe the effects of male violence, for instance in mass shootings, terrorist attacks, and urban gang brutality. Apocalypse also means an uncovering or disclosure of knowledge. In that sense, it stands for revelation, as in the *New Testament's Book of Revelation*, which portrays the final judgment of humankind. This dual meaning of apocalypse encompasses psychic boundaries of inside and outside, which can become confused in many boys and men, leading to extreme alienation and destructive acts.

Alienation once meant insanity, and the word alienist indicated those who worked with the insane. Today, alienation is frequently understood as being isolated from others, lonely and marginalized. As analysts, we can appreciate that it also refers to being distanced from the inner world, cut-off from the vital life of psyche. It is this barrier to internal processes that interests me in what many males describe when saying, 'I'm broken.'

One more term pertains to *video games*. The video games I hear about fall into a category called *MOBA*, or multi-player online battle arena games. These are point-and-shoot games, in which a player has a weapon and tries to maximize his score by killing as many enemies as he can. These games are mostly played on the Internet. When I refer to video games, I mean this kind of game. Two examples are *League of Legends*, released in 2009, and *Fortnite*, released in 2017. Almost 80 million people play *Fortnite* each month, and this game generates revenues of over $300 million monthly (www.polygon.com, 2018). Over 70% of the players are male (www.statistica.com, 2019).

Herman – Early Work

When Herman came to see me, he presented as a dishevelled, silent 15-year-old boy who looked very depressed[1]. His parents told me that he had become socially isolated for reasons they could not explain since he had been previously popular at school. All they knew was that there had been some incident, after which Herman was shunned by his peers. He spent long hours playing video games and hung black curtains over the windows of his room. He stayed in his room ten or more hours daily and refused to take part in any enjoyable family activities. Herman's parents told me that he had recently broken up with a girlfriend.

Herman was adopted at age five by a white heterosexual couple. He was Latino. He had been in foster care because of severe parental abuse that included being tied up with a noose around his neck. His father had gone to prison for what he had done to Herman, and since then, Herman had only sporadic contact with his mother. Herman told me that his ex-girlfriend hacked his social media accounts to spread rumours about his supposed sexual exploits, which he maintained were untrue. This was a harsh form of what online is called 'trolling', and is cyberbullying. His friends abandoned him, and he quit the basketball team, even though he had been a skilful player. Herman told me that he felt crushed by what his ex-girlfriend had done, and he collapsed, having no will to defend himself against the online lies. Being scapegoated at school precipitated a regression, in which he withdrew into darkness and videogaming.

Herman's depression brought back to him feelings and memories of his earlier abuse and abandonment. When he described what his girlfriend had done to him, he said, 'She dumped me, and that wasn't enough. She had to beat me when I was down.' He spoke at length about their relationship 'drama', which entailed many breakups and reunions. He was surprised by how hard he took the final separation: 'You'd think I'd have been prepared by everything we'd been through.'

I mentioned to Herman that feeling dumped and not able to fight back were difficult feelings that sometimes resonate with earlier

---

[1] Details of this case have been disguised. Parts appear in Ch. 7 of *Male Alienation at the Crossroads of Identity, Culture and Cyberspace*, by Robert Tyminski. (2019). London & New York: Routledge.

events in a person's life. He thought about this, and replied that he was angry his biological parents had 'dumped' him. During these sessions, Herman began to work through his depression and helplessness. He recalled for me horrible incidents of abuse that his father had inflicted on him, including being burned, strangled, and nearly drowned. I reinforced to Herman how brave he had been, that he was a survivor, and that telling me his story was important. I saw both an abused child and a resilient one.

During this initial period of analysis, Herman was consumed by the video game *League of Legends*, which he told me he played over 25 hours weekly. *League of Legends* takes place in a fictional land named Runeterra. Players are individually and publicly ranked by the number of levels each of their characters achieves, and some of the characters, called champions, are a marksman, a mage, and a slayer. Gaming a battle, players seek similarly ranked players so that winners can obtain special weapons, armour, powers, and treasure. Recently, *League of Legends* had nearly 100 million players worldwide and up to 27 million playing monthly (Heimer 2019). The company making it, Riot Games, organizes official world championships, televised online, where the winners are awarded cash prizes.

Herman reported that he liked feeling powerful, gaining trophies, and killing enemies. Sometimes, he talked as if these achievements were more than success in a video game. Although his play was real, I wondered if he was capable of separating himself from what happened in it. This game is violent in content and accompanied by players' commentary full of racist, homophobic, and misogynistic slurs. Other boys and young men in my practice confirm that such language is common while videogaming. It was difficult to hear Herman tell me about these, and I shared my reaction, yet he was only minimally surprised. The part of him that believed he was strong and powerful did not like what I had to say about this hateful language. Herman had a fantasy that he might earn a living playing the game. He saw the sponsors, often major corporations marketing to adolescents and young adults, that the most successful players have, and figured he could do the same. He sometimes realized he was not at their skill level. The fantasy of earning a living this way interfered with his focus at school where he daydreamed about videogaming. I tried various approaches to help him with reality testing, including limits on exposure to the game, and these were only modestly effective.

Herman Becomes a Monster

After his depression improved, Herman continued to play *League of Legends* for many reasons. This game made him feel strong. It gave an alternative to his lack of success at school; and it provided a refuge and escape, similar to getting lost in a good book. Sometimes, after playing for hours, Herman was so agitated that he became aggressive at home, throwing things and breaking them. This loss of control was as if the game had intoxicated him. This is a point at which analysts question when an activity is no longer escapism, but now an addiction. Herman viewed himself as a fighter, although this self-image didn't match his anxious persona. There was a noticeable gap between his idealized self-concept and what others saw. Videogaming contributes to feelings of being unreal and disembodied. Herman often complained that he felt muscle tension after sitting for hours, yet he resisted recognizing that his bodily discomfort had anything to do with his rages after he was online.

He had a limit on how much his parents allowed him to play, but he played much more through deception, sneaking, lying, and trickery. During one period, he stole the family's Wi-Fi codes, and he played through the night for several days. He felt deprived that his parents tried to limit his time on *League of Legends*, while asserting his friends had no limitations on their playing time. This perception of being treated differently fed his anger and led to arguments that escalated into shouting matches. His parents asked me, how much should they allow him to play online? This is a question that parents regularly ask child and adolescent psychotherapists.

The *American Academy of Pediatrics* now recommends the following for children ages 6 to 18: 1) parents and caregivers place consistent limits on the time spent using media, and the types of media, and make sure media does not take the place of adequate sleep, physical activity and other behaviors essential to health; 2) parents designate media-free times together, such as dinner or driving, as well as media-free locations at home, such as bedrooms; and 3) parents have ongoing communication about online citizenship and safety, including treating others with respect online and offline (American Academy of Pediatrics, 2016). These guidelines are helpful markers for containment, because they delineate temporal, spatial and relational limits that parents can readily conceptualize themselves.

Many parents, however, find it difficult to follow through with limits on screen time, because they report being worn down by angry protests when they try to enforce them. They wonder what the point is of being strict about screen time, when they rightly suspect that their children will find ways to get online despite trying to regulate their access. Many feel they are fighting a losing battle, because the Internet permeates our lives.

During this period, Herman, now 16, became contemptuous of his parents, teachers and me. He insulted his mother, 'You're fat and too old to change'; this occurred at a time when he had a growth spurt and suddenly looked more like a young man than a boy. He was suspended from school after telling a teacher, 'Fuck off', because he thought she was singling him out unfairly. I brought up his aggression and tried to establish various links, for example with his emerging young adult strength that wanted no part of his history of abuse and feeling weak. These ideas helped sometimes, but often they brought out his contempt of me. 'Rob, that's lame', or 'You're repeating yourself. Isn't that what happens to old people?' I labelled his belittling remarks as his wish to cut me down. He would sometimes nod, but often rolled his eyes and shook his head with a smirk, as if I were a dummy. One day, he mocked a younger boy leaving my office, a boy with a physical disability. I became angry, and Herman noticed. With a superior-sounding tone, he scolded me, 'Keep your cool, dude. It's just a joke. Maybe you need a vacation.' I kept silent for a while, then said to Herman, 'You like that you can upset me. That's going to become a bigger problem for you if you can't get a handle on it – that you like being mean to people.' I felt it important to address the sadism within his contempt.

Around this time, Herman's father called me. He told me that he'd been upgrading Herman's computer with a new one, and he discovered that Herman had been searching Dark Web sites that sold guns. The Dark Web is typically accessed through browsers such as Tor, which are harder to trace, but any browser can work. His father had checked Herman's web browsers and found that Herman had been viewing many *YouTube* videos of jihadists, who were committing atrocities in Syria and Iraq. He confronted Herman, and they argued until Herman stormed out and didn't return home until the next morning.

After this news, when I went out to meet Herman for his session, he was sitting in a chair across the waiting room in a nook, almost hiding. Once in my office, I noted he was in a different spot than usual. He nodded. The tension between us was obvious. I said, 'I wonder if you're feeling everything has changed and now, you're in a way different spot than either of us expected – in fact, in a very difficult spot than before.' He replied quietly, 'Yes, I guess you could say that.' We spoke more openly about his troubles with videogaming, violent videos, and searching for real guns. While I offered him a containing space, I was still firm in telling him that I thought he had crossed a line because videogaming over-stimulated him to a point where he felt a need for really violent outlets for his imagination. I said I was worried where this desire would take him. He slowly replied, 'I think I have to not play as much.' I encouraged him to say more, and he added, 'I'm afraid I'm going to mess up even more… that I could hurt myself … or maybe another person.' He looked frightened and cried some.

Herman worked with me over the following months to curb his videogaming. He took up swimming, and joined a swim team, which had afternoon practices that kept him off screens. Concurrently,

I encouraged Herman's parents to talk more with him about his future. They took on an important parental function of helping him set reasonable goals for himself. Herman loved his adoptive parents, although he challenged them in fits of rebellion that they experienced as destabilizing. I worked with his parents to help them differentiate the normative part of Herman's rebellion from when he needed limits to rein in his aggression. Within his psyche, there was a heated struggle between the boy who'd been an abused victim and the young man who wanted to avenge him. Herman got along better with his father than his mother. This situation often happens during a boy's adolescence, when he wants to separate from feelings of needing his mother. I knew from Herman that his mother had a complicated family background. Her father had been involved in the military during a terrible genocidal war. Within her family, there appeared to be an unconscious intergenerational problem about the consequences of aggression. She repeatedly told me that she was afraid of Herman's potential for violence.

Complexities in containing and limiting aggression are typical during adolescence and early adulthood. When parents struggle with holding limits, this can add to psychological difficulties for internal containment. As a result, a young person may feel unable to metabolize his psychic experiences. I find the work of the French psychoanalyst Didier Anzieu (1989) to be helpful in conceptualizing these problems of internal containment during adolescence. Anzieu developed a theory of the skin ego, originating in the earliest infantile experiences, to understand the mind as a container. This container holds the Self; it protects the psyche; and it operates as a filter for exchanges with others. It makes symbolization possible by separating inner from outer. According to Anzieu, when the skin ego fails, primitive anxieties escalate, and aggression is often discharged. A person in this mental state will usually *search for an alternative container*. He might present psychologically as phobic, panicked, or overtly hostile with destructive behaviours. Many boys and young men engage with video games as substitute containers for their destructive projections. Other aspects of cyberspace also function like containers for projections, for example, social media, Internet pornography, and shopping websites. Vulnerable psyches can be seduced by an apparent solution to inadequate inner containment believing they will find it in the non-human webs of cyberspace.

Herman – Later Work

Because of Herman's history of traumatic early abuse, the fate of the boy who could have been killed stayed on my mind throughout my work with him. After his first weekend trip away with another young man – Herman was now 18 – he came into his session smiling and asked me if I could guess why. I said no, but could see that he was excited to tell me. 'I got a tattoo!' Before I could say a word, he pulled down the collar of his t-shirt to show me a tattoo *over his heart* of a dark, hooded figure with a scythe.

I asked, 'Do you realize what that is?'

Herman laughed, 'Yeah, it's the reaper guy. It's cool. It's like my heart is protected by him now.' Although Herman saw this image as a shield, I wondered if it represented his murderous father getting too close.

I told him that it reminded me of the close calls he'd had when he was a young boy. I added that I felt worried because he seemed to want to turn those horrible memories into a badge of courage. He took in what I said and didn't argue, although he focused more on the fact of having a tattoo than what it symbolized. The Pew Research Center documents the increased popularity of tattoos among Millennials with nearly 40 percent having a tattoo and half of them more than one (Pew Research Center 2010, p. 1). Almost 25 percent have a body piercing that is not on the ear (ibid., p. 58).

Alessandra Lemma (2010) discusses the psychoanalytic meanings of body modifications to show an identity and to protest, and she points to an archetypal underpinning for them. During a presentation with her (Lemma, Brady & Tyminski 2012), I mentioned the Jungian concept of initiation, which often involves a visible change to our bodies. Jung writes that initiation, in the case of an adolescent, means separation from the parents and that 'there must be a drastic ceremony that looks very like sacrifice' (Jung 1927, pp. 374-75). Tattoos are a way for a young man to emphasize a passage requiring something like sacrifice. I kept these ideas in mind as I spoke with Herman about his tattoo.

Two weeks later, Herman was in a car accident that totaled his vehicle. He was not high or drunk, but an inattentive young driver, who crashed into a truck stopped in front of him. No one was hurt, and Herman was mostly upset about what he'd done to his first car. He admitted responsibility, although he mixed his acknowledgement with grumbling about heavy traffic and slow drivers. I wondered if he could think of any other reasons why he might have had this accident. I had an intuition about his tattoo, and I felt unsure how to bring it up. Herman told me no, then asked, 'You got an idea?'

I said that it was worth thinking about. I commented that it seemed like irony that soon after getting a fearsome tattoo, which he thought would protect him, he had this bad accident.

He replied, 'Wicked, Rob, irony!' He hesitated before adding, 'I guess that's harsh but true.'

Herman went on to say that his belief about protection was 'busted', and he wondered if he hadn't needed to correct that. I thought that he recognized he'd been inflated about the tattoo, and now he accepted a realistic limit to it. Herman reviewed the accident many times with me; he wanted to understand why his mind had 'tricked' him into distraction. This effort on his part felt promising, because it suggested he could recognize an unconscious force thwarting his intentions, in other words, his shadow. His attitude about the tattoo changed during these discussions. 'It's just ink – I can't rely on ink.'

Although I chose not to bring up his early history in relation to this image of the Grim Reaper, I thought about it for a long time. I believe that Herman's tattoo, placed significantly over his heart, was partly a symbol of the dangers around his early survival. It expressed something similar at this later stage of life: a reactivated fear of survival around finishing high school and separating from his adoptive family. During this time, we spent many sessions discussing his worries about being on his own, as well as planning together what he would need to become independent. This combination of encouraging him to express his feelings and thinking about plans worked well with Herman because he was open to both. Not every young man is.

Videogaming toward Apocalypse

Before discussing how I understand the analytic process between Herman and me, I want to comment briefly about videogaming by sharing some images of *Fortnite* with you. I am interspersing them with images from Western art to amplify archetypal aspects. Notice the glow apparent within each scene. What does it mean? Is it an expression of destructiveness? Could it convey a glimmer of hope within apocalyptic imagery? It is noteworthy how many video games portray war within apocalyptic settings. Although it can be difficult to listen to many details about videogames, I believe an open attitude toward them is important, and in a way, I try to regard them as fantasy tales and even dream-like portrayals of something a boy or young man wants to see more clearly in himself.

Teams of video gamers now compete for money in what *The Economist* calls 'an adrenalin-filled corollary to social media', as if there is a demand to intensify what occurs online (*Economist* 2019, p. 54). Citing marketing revenues of $150 billion, they write, 'Trigger-happy 15-35 year-olds are literally calling the shots' (ibid.). Many mass shooters are reported to have had compulsive or addictive behaviours around videogaming. In my work with Herman, I often listened to fantasies about how he hoped to earn a living playing video games. I have heard similar fantasies from many boys and young men in my practice during the last five years. Such aspirations appear to be a new sociocultural trend. A 16-year-old boy recently won $3 million in an international *Fortnite* competition (Humphries 2019).

Figure 1: Player on Fortnite, by madam F / Shutterstock.com, 2019.

The Meanings of Apocalypse

I think that extreme alienation in boys and young men is often associated with apocalyptic fantasies that many combat video games reinforce. Apocalyptic themes are also prevalent in many doomsday films, for instance the zombie genre, and in other popular media, especially graphic novels. Apocalyptic references show up in political discourse, terrorist imagery, predictions about climate change, and forecasts of economic disaster. Apocalyptic art is spread across centuries of Western visual media, and its iconography is typically based on apocalyptic manuscripts that refer to the *Book of Revelation*, often proliferating before or after a millennial date, such as 500 CE, 1000 CE, and 1500 CE (O'Hear 2011). A place where we can find religious details of apocalypse is in the *Book of Revelation*.

Here, a reader encounters the four horsemen of the apocalypse, who bring devastation before the Last Judgment. 'And I saw, and behold a white horse: and he that sat on him had a bow; and a crown was given unto him: and he went forth conquering, and to conquer' (*Bible*, KJV 1997, p. 304). The first horseman with his bow and arrow is thought to represent both conquest and plague. Psychologically, this symbolism signifies triumph and then a deadness following it. Such deadness occurs in psychic states of emptiness and desolation. I think that the four horsemen can help us understand the destructive fantasies that preoccupy many alienated boys and men. For example, the rider of the white horse can be viewed as symbolizing what happens in compulsions and addictions.

Figure 2: Albrecht Dürer, The Four Horsemen, from the Apocalypse, *1498.*[2]

When I worked with Herman around his addiction to video games, I saw an inflation-deflation cycle that gripped him, and in a way, plagued him. His desire to be strong became a kind of megalomania. Herman's desire turned from play to domination, and later became the obliteration of his opponents. This period of his analysis, when his video game addiction was acute, was one in which Herman was deeply alienated from his family, peers, and teachers. I wondered how connected to me he felt, because there were many moments when I thought I could be cast aside like the dead players in his video game.

Albrecht Dürer's woodcut of the Four Riders shows the terror that they bring forth. He depicts them spurred on by an angel and trampling over miserable victims. Some believe he made his apocalypse series after an apocalyptic dream that he had (O'Hear 2011, p. 147). Erwin Panofsky, a scholar of Dürer, writes, 'Like Leonardo's

---

[2] This file was donated to Wikimedia Commons as part of a project by the Metropolitan Museum of Art. This file is made available under the Creative Commons CC0 1.0 Universal Public Domain Dedication.

Last Supper, Dürer's *Apocalypse* belongs among what may be called the inescapable works of art' (Panofsky 1943/2005, p. 59). He notes that Dürer's illustrations of the apocalypse were copied extensively and their influence was far reaching. His description 'inescapable' tells us that there is something archetypal in this image.

The next horse in St. John's vision is red with a horseman carrying a sword (*Bible*, Rev. 6:4, p. 304). This red horse and rider represent war, violence, and killing. From a psychological perspective, this figure perpetrates aggression, lives it out, and inflicts pain on others, perhaps like the shooters at Columbine, Virginia Tech, Sandy Hook, Orlando, Parkland, Christchurch, Dayton, and El Paso. Herman had many destructive fantasies from videogaming, and once told me that he played because he liked destruction. His identification with powerful destructive forces became alarming when he left the parameters of the game and looked into buying a gun. During this time, his rage was evident to many around him. Importantly, a *revelation,* or uncovering, occurred when Herman's father found out just how disturbed Herman's preoccupations had become.

The third horse is black, and its rider holds a set of scales used to weigh. He is thought to represent famine and greed, when appetites spin out of control. Psychologically, this figure represents internal famine coming from emotional deprivation. He evokes the idea of craving, when appetites cannot be contained, and moderation is impossible. For example, Herman protested loudly that his parents deprived him of access to videogaming, showing a greediness intolerant of limits. His complaints about other deprivations extended to school, where he viewed teachers as withholding and stingy. He felt similarly about me when I couldn't resolve his grievances. During these encounters, Herman frequently expressed contempt, for instance by mocking other patients I saw. He insulted me for not having a practice with people he thought looked strong or powerful. The implication was clear: how could I possibly satisfy him? Holding analytically in mind Herman's greediness and his history of deprivation and abuse was one of the hardest aspects of working with him. Such greediness can be aggressively alienating when it creates a ruptured chasm between an analyst and his patient.

St. John sees a fourth horse, a pale horse, and 'his name that sat on him was Death, and Hell followed with him' (*Bible*, Rev. 6:8, p. 304). This rider is commonly depicted as carrying a scythe like the Grim Reaper. Both Joseph Turner (c. 1825) and William Blake (c. 1800) drew this rider, who denotes the final end, dying and dissolution – our mortality. He further symbolizes a quest for meaning, a desire for faith and spiritual enlightenment. The pale horse reminds us that our time is limited and that individuation entails giving this finality a meaningful shape in our psyches. How do we respond, with despair or with integrity?

Herman's despair became clearer at the moment when he hid from me in the waiting room. Would I find him, or would I give up? Through my calling attention to this enactment, he became able to discuss his videogaming as an addiction, with despair implicit in this admission. Later, however, he seemed to imagine his reaper tattoo was a way to repudiate despair. He thought it would magically protect him. He had to re-evaluate this magical thinking when his car accident made real how close he could still get to despair. In so many ways, his childhood story is full of despair, although also of survival and resilience.

After his break with Freud in 1913, Jung experienced deep alienation, and he struggled with despair. 'After the break with Freud, all my friends and acquaintances dropped away. My book was declared to be rubbish; I was a mystic, and that settled the matter' (Jung 1965, p. 167). He often referred to this as a period of 'disorientation', and it led to his active imaginations that resulted in *The Red Book*. In his introduction, Sonu Shamdasani notes how prevalent apocalyptic imagery was at that time (2009, p. 199). Probably most of us know Jung's apocalyptic vision from 1913 in which a flood covers much of Europe and turns into a bloody sea (Jung 1965, p. 175). The pale rider represents overwhelming dissolution like Jung's vision. Even Jung's description of yellow waves conjures the pale rider – in Greek, the horse's colour is described as greenish-yellow, the colour of a corpse. WWI broke out the following July.

Concluding Observations

I called attention to the glow in the apocalyptic images I showed; these are also evident in the video game pictures. I wonder if this glow is a hope for revelation that leads to healing. It is perhaps an indicator of soul waiting to be reclaimed, and to do that, a spiritual perspective is important. For Herman, this took the form of his deciding to do something where he could help others. In his 20s, he attended a vocational school, continued his analysis by travelling weekly to meet with me, and completed his studies. Yes, he still videogamed, but he looked back on his tendency to become inflated, and felt regret at choices he made that undermined his relationships. He had a deeper appreciation of his inner life and for what he called 'looking after the boy inside.'

Figure 3: Young man playing Fortnite. Jenny Book / Shutterstock.com, 2018.

Many, not just boys and men, search for a numinous glow on their screens. I fear for them, because they will not find anything soulful there. Being online pulls for two-dimensional thinking and it flattens our relating, somewhat appropriate consequences, given that most computer source code is binary. I cite examples of this lack of depth in my book about male alienation (Tyminski 2019). Cyberspace is effective at reinforcing alienation, specifically when it indoctrinates us to transactional values. Consider that it:

- Degrades the symbolic
- Gives wide latitude to magical thinking
- Narrows appreciation of otherness
- Reinforces splitting
- Concretizes exchanges
- Distances us from one another (virtual is unreal and disembodied)
- Appears to create greater risks for boys and men
- Spreads restricting definitions of masculinity and gender

These considerable risks interfere with an individuation process, especially its spiritual dimensions. A recent *Washington Post* article explains the further risks for alienated boys being recruited online by extremist groups such as white supremacists (Gibson 2019).

What Jung refers to as numinous William James calls 'an element or quality ... which we can meet nowhere else' (James 2002, p. 52). He explains that this establishes a capacity 'for union with *something larger than ourselves*', and such union provides us quiet, peace and calm (ibid., p. 570). The sense of feeling whole implicit in this union is foreign to alienation, the more severe forms of which are characteristic of paranoid-schizoid functioning. When, however, suffering is not externalized, a possibility emerges of the depressive position, in which internal objects can reach toward mysteries beyond an individual psyche. Soulful union belongs to another path from that pointing to apocalypse.

The following verse by T.S. Eliot (1934) expresses a bit of this wonder:

> 'We thank Thee for the light that we have kindled,
> The light of altar and of sanctuary;
> Small lights of those who meditate at midnight
> And lights directed through the coloured panes of windows
> And light reflected from the polished stone,
> The gilded carven wood, the coloured fresco.
> Our gaze is submarine, our eyes look upward
> And see the light that fractures through unquiet water.
> We see the light but see not whence it comes.'

(*The Rock*, pp. 84-85)

References

American Academy of Pediatrics. (2016). Guidelines for online and screen time. www.aap.org

Anzieu, D. (1989). *The Skin Ego*, trans. C. Turner. New Haven: Yale University Press.

Bible, King James Version. (1997). Oxford: Oxford University Press.

Economist. March 2, 2019. 'Video gamers v couch potatoes.'

Eliot, T.S. (1934). *The Rock*. New York: Harcourt, Brace and Company.

Gibson, C. (September 17, 2019). 'Do you have white teenage sons? Listen up. How white supremacists are recruiting boys online.' *Washington Post*, online version, accessed September 17, 2019.

Heimer, R. (2019). www.unrankedsmurfs.com/blog/players-2017 Accessed June 15, 2019.

Humphries, M. (July 29, 2019). '16-year-old wins $3M in first every *Fortnite* world cup.' www.pcmag.com/news/369799/16-year-old-wins-first-ever-fortnite-world-cup-and-3m Accessed September 17, 2019.

James, W. (2002). *The Varieties of Religious Experience: A Study on Human Nature*. New York: The Modern Library.

Jung, C.G. (1927). 'Analytical psychology and Weltanschauung', *CW* 8.

– (1965). *Memories, Dreams, Reflections*. Ed. A. Jaffe. New York: Vintage Books.

– (2009). *The Red Book. Liber Novus*, ed. S. Shamdasani. New York & London: W.W. Norton & Co.
Lemma, A. (2010). *Under the Skin: A Psychoanalytic Study of Body Modification*. London: Routledge.
Lemma, A., Brady, M. & Tyminski, R. (2012). 'Ink, hole, and scars: The stories our bodies narrate.' Panel discussion at the Northern California Society for Psychoanalytic Psychology, Annual Conference, Berkeley, California, March 10, 2012.
O'Hear, N.F.H. (2011). *Contrasting Images of the Book of Revelation in Late Medieval and Early Modern Art: A Case Study in Visual Exegesis*. Oxford: Oxford University Press.
Panofsky, E. (1943/2005). *The Life and Art of Albrecht Dürer*. Princeton: Princeton University Press.
Pew Research Center. (2010). 'Millennials: Confident. Connected. Open to change.' www.pewsocialtrends.org/2010/02/24/millennials-confident-connected-open-to-change/ Accessed February 15, 2019.
www.polygon.com/fortnite/2018/9/20/17884036/how-many-fortnite-monthly-players-2018 Accessed February 15, 2019.
www.statista.com/statistics/865625/fortnite-players-gender/ Accessed February 15, 2019.
Tyminski, R. (2019). *Male Alienation at the Crossroads of Identity, Culture and Cyberspace*. London: Routledge.

Tuesday, 27 August 2019

Panel
Encountering the other within: Dream research in Analytical Psychology and the relationship of ego and other parts of the psyche

Jungian theory of dreaming and contemporary dream research findings from the research project 'Structural Dream Analysis'

Christian Roesler
(DGAP) Freiburg, Germany

To provide empirical support for analytical psychology's main concepts is difficult in some fields, namely archetype theory, but regarding Jung's theory of dreaming there is a surprisingly large amount of support coming from empirical dream research. I have been investigating the connection between dreams and the course of psychotherapy in Jungian analysis, and I have found that there is strong empirical support for our Jungian perspective on the role of dreams.

We know that Freud's and Jung's perspectives differ in many aspects, and so they do regarding dreaming and dream interpretation. Whereas Freud (1900) was convinced that dreaming serves the function of protecting sleep by distorting the unconscious meaning of the dream, Jung saw the dream as a total picture of the current situation of the psyche including unconscious aspects; later he added that the dream compensates the attitude of ego consciousness. So, in a certain sense Freud sees the dream as covering its meaning, whereas Jung believes that the dream uncovers the unconscious. A specific contribution which Jung made to the theory of dreaming is that, in dreams, parts of the personality which are not yet integrated or even being manifest through conflict (in the sense of complexes), can appear personified. From the Jungian point of view the interesting question is: what is the relationship of dream ego, as representing the ego complex and the strength of consciousness, and these other parts of the psyche? Is the ego in the dream capable of dealing with these parts or even integrating them or will they appear as a threat to the ego?

Parallel to these psychoanalytic approaches to dreaming, an independent tradition of empirical dream research has developed following the discovery of rapid eye movement (REM) (Aserinsky

& Kleitman 1953), which has produced a large corpus of empirical findings on the functions of dreaming and its connection to waking life. I will first give an overview of these findings of empirical dream research and describe how they support or contradict psychoanalytic theories of dreaming, and will then present findings from my own research on dreams in psychotherapy using the method of Structural Dream Analysis.

Empirical dream research

Hall and Van de Castle (1966), who developed a coding system for the content of dreams, argued that it is possible to draw a personality profile based only on a person's dreams. Furthermore, there is substantial continuity in the themes in a person's dreams over a long period of time (Levin 1990). And Cartwright (1977), found that the themes in the dreams change when a person goes through psychotherapy. In a study on the dreams of persons with multiple personality disorder, Barrett (1996) was able to demonstrate that the split-off parts of their personalities appeared personified in their dreams. Greenberg and Pearlman (1978) compared the content of dreams of patients currently in psychoanalysis with the protocols of their therapy sessions that coincided with the time of the dream, and found a strong connection between the themes in the dreams and their psychotherapy. The dream could be read as a report about the current conflictual themes in the waking life of the dreamer. Palombo (1982) could show that clients reprocess contents from their last analytical session in their subsequent dreams and Popp, Luborsky and Crits-Christoph (1990) found that both therapy narratives and dreams were structured using the same unconscious relationship patterns. Therefore, today's most prominent theory of dreaming derived from empirical research is the so-called continuity hypothesis, which says that there is a continuity in mental functioning from waking life to sleep (for a more detailed discussion see Roesler 2018a).

According to Barrett and McNamara (2007), the results of empirical dream research can be summarized in the following way: in the dream, the brain is in a mode where it does not have to process new input but can use larger capacities for working on problems and finding creative solutions. The dream especially focuses on experiences in waking life that have emotional meaning for the dreamer. The dreaming mind can find solutions for problems more readily compared to waking consciousness because it is able to connect different areas and functions of the brain. This supports the view taken by Jung (1971), which sees the psyche as a self-regulating system and the dream as a spontaneously produced picture of the current situation of the psyche in the form of symbols. It seems that empirical dream research, though not having any intention of testing Jungian theory, has become quite supportive of Jung's theory of the dream.

Jung differentiates between a 'subjective' level and an 'objective' level to dreams. In the first perspective, the figures and elements of the dream are interpreted as representing parts or qualities of the dreamer's personality (especially conflictual parts, i.e. complexes), whereas in the objective perspective, they are seen as representing persons or entities existing in reality. In dreams, the unconscious psyche attempts to support ego consciousness and foster a process of personality integration by pointing to parts of the psyche not yet integrated into the whole of personality, or to indicate unresolved conflicts. Through dreams, the unconscious, because it contains a more holistic knowledge about the development and integration of personality, brings new information to consciousness, which can then be integrated, if a conscious understanding of the information is possible. This is the aim of dream interpretation in psychotherapy. So Jungian dream interpretation focuses on the relationship of the dream ego (i.e. the figure in the dream which experiences the dreamer as 'myself', psychoanalytically representing ego consciousness) to the other figures in the dream, which gives an indication, through the imagery, of the ability of the ego to cope with emotions, impulses and complexes (being represented in this symbolic form in the dream), and the strength of ego consciousness. Since the information in dreams comes in the form of symbols and images, it needs translation to be understood by the conscious ego.

Contemporary conceptualizations of dreaming based on empirical research strongly question the assumptions in Freud's classic theory on dreaming and dream interpretation: there is no evidence for a process of distortion which leads to a difference between manifest and latent meaning and also the dream is not 'the keeper of the sleep' etc. (Fiss 1995). In the last decades, there has been development in the reconceptualization of psychoanalytic dream theories influenced by insights from empirical dream research. This has led to a convergence of contemporary Freudian dream theories, moving towards Jung's understanding of the dream (e.g. Fosshage 1987; Levin 1990). As a result of this research, some contemporary Freudian dream theories have incorporated a number of aspects of Jungian dream theory. An example of this convergence can be found in the dream theory of Fosshage (1987, 1997), which focuses on the functions of the dream as a regulator of emotions and integrator of psychological organization. On the other hand, scholars and researchers from the Freudian tradition (even though quoting the empirical evidence speaking against Freudian assumptions), still argue for a process of censorship in dreaming – which results in a distortion of the latent content – and also for the theory of wish fulfilment of dreams. The overall function of dreaming is still supposed to be protecting the sleeper from being alarmed by repressed impulses (Werner & Langenmeyer 2005; Fisher & Greenberg 1977, 1996).

The research project 'Structural Dream Analysis'

There is also a long tradition of clinical research on dreams in psychoanalysis (Fonagy et al. 2012). A problem with these approaches is that they often include assumptions taken from psychoanalytic theories, e.g. that the dream serves as a guardian of sleep. We attempted to prevent the research method from implicitly including any theoretical psychodynamic assumptions about the dream. Consequently, Structural Dream Analysis (SDA) was developed as a method to investigate dreams from a structuralist point of view.

The usual research approaches investigating the meaning of dream content make use of coding systems, e.g. the well-known coding system of Hall and Van de Castle (1966). Furthermore, in psychoanalytic dream research, elaborated coding systems for dream content have been developed and used in studies investigating the process of psychotherapy (e.g. Moser & von Zeppelin, 1991). In psychoanalytic research on dreams (see Fonagy et al. 2012, for a current overview), there is often the problem that basic assumptions about the function of dreams are taken for granted. For example, the Moser and von Zeppelin coding system is based on the assumption that the function of dreaming is to protect sleep and so investigates the changing positions of elements in the dream which 'evidences' this function. But as it is, this coding system is not able to falsify any Freudian assumptions.

In our study, we attempted to prevent the research method from implicitly including any theoretical psychodynamic assumptions about the dream. Consequently, Structural Dream Analysis, was developed as a method to investigate dreams from a structuralist point of view. The assumption is that the meaning of a dream consists not so much in it containing certain symbols or elements but more in the relationship between the elements and in the course of action which the dream takes, i.e. its structure. The aforementioned coding systems, which count the appearance of certain elements and symbols in dreams, from our point of view, are not able to identify the meaning of dreams, since meaning is the result of interpretation. An example is the famous system built on content analysis of over 50,000 dreams by Hall and Nordby (1972). Typical dreams reported in this classification involved aggression, predatory animals, flying, falling, being persecuted by hostile strangers, landscapes, dreams of misfortune, sex, getting married and having children, taking examinations or undergoing some similar ordeals, travelling, swimming or being in the water, watching fires, and being confined in an underground place. The problem with this kind of classification, from my point of view, is that these typical dream motifs describe very different entities, from objects and beings to action patterns and story structures. There is no theoretical model behind such a classification which could connect the dream motifs with a meaning for the dreamer. This position has already criticized by Stevens (1995), who gives the following example: 'Simple content analyses reveal that agonistic dreams are more common among males of all ages and hedonic dreams more common among females, but both types of dreams occur in both sexes. A more significant variable than gender in determining the relative incidence of such dreams is the kind of family the individual grew up in' (p. 249).

Structural Dream Analysis is a qualitative, interpretive research method that attempts to formalize the process of interpretation of the dream in a way that the conclusions are independent from the interpreter. In our study, a reliability test found an interpreter agreement for the results coming from the same case of $k = .70 - .82$. Structural Dream Analysis sees the dream as a narrative. In narratology, a narrative is defined as a development from a starting point, which often is a problem that needs repair or solution. The narrative goes through ups and downs leading to the solution of the problem or a valued endpoint to the story (Gülich & Quasthoff 1985). Similarly, the dream is a short story about how the protagonist, in most cases the dream ego, processes a problem. Structural Dream Analysis thus makes use of analytic tools developed in narratology. Two earlier methods of narrative analysis were incorporated: a) Vladimir Propp's (1975) structuralist method of Functional Analysis used to investigate the structure of fairy tales. Each fairy-tale is divided into its functional parts (e.g. 'The King is ill and needs healing'; 'The hero fights the Dragon') and each functional part receives an abstract symbol, e.g. a letter or number. As a result, each fairy-tale can be written as an abstract formula of symbols and then different fairy-tales can be compared regarding their structure. b) Boothe's (2002) narratological method JAKOB, used in analytical psychotherapies for the analysis of patient narratives and their development over the course of the psychotherapy. This method focuses on the role the narrator takes in the narrative in terms of activity vs. passivity and his/her relation to other protagonists in the narrative, as well as on different episodic models which describe the course the narrative takes.

The meaning of symbols in the dreams we investigated was analysed by a systematized form of amplification. In psychotherapy, the analyst assumes that the series of dreams presented by the analysand follows an inner structure of meaning. Structural Dream Analysis aims at identifying this inner structure of meaning from the series of dreams alone, without referring to additional information about the dreamer, their psychodynamics or the course of psychotherapy. The meaning conveyed by the dream is analysed in a systematic series of interpretive steps for which a formalized manual is available (for more details see Roesler 2018b). The interpreters, who have no information about the dreamer, are given a series of 10 to 20 dreams covering the whole course of the psychotherapy and which ideally mark the core points and topics of it. The dreams are provided by practising analysts who also write a case report about the psychopathology and psychodynamics of the patient involved, as well as about the development of core conflicts and themes in the course of the therapy. Only when the dream series are completely analysed using Structural Dream Analysis are the results compared to the reports by the therapists.

Structural Dream Analysis allows for systematic and objective analysis of the meaning of dreams produced by patients in psychotherapies. The method focuses especially on the relationship between the dream ego and other figures in the dream and the extent of activity of the dream ego. The following questions are investigated: Are generalized structures to be found in the development of dreams in successful psychotherapies compared to failed ones? Are there connections between type of psychopathology, e.g. depression, and the symbols and structures in the dreams?

Results

A major finding is that a high percentage of all dreams from all cases can be categorized by a very limited number of structural patterns. The most general pattern can be described as: the ego is confronted with a requirement, has to cope with a challenge, has to fulfil a plan or task. This general pattern can be differentiated into five more specific patterns regarding the extent of agency of the dream ego:

Whereas in Pattern 1 there is no ego present at all, in Patterns 2 and 3 the dream ego is present but under pressure from other forces in the dream and the initiative is not with the ego but with others. The ego is subjected to their activity, power and control. In Patterns 4 and 5 the ego has taken over the initiative and attempts to follow a personal plan but may be confronted with difficulties. In Pattern 5 this activity focuses on a social relationship.

Pattern 1: No dream ego present

In the dream there is no dream ego present, the dreamer just observes a scene as if watching a movie and does not actively take part in the dream. In some cases, the dream ego flies above and looks down on a scene or happenings in the dream.

Pattern 2: The dream ego is threatened

In dreams of this kind the dream ego is threatened, e.g. attacked or injured, and usually tries to escape or protect itself against the threatening figures. In b) to d) below, the dream ego very often reacts with panic and either feels powerless or tries to escape from the threat. Often this results in the dream ego being chased by the threatening figures. The dreams in this pattern can be differentiated depending on the severity of the threat.

a) the dream ego is damaged, e.g. severely wounded, or even killed. In some cases, the killing has already happened and the dream ego is found as a dead body.

b) the threat to the dream ego comes from a force in nature, e.g. a natural disaster, earthquake, fire, flooding, storm etc.

c) the dream ego is threatened by (dangerous) animals.

d) the dream ego is threatened by human beings, e.g. criminals, murderers or 'evil people', or human-like figures, e.g. ghosts, shadows etc.

Pattern 3: The dream ego is confronted with a performance requirement

The dream ego is confronted with a performance requirement, which is set by another figure or agency in the dream. The dream ego is confronted with a task which it has to fulfil, or is required to find something or to give something to another person in the dream so that they can fulfil a task etc. The most common form of this pattern is the examination dream. An important part of this pattern is that the initiative is not with the dream ego but with other figures confronting the dream ego with a requirement. The dream ego is subjected to their control and power.

a) Examination in a school or university setting.

b) The dream ego is subject to an inspection by an official person, e.g. a ticket inspection on the train where the right of the dream ego is questioned.

c) the dream ego has the task to find something (which was lost before), get something, produce something etc.

A very typical pattern in these kinds of dreams is that the dream ego does not feel capable of performing the task, does not possess the right tools or capabilities, or has failed to bring these devices, has lost them on the way etc. For example, the dream ego is not prepared for the examination, or arrives too late for it.

Pattern 4: Mobility dream

The dream ego is moving towards a specified or unclear destination, e.g. travelling and making use of different forms of transportation, like a bicycle, car, bus, train, airplane, ship etc. An interesting differentiation is the question of whether these transportation devices are public or individual. Again, this form of dream can be differentiated depending on the extent of the dream ego's agency, which shows in the extent to which the dream ego determines its own movement.

a) disorientation: the dream ego has no idea where to go, even where it is and there are no signs of direction etc.

b) the dream ego is locked up in a closed space, imprisoned etc., and is looking for a way to get out.

c) the dream ego wants to move, travel etc. but has no means to do so, e.g. it misses the train

d) the dream ego attempts to move and has some means of transportation but cannot control the movement, e.g. it cannot steer a car.

e) the dream ego is moving but the way is blocked or the means of transport breaks down or crashes and movement cannot be continued.

f) the dream ego is moving, making use of some means of transportation but it is going the wrong way, is in the wrong train or bus, or is not authorized to use it (e.g. has no ticket) and therefore cannot continue the journey.

g) In the positive form, the dream ego succeeds in moving towards and reaching the desired destination.

Pattern 5: Social interaction dream

The dream ego is occupied with making contact or communicating with another person or figure in the dream. The dream ego wants to get in contact with another person, or is in communication and attempts to communicate something to the other person, or is more generally occupied with creating a desired contact with the other person which can include sexual contact. This dream pattern can be differentiated depending on the dream ego's activity and how successful it is in reaching its desired contact.

a) the dream ego wants to get into contact but is ignored by others.

b) the dream ego is criticized, devalued or made ridiculous by others and feels shame.

c) the dream ego is successful in creating the desired contact.

d) a special case: the dream ego is aggressive towards others (even kills others) which expresses the will of the dream ego to be separated and autonomous.

There is a strong correlation between dream content and repetitive patterns in dream series on one side and the dreamer's personality structure and psychological problems on the other. Additionally, changes in the course of psychotherapy are paralleled by a transformation in the dream patterns of the patient. The five patterns detected can be interpreted psychologically as an expression of the capacity of the dreamer's ego, on different levels, to cope with and/or control emotions, motivations and complexes. The extent of agency of the dream ego is equivalent to that which psychoanalysis calls ego strength or maturity of the personality, as well as the degree of integration of ego and other parts of the psyche into the whole of the personality and the capacity of ego functioning.

Patterns of change in the structure of dreams over the course of therapy

In this study we not only found typical patterns in the structure of the dreams but also across the whole series of dreams. A general finding was that in those cases where the psychotherapeutic intervention was successful such that there was an improvement in symptoms, psychological well-being, regulation of emotion and, from a psychoanalytic point of view, a gain in psychological structure and ego strength, we found a typical pattern of transformation in the structure of the dreams. Typically, the first half of the psychotherapeutic process was dominated by a repetitive pattern in the dreams, which was connected with the psychological problems of the dreamer, in the sense as described above. Generally, in the middle of the dream series there appears a dream or dream symbol which marks a change in the pattern (see more details below). The second half of the dream series is then typically characterized by a change in the repetitive pattern:

In Pattern 2 (the dream ego is threatened), the dream ego changes its reaction to the threat. Instead of escaping, it confronts the threatening figures, fights actively, finds constructive strategies to cope with the threat and, towards the end of the dream series, succeeds in overcoming the threat.

Example: In case 7, the dream ego in the first half of the series is threatened by water in the form of giant waves, flooding etc. and usually drowns in the flood. In the second half of the series, however, the dream ego more and more succeeds in moving to a safe place on dry land. Furthermore, a transformative pattern emerges in which the dream ego realizes that the seemingly threatening figures are not as dangerous and even makes friends with these figures.

Typical examples of the second transformative pattern are seen in cases 5 and 6: in case 5, in the first half of the series, the dream ego is threatened by snakes. Then in the midst of the dream series, a golden snake appears which is not dangerous. In the next dream the threatening figure changes into a salamander, then into a dark man. In case 6, the dream ego in the first half of the series is chased by dogs and tries to escape, then in the midst of the series there appear helpless and wounded dogs which need the dream ego's support but the dream ego reacts with disgust. Finally, the dream ego finds a helpless baby which needs care and support.

To summarize, in the dream series dominated by Pattern 2, the threatening figures tend to change from natural disasters or threatening wild animals to less dangerous animals and then into human beings. A similar pattern of transformation in the series of dreams can be found for those cases which are dominated by Patterns 3 and 4.

In Pattern 3 (performance requirement), the first half of the series is typically dominated by the dream ego failing to fulfil the required task. This is seen in cases where the dream ego is repeatedly confronted with an examination, is not prepared, is too late or even forgets about the examination, thereby fails and escapes etc. Change in this pattern is characterized typically by the disappearance of examination dreams in the second half of the series.

Pattern 4 (mobility): typically, in the first half of the series, the dream ego is not able to reach the desired aim, is on the wrong bus or train or has no ticket etc., the road is blocked, or the dream ego is not capable of controlling the car. In some cases, the dream ego is even walled-in and not able to escape. In the second half of the series this typically changes into the dream ego succeeding in reaching the desired aim and controlling the means of transportation.

Pattern 5 (social interaction): the cases dominated by this pattern are usually characterized by failed attempts (or passivity) of the dream ego to get into a desired contact or communication with others in the first half of the series – the dream ego is ignored by others, others forget about the ego's birthday, or the dream ego is even criticized and devalued by others. Towards the end of the dream series, the dream ego is more and more capable of creating satisfying interactions with others or it experiences care and support from others. In those cases with successful therapeutic change, the second half of their dream series is dominated more and more by Pattern 5, that is, the dream ego becomes occupied with creating a desired social interaction. And this occurs after the dream ego has succeeded in overcoming a repetitive negative pattern of being threatened or having failed mobility or negative examination dreams.

These transformative patterns were only found in cases where the therapists reported improvement on the symptom level as well as positive changes in personality structure. By contrast, there are two cases in the sample where the therapists delivered dream series to the researchers even though the therapy was not yet completed (and this information was not given to the interpreters). In these cases, repetitive patterns can also be found but with no change in the repetitive pattern in the way described above: e.g. the dream ego in most of the dreams is in a movement, usually by public transport but fails again and again to reach the desired aim because it has no ticket, or the train or tram breaks down etc.

These transformative patterns in the dream series are interpreted from a psychodynamic perspective and are seen as speaking to the fact that an initially weak ego structure, which fails to regulate and integrate threatening emotions, impulses and complexes, gains in ego strength over the course of the therapy and increasingly succeeds in coping with initially suppressed or split-off parts of the psyche and integrating these into constructive interactions with others. As a result of such gains in ego strength, the dream ego is increasingly capable of executing willpower, conducting its plans, reaching aims and expressing its needs in social interactions. This interpretation is supported by the findings from the two cases where there is no therapeutic change and where there is also no transformation of the repetitive dream pattern.

Dream patterns and symbols are connected with psychological problems of the dreamer

As a result of our study we not only found a clear correlation between therapeutic change and a transformation of patterns in the dream series, but also a clear connection between the patterns that dominate the dream series (or at least the first half of the series) on the one hand and the psychological problems and the personality structure of the dreamer on the other. The five patterns can be interpreted psychologically as imaging the capacity of the ego to cope with and/or control emotions, motivations and complexes (as unintegrated parts of the psyche). The extent of agency of the dream ego is equivalent to that which in psychoanalysis is called ego strength or maturity of the personality, that is, the degree of integration of the ego and other parts of the psyche into the whole of the personality, thus enabling positive ego functioning.

There is only one case in the sample in which Pattern I (no dream ego present) is found in its full form. In the first five dreams of the series, this dreamer just observes a scene as if watching a movie. This case is a Japanese male student, 18 years of age, who was treated because of severe school refusal over several years. The patient had retreated into total passivity and several attempts of psychotherapy, including in an inpatient setting, had failed to change the situation. This storyline in his dreams can be interpreted as an imaging of a deeply regressed personality structure and lack of a clear identity, where ego strength is at a very low level. There is an interesting parallel to another case, again a male student 18 years of age with the diagnosis of school refusal and where ego strength and identity structure are at a comparably low level. In this latter case, in several of his dreams there is a dream ego but it is hovering above the actual happenings in the dream and does not participate or is not active in any way.

Pattern 2 (the dream ego is threatened) is found in those cases diagnosed with a narcissistic disorder, connected with a very weak ego structure, where there is an unclear personal identity or blocked identity development and low self-esteem. Often such patients have developed a compensatory 'false self' whilst splitting-off unaccepted parts of their psyche. Dream images of an injury or damage to the dream ego, the dream ego being murdered or found as a dead corpse seem to be connected on the psychological level with more severe cases of low self-esteem, a 'narcissistic wound' or even traumatization. From a psychodynamic point of view, such motifs in the dreams can be interpreted as a weak ego struggling with overwhelming forces derived from split-off emotions, impulses and complexes, as well as devaluing introjects that continually threaten the functioning of ego consciousness. Development in psychotherapy – and in the dreams – is characterized by a growth in ego strength, which becomes more and more capable of coping with the threatening parts of the psyche and accepting them as integral parts of the personality.

Pattern 3, especially examination dreams, and Pattern 4, where the dream ego attempts to move in a desired direction, is found to occur in those cases with a more stable ego structure (as diagnosed by the therapist), but where the patient has problems with making decisions and taking progressive steps in life, such as completing exams and deciding on a professional career.

Pattern 5, where the dream ego is involved in social interactions, characterizes those cases where a stable ego is diagnosed by the therapist but where the patient struggles with neurotic problems around interpersonal relationships, such as finding an intimate partner and creating a satisfying, intimate and erotic relationship. This pattern can be interpreted as imaging a more mature personality structure, which is not so much struggling for integrity of the ego but rather more with interpersonal relationships. This interpretation is supported by the finding that in positively developing psychotherapies/dream series, often a repetitive pattern on a lower level is overcome and replaced by dreams following Pattern 5 in the second half of the therapy.

It is also found in a number of cases that a dominating symbol, which appears repeatedly as part of a repetitive pattern, usually of Pattern 2 (where the dream ego is threatened by this symbol), is strongly connected with the psychological situation or problem of the dreamer, e.g. in one case, the female dreamer is repeatedly threatened by snakes. In this case, the therapist diagnosed a strong tension in the personality between a very moralistic superego, on the one hand, and very lively erotic and sexual desires, on the other. The snake can clearly be interpreted as a sexual, phallic symbol, which appears threatening to an ego under the pressure of the moralistic superego. But there is also clear evidence from the dreams in this study that the meaning of a symbol can be totally different in other cases; e.g. the snake in case 8 has the role of a helper. In the case described above, the threatening dogs are symbolically summarizing the unresolved problems of the dreamer concerning violence, sadism, sexual obsessions and a deeply wounded self-esteem. In summary, symbols appearing repeatedly in dream series can often be interpreted as symbolic images for parts of the psyche, its impulses and complexes, which are not yet integrated into the personality as a whole and which therefore appear threatening to ego integrity.

Transformative dreams

In those cases which were considered as successful therapies from the viewpoint of the therapist, that is, with improvement or even fundamental changes in the personality structure of the patient, certain changes in the dream stories coincided with positive shifts in the therapy. Usually such transformative dreams were found in the middle of the dream series following a series of dreams with a repetitive pattern, e.g. threat and escape imagery which was not continued after the transformative dream. These transformative dreams stand out as they show a great variety of images and structures and are usually experienced with positive emotions in the dreamer.

Nevertheless, a similar motif was found in about half of the cases who had transformative dreams: a baby or young child, which needed help and support, played a major role in these dreams. The dream ego was asked to care for and give support to the child but had initial difficulties in turning towards and taking appropriate care of the child (see case example above). This motif is interesting insofar as Jung pointed out that the archetype of the child is connected with transformation in psychotherapeutic processes (Jung 1981) and, further, a number of models of psychotherapy focus on supporting the patient to turn towards and take care of his or her 'inner wounded child'. Other motifs in these transformative dreams included: the appearance of helpers who support the dream ego in coping with threatening figures; the dream ego succeeding in working its way through narrow tubes or tunnels and the dream ego celebrating freedom with a dance.

Discussion

As a result of our findings we form this hypothesis: the relationship between the dream ego and threatening figures, and the reaction of the dream ego to the threat, is imaging the relationship between actual ego strength and unintegrated or conflicted parts of the psyche, unconscious and repressed needs, motivations and complexes. The special form the threatening figure takes in the dream can be seen as symbolizing the psychological problem, the complex or repressed impulse with which the dreamer is struggling, especially if the dream pattern is repetitive. Patients whose dreams are shaped mainly by the threat / escape pattern, usually struggle with structural problems around an unstable ego and personality with unclear boundaries, whereas patients with dreams of mobility and interpersonal relationships seem to have more integrated personalities and higher ego strength and are preoccupied with more neurotic and interpersonal problems.

We would also hypothesize that there is a typical change in dream patterns over the course of successful therapies. Typically, the first half of the psychotherapeutic process was dominated by a repetitive pattern in the dreams, which was connected with the psychological problems of the dreamer. Generally, in the middle of the dream series, there appears a dream or dream symbol which marks a change in the pattern. The second half of the dream series is then typically characterized by a change in the repetitive pattern: dreams move from Patterns 1, 2 and 3 in the first half of a successful therapy process, where there are failed attempts by the dream ego to move and create relationships in a desirable way, to Patterns 4 and 5 where successful activities and control by the dream ego are seen.

These transformative patterns in the dream series are interpreted from a psychodynamic perspective and are seen as speaking to the fact that an initially weak ego structure, which fails to regulate and integrate threatening emotions, impulses and complexes, gains in ego strength over the course of the therapy and increasingly succeeds in coping with initially suppressed or split off parts of the psyche and integrating these into constructive interactions with others (see also fig. 1). As a result of such gains in ego strength, the dream ego is capable of increasingly executing willpower, conducting its plans, reaching aims and expressing its needs in social interactions. This interpretation is supported by the findings from two cases where there is no therapeutic change and where there is also no transformation of the repetitive dream pattern.

Since these findings are based on cases from Jungian psychotherapies, we attempted to test the hypothesis with a classical Freudian case, the so-called specimen case Amalia X. This is a Freudian psychoanalysis of more than 500 sessions, which was fully documented on video and was subject of more than 100 scientific investigations (Kächele 2012; Kächele et al. 1999, 2006). This case included 93 dreams which were discussed over the course of therapy. As it is considered to be a very successful therapy, we assumed that we would find a movement from patterns 1 and 2 to patterns 4 and 5 over the course of therapy. This hypothesis could be empirically confirmed.

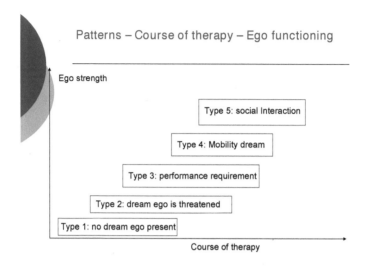

Fig. 1: *Changes in dream patterns over the course of therapy in connection with improvements in ego strength*

The findings of this study also support the hypothesis that dreams can be understood as an image of the current situation of the dreamer's psyche as a whole, including aspects and processes which are unconscious and not accessible to waking life consciousness. The findings of this study show no evidence of a process of censorship in the sense of Freud. Even though psychological problems and the state of ego integrity of the dreamer were symbolized in the dreams in the form of images as well as in the form of patterns, no distortion could be found. Instead, the manifest content of the dream was clearly picturing the psychological situation of the dreamer, in most cases even dramatically. Our findings also refute the hypothesis of wish fulfilment of dreams. Instead, most of the dreams, especially in the first half of the psychotherapy process, were putting the strongest fears of the dreamer into clear images.

Insofar as the extent of ego functioning and the psychological problems of the dreamers are mirrored in the dream patterns and symbols, these findings support the continuity hypothesis (Domhoff 2017).

The Jungian view of dreams could also provide a synthesis for the debate around continuity versus discontinuity of dream content and waking life experience. As Hobson and Schredl (2011), in their discussion of the continuity hypothesis point out, dreams actually contain elements of waking life on a thematic level but this does not explain the occurrence of elements in dreams which dreamers have never experienced in their waking life. As they say, 'This raises the intriguing question: If dreaming is not entirely derived from waking experience, then just what is the source of the anomalous content and what is its function?' (p. 3). Hoss (2011) in his commentary on the debate, argues, following Jung, that the distortions of waking content are not misrepresentations but are rather the 'unconscious aspect' of the waking event expressed in the dream not as a rational thought but as a symbolic image.

Based on my own findings and those from earlier studies, I would say that there is no real evidence for a compensating activity in dreams, as Jung claims. There is more evidence for Jung's first theory, that the dream presents a more holistic picture of the total situation of the psyche, including unconscious aspects. In this sense, the function of dreams could be called not so much compensating, but more of completing the picture by adding aspects that are not accessible for waking life consciousness. Of course, in a case where there is a strong split between the conscious attitude of the ego and unconscious processes, this can lead to a compensating effect. Nevertheless, in our study, the function of the dreams, e.g. in Pattern 2 (threat and escape), seems more to be to present the full reality of the inner world to ego consciousness.

In the future, we will try to strengthen our hypothesis regarding the five patterns and their connection with psychopathology and the development of psychotherapy. We will do so by analysing 150 cases we received from the Jung Institute Stüttgart. We will also investigate the appearance of the child symbol and whether it has a transformative character for the whole series of dreams. I believe that this kind of research is capable of providing support for one of the most important concepts of analytical psychology, the theory of dreaming.

References

Aserinsky, E. & Kleitman, N. (1953). Regularly occurring periods of eye motility and concomitant phenomena during sleep. *Science* 118, 273-74.

Barrett, D. 1996. 'Dreams in multiple personality'. In *Trauma and Dreams*, ed. D. Barrett. Cambridge, MA: Harvard University Press.

Barrett, D. & McNamara, P. (eds.) (2007). *The New Science of Dreaming. Vol. 2: Content, Recall and Personality Correlates*. Westport: Praeger.

Boothe, B. (2002). Kodiermanual zur Erzählanalyse JAKOB. *Berichte aus der Klinische Psychologie, Nr.52*. Zürich: Universität Zürich, Psychologisches Institut.

Cartwright, R. D. (1977). *Night Life. Explorations in Dreaming.* Englewood Cliffs: Prentice-Hall.
Domhoff, G. W. (2017). The invasion of the concept snatchers: The origins, distortions, and future of the continuity hypothesis. *Dreaming,* 27, 1, 14-39.
Fisher, S. & Greenberg, R. P. (1977). *The Scientific Credibility of Freud's Theories and Therapy.* Hassocks: Harvester Press.
— (1996). *Freud Scientifically Reappraised. Testing the Theories and Therapy.* New York: Wiley.
Fiss, H. (1995). 'The post-Freudian dream. A reconsideration of dream theory based on recent sleep laboratory findings'. In *The Significance of Dreams: Bridging Clinical and Extraclinical Research in Psychoanalysis,* eds. P. Fonagy, H. Kächele, M. Leuzinger-Bohleber & D. Taylor. (2012). London: Karnac.
Fosshage, J. L. (1987). 'New vistas on dream interpretation'. In *Dreams in New Perspective. The Royal Road Revisited,* ed. M. Glucksman. New York: Uman Sciences Press.
— (1997). 'The organizing functions of dreaming mentation'. *Contemporary Psychoanalysis,* 33, 429-58.
Freud, S. (1900). *The Interpretation of Dreams.* SE 4 & 5.
Greenberg, R., Pearlman, C. (1978). 'If Freud only knew. A reconsideration of psychoanalytic dream theory'. *International Review of Psycho-Analysis,* 5, 71-75.
Gülich, E. & Quasthoff, U. (1985). 'Narrative analysis'. In *Handbook of Discourse Analysis, Vol. II: Dimensions of Discourse* (pp. 169-97), ed. T. A. van Dijk. London: Academic Press.
Hall, C. S., & Nordby, V. J. (1972). *The Individual and His Dreams.* New York: New American Library.
Hall, C. S., & Van De Castle, R. L. (1966). *The Content Analysis of Dreams.* New York: Appleton-Century-Crofts.
Hobson, J. A., & Schredl, M. (2011). 'The continuity and discontinuity between waking and dreaming: A dialogue between Michael Schredl and Allan Hobson concerning the adequacy and completeness of these notions'. *International Journal of Dream Research,* 4, 1, 3-7.
Hoss, R. J. (2011). 'The continuity and discontinuity between waking and dreaming from the perspective of an analytical psychological construct'. *International Journal of Dream Research,* 4, 2, 81-83.
Jung, C. G. (1971). *Allgemeine Gesichtspunkte zur Psychologie des Traumes.* GW Bd. 8. Olten: Walter.
Jung, C. G. (1981). *Die Archetypen und das Kollektive Unbewusste.* GW Bd. 9/I. Olten: Walter.
Kächele, H., Eberhardt, J., & Leuzinger-Bohleber, M. (1999). *Expressed relationships, dream atmosphere and problem solving in Amalia's dreams—Dream series as process tool to investigate cognitive changes—A single case study. Psychoanalytic process research strategies II.* Ulm: Ulmer Textbank.
Kächele, H., Leuzinger-Bohleber, M., Buchheim, A., & Thomä, H. (2006). 'Amalie X – ein deutscher Musterfall (Ebene I und Ebene II)'. In *Psychoanalytische Therapie* (pp. 121-74). Springer, Berlin, Heidelberg.
Kächele, H. (2012). 'Dreams as subject of psychoanalytical treatment research'. In *The Significance of Dreams. Bridging Clinical and Extraclinical*

Research in Psychoanalysis; (pp. 89-100), eds. P. Fonagy, H. Kächele, M. Leuzinger-Bohleber & D. Taylor. London: Karnac.
Levin, R. (1990). 'Psychoanalytic theories on the function of dreaming. A review of the empirical dream research'. In *Empirical studies of psychoanalytic theories*, ed. J.M. Masling. Hillsdale NJ: Erlbaum.
Moser, U. & v. Zeppelin, I. (1991). *Cognitive-Affective Processes*. Berlin, New York: Springer.
Palombo, S.R. (1982). 'How the dream works. The role of dreaming in the psychotherapeutic process'. In *Curative factors in dynamic psychotherapy* (pp. 223-42), ed. S. Slipp. New York: McGraw Hill.
Popp, C., Luborsky, L. & Crits-Christoph, P. (1990). 'The parallel of the CCRT from therapy narratives with the CCRT from dreams'. In *Understanding Transference. The CCRT method* (pp. 158-72), eds. L. Luborsky & P. Crits-Christoph. New York: Basic Books.
Propp, V. (1975). *Morphologie des Märchens*. Frankfurt a.M.: Surkamp.
Roesler, C. (2018a): 'Jungian dream interpretation and empirical dream research'. In *Research in Analytical Psychology*, ed. C. Roesler. London: Routledge.
— (2018b): 'Structural Dream Analysis: a narrative research method for investigating the meaning of dream series in analytical psychotherapies'. *International Journal of Dream Research*, 11, 1, 21-29.
Stevens, A. (1995). *Private Myths: Dreams and Dreaming*. London: Hamish Hamilton.
Werner, C. & Langenmayr, A. (2005). *Der Traum und die Fehlleistungen. Psychoanalyse und Empirie* (Bd. 2). Göttingen: Vandenhoeck und Ruprecht.

On the relationship between the sense of self and the structure of dreams examined through questionnaire research for Japanese university students

Yasuhiro Tanaka
(AJAJ) *Kyoto, Japan*

Focusing on the 'structure' of dreams

Conventional researches on dreams have mainly focused on the 'content' both quantitatively and qualitatively. However, when reflecting on Jung's emphasis on the importance of 'interpretation on the subjective level' (Jung 1953, para. 131), that is, self-relation expressed in dreams, or his observation that there are '…a great many "average" dreams in which a *definite structure* can be perceived' (Jung 1960, para. 561, italics added), it could be seen as natural and appropriate that psychotherapists have recently noticed the importance of the structure of dreams (e.g. Roesler 2018, Konakawa 2018).

Following this stream, my colleagues and I focus on the following three viewpoints in this research: 1) relationship between dream-ego and others (self-relation) in the dream, 2) sense of agency of the dream-ego, and 3) continuity of the place and time where the relationship (self-relation) develops and the viewpoint of dream-ego.

Structural changes of youth mind in Japan, or all over the world

Many psychotherapists in Japan, especially those working in school counselling services, have experienced over ten years that young people have difficulty holding, or sustaining anxiety; they have trouble with 'their disability to suffer a torment persistently' (Takaishi 2009). In the 1960s and the 1970s, however, there were many case reports and studies on anthropophobia. It is a peculiar neurosis in Japan, regarded as a clinical state that occurs frequently during puberty and adolescence, where one backs away from interpersonal relationships as much as possible because of unreasonably high levels of anxiety in interpersonal situations. Young people suffering anthropophobia in this group could *neurotically* suffer a torment, or keep their initial psychological problem, for which they sought psychotherapy. However, according to Hirosawa (2015), a Japanese psychiatrist working for a university counselling centre, young people today have persistent difficulty implicating and orienting their experiences by themselves

Three viewpoints to see dream-structure	Detailed check items
1) Relationship between dream-ego and others	a. Is approach from dream-ego, or from others?
	b. Is interaction between dream-ego and others established or not? (Is there only dream-ego or only others?)
	c. Quality of approach from others (direct or indirect, predictable or unpredictable, friendly or unfriendly?)
	d. Which has the initiative, dream-ego or others?
	e. Does some trouble happen, involving dream-ego? Even under such situation, does dream-I have the initiative?
2) Sense of agency of dream-ego	f. Does dream-I have some intention, or not? If so, does dream-I actualize it, or not?
	g. To what extent does dream-I cope with a given situation on his or her own initiative? (Dream-I's agentic coping or others' coping? Is dream-I passive there, or not?)
	h. To what extent is dream-I's action spontaneous? (Can dream-I control his or her action? Does dream-I nip an evil in the bud?)
	i. Result of dream-I's action (Is his or her action effective or a failure?
	j. Dream-I's emotional stability (How unstable? How conflictual? Does dream-ego sustain conflict persistently?)
3) Continuity of place, time and viewpoint of dream-ego	k. Continuity of place (Unambiguous boundary of dream-ego, objects, and places, discontinuity of states of objects, ambiguity of substance of objects)
	l. Continuity of time sequence (Does dream have the "introduction, development, turn and conclusion"?
	m. Continuity of dream-ego's perspective (Is there detailed description from dream-ego's viewpoint? Is dream-scenery comprehended well or in detail? Is the continuity of dream-ego's state maintained?

Table 1. Check items included three viewpoints to see dream-structure

due to their *weak sense of self*. We may say that the situation has completely changed.

Of course, it is hard for psychotherapists to practise psychologically with clients who are not able to sustain their anxiety or suffer torment persistently because conventional psychotherapy has presupposed clients' ability to do so and to come and see us with their problems, torments, or distresses. But they are in the status of 'before-anxiety', or 'before-suffering'; they just come to see us without their own peculiar problem. This kind of tendency is very typical in the young generation, but it can also be observed in a wider age group in our practice.

As Jung described, 'the dream is a spontaneous self-portrayal, in symbolic form, of the actual situation in the unconscious' (Jung 1954, para. 505) or 'a symbolical representation of an unconscious content' (ibid., para. 506), therefore we may gain an understanding of the psychic structure of young people today by conducting a questionnaire of their dreams, anthropophobia mentality, and sense of self. In dealing with their dreams, we focus on the structure.

Survey method

Outline

This survey was sent to students of a university in Kyoto, Japan, in January 2016. A total of 230 responses were received and 212 were assessed to be valid responses (Konakawa et al. 2018). The questionnaire consists of items concerning dreams, an anthropophobia mentality scale (Horii 2012) to investigate the tendency to worry about relationship with others, and a sense of self scale (Matsuoka 2015) to investigate phases of sense of self. The items concerning dreams asked for a free response on contents of 'impressive dreams in childhood', 'recent impressive dreams', when these dreams occurred, and what happened in reality.

Procedure

After a lecture was given to students at the university and before the study was conducted, students were informed that they were free to answer or not answer the questionnaire and that anonymity was assured. Students who agreed to participate were then asked to answer the questionnaire. All data were analysed anonymously.

Analysis

All participants were classified into high and low groups based on the means of scores of each scale. Then, the four groups were built with the combination of high and low groups of each scale as shown in Figure 1. As already mentioned, 'childhood' and 'recent' dreams of each group were compared in their 'structure' from the three viewpoints described above and summarized in Table 1 (see previous page).

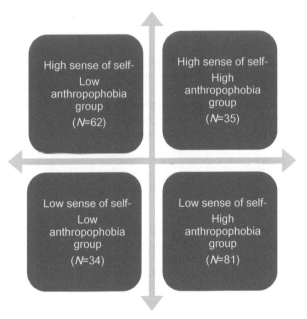

Figure 1: Four groups and each number

Discussion

Relationship between the sense of self and the structure of dream

The characteristics of dreams from participants classified in the low sense of self group could be found in the following ways: 1) the dream-ego does not respond to the object's approaches, 2) the dream-ego could not be related to the events in the dream and the narrative in the dream is not based on the perspective of the dream-ego due to the weakness of its sense of self-agency, 3) the dream has no organization which includes its introduction, development, turn and conclusion. On the other hand, we found in the dreams from participants classified in the high sense of self group: 1) the dream-ego actively deals with situations, 2) while keeping the perspective of the dream-ego, the events in the dream develop in the mutual relations between the dream-ego and objects, 3) the dream could be narrated as a story with its introduction, development, turn and conclusion.

Moreover, there is a difference in the way in which the dream-ego's way of experiencing conflicts between the high and the low sense of self groups. In the dreams from participants classified in the high sense of self group, we can find a tendency that the dream-ego sustains conflicts more persistently than the low sense of self group. In this research, we can only find much less coherence between the anthropophobia mentality and the structure of dreams in this research. This result may suggest the strong connectivity between the sense of self and the structure of dream.

Characteristics of dream in each group

Here I would like to only introduce 'recent' dream samples and discuss the characteristics of dreams in each group.

Low sense of self – low anthropophobia group

Based on their scores of the two scales, the students in this group can be described as having fragile self-consciousness and being less aware of their own torments in interpersonal relations or everyday life. They are adaptive in school life but tend to cope with a given situation by making use of their divided self-image. Since they are not worried about their weak sense of self, they are less aware of their divided self-image and hardly have any conflict about that.

Their dreams could be characterized as follows: while having a tendency that the dream-ego could not be related to the events in the dream and the behaviours of the dream-ego are not clearly mentioned, problem situations occur more frequently than in their 'impressive dreams in childhood'. However, in such dreams, we cannot observe the dream-ego's active coping with each problem situation. In some cases, the dream-ego does not have to cope with it; both the dream-ego and the object (other) have no clear will, everything is determined without reason, as shown in the following dream:

> My father was placed in a situation in which he could not help but eat a human to survive. I moved into an unknown house with my mother. On our way to the house, I got out of the car alone and prowled forest and rivers. On my way, I met someone and went with them.

In addition, there is a tendency in their dreams that the boundaries between the dream-ego, objects, and locations become more obvious than in their 'impressive dreams in childhood', but in comparison with the other groups, the objects are more frequently inanimate, neither human, animal, nor natural object, as shown in the following dream:

> I can observe myself lying on the bed from a viewpoint of a surveillance camera. The concept of 'face' was drawing nearer to me. When the 'face' was about to touch my body, the point of view changed from above to the subject, and I woke up.

Low sense of self – high anthropophobia group

The students in this group have some worries, or sufferings, in their actual life, although having little awareness of self-agency or self-image. Takaishi (2009) described the new typical figure of students to use the counselling service at university as 'vaguely complaining their mal-conditions without any awareness of their own problem', 'subjectively suffering as students in former days', but 'not being able to hold discourse about their inside'. This description can be best applied to the 'low sense of self – high anthropophobia group' among the four groups which we studied. The characteristics of dreams in this group is that, while having the will, the dream-ego does not come to carry it out, thereby does not have a mutual relationship with the object, as shown in the following dream:

> I met actress A by chance. I wanted to speak to her, but could not do it, which made me regret.

Since the dream-ego's motivation, or will, was not strong, his or her conflicts could not be sustained consistently. Also, as is describe in the following dream, the unstable status of objects and the incoherent ideas of the dream-ego stood out more than in the other groups and many changes took place in the dreams:

> After taking a bath, I went to bed without drying my body carefully. A bud of a cactus came out of my knee. It didn't hurt me specially and I was wondering what to do. Meanwhile, the cactus turned out to be haircap moss.

High sense of self – low anthropophobia group

The students in this group hold consistent self-consciousness, or self-image, and are not emotionally troubled so much. In that sense, we can regard the group as the most mentally stable in their subjective evaluation. However, as far as this research used the questionnaires, it may be assumed that this group would include those students who are not aware of their problems as they are without an adequate capacity for self-reflection, as well as those who are well adapted to their everyday life.

In the dreams of this group, we can find a tendency that the dream-ego has a mutual relationship with the object. In comparison with the dreams in the low sense of self group, there are more dreams in which the dream-ego is helped by a friendly other, as shown in the following dream:

> I was tied with rope. I could not move, but someone rescued me.

Additionally, in comparison with their 'impressive dreams in childhood', the dream-ego's coping strategy is not successful and thereby his or her conflicts are sustained in the dreams, for example:

> My paternal grandfather died. I was wailing.

In general, while keeping the perspective of the dream-ego as a protagonist, the dream was narrated as a story with its introduction, development, turn and conclusion.

> I became Hagrid, a character in Harry Potter (a giant). My attention was attracted by something sent by a really bad scientist. Meanwhile, I was injected with poison into my mouth by the scientist and I had a bad stomach-ache. I stand, but it is seen through, then I was finished off by a stab with a knife.

High sense of self – high anthropophobia group

The students in this group have consistent self-consciousness, or self-image, but they have some worry, or suffering, in their interpersonal relationship and everyday life. With this, we may assume that they have reflective self-consciousness and thus have troubles and conflicts. That is similar to the status of 'modern consciousness' having the ego as a centre and *being able to* hold troubles within itself. The main characteristic of dreams in this group is that the dream-ego actively copes with, or acts for, problem situations. In some cases, the behaviours of the dream-ego were directed towards problem-solving, as shown below:

> I forgot my part-time job, which I realised two hours after the start of my job. I called my workplace and said, 'I'm coming right now'. Store manager quitted. Then I apologized to a new manager who I met for the first time.

In this dream, we can also observe that while keeping the perspective of the dream-ego, the dream was narrated as a story with an introduction, development, turn and conclusion and that the dreamer can recall and report the details including the location, background, and so on. In addition, the dream-ego often attempts to nip an evil in the bud, which means that the dream-ego attempts to immediately recover from something bad or troubled. I tend to think that this tendency is compensation for their excessive anxiety, as shown below:

I dived into the ocean. I sometimes rose to the surface and throw something like a hand grenade at a battery of a battleship (I was seized by some sense of crisis and I did it frantically).

Conclusion and more...

This research suggests that there is a prominent difference in the structure of dreams between the high and low sense of self groups. The sense of self has an influence not only on the behaviours of the dream-ego but also on the time and space in which the events develop themselves in the dreams and the continuity of the dream-ego's perspectives. From this, we may assume that the difference in sense of self should reflect on various aspects included in the structure of dreams.

Although Jung said, 'there are a great many "average" dreams in which a definite structure can be perceived, not unlike that of a drama' (Jung 1960, para. 561), in the dreams of the low sense of self group, we could often observe that there were only superficial descriptions for each scene and then the scene changed into another one. It was certainly pointed out that, in Japanese dreams, there is a tendency that a shift of scenery happens in some difficult and painful situation that the dream-ego cannot endure, in which the dream-ego has a bird's-eye view (Kawai 1976). However, in the dreams of the low sense of self group, the dream-ego does not have any sense of incongruity, just mentioning 'without knowing why' or 'like a mystery', in some *sudden* shifts of scenery. Therein, such detaching from the dream events seems to be very natural for the dream-ego, which is quite different from the above-mentioned tendency of Japanese dreams in former days. Something new happens in our mentality!

In this context, I would like to point out the necessity of cross-cultural studies in this field. Together with Dr. Roesler we attempted to examine the cultural differences between German and Japanese dreams reported in psychotherapy. I am very interested in the result that, among the five patterns that Dr. Roesler described in his previous study (Roesler 2018), 'Pattern 4: Mobility Dream' has a significantly high frequency amongst the German dreamers in his study, whereas 'Pattern 3: The Dream Ego Is Confronted with a Performance Requirement' had a high frequency amongst Japanese dreamers in my study. Moreover, it was observed that, in the process of the psychotherapies, the dream-ego was strengthened in moving and thereby increasing his or her mobility in the German dreams, while on the other hand, the Japanese dreamers worked on his or her own psychological theme through the dream-ego's relationships with the dream-others, in which they themselves had a rather *subjective* role.

In addition, why do we Japanese have fewer 'mobility dreams' than German dreamers? One of my co-researchers, Dr. Konakawa, pointed out its relation to the shift of scenery in Japanese dreams mentioned above. Therein, the dream-ego does not *actively* move, but the scene changes. This difference can be found in similar research for students in European universities. As mentioned before, in the Japanese students' dreams, the shifts of scenery happened without any sense of incongruity, whereas in the European students' dreams the dream-ego runs away and moves to another place and then a new scene starts. This would be related to the difference in the status of our consciousness, such as its continuity, strength, and flexibility. This cross-cultural observation is just a trial having very limited participants at this point, still less than 20. But we noted with interest that all European participants scored more highly for sense of self than the Japanese students' average; all European students were classified into the high sense of self group in this paper.

We are quite different. However, through this kind of research, we can meet the others within ourselves certainly and deeply.

References

Hirosawa, M. (2015). *Gakusei-soudan kara mita 'kokoro no kouzou'* (in Japanese), (*Structure of psyche seen from student counselling*). Tokyo: Isawaki gakujutsu shuppan.
Jung, C.G. (1953). *Two Essays on Analytical Psychology*. CW 7.
— (1960). *The Structure and Dynamics of the Psyche*. CW 8.
— (1954). *The Practice of Psychotherapy*. CW 16.
Kawai, H. (1976). 'Yume no naka no "watashi"' (in Japanese), ('"I" in dreams'). *Risou*, 516, 65-80.
Konakawa, H. (2018). 'Research on the meaning of dreams appearing in psychotherapy'. Doctoral thesis of the Graduate School of Education, Kyoto University.
Konakawa, H., Matsuoka, T., Tanaka, Y., Kawai, T., Hatanaka, C. & Umemura, K. (2018). 'The relationship between the style of sense of self of dreamers and the structure of dreams' (in Japanese). *Archives of Sandplay Therapy*, 31, 2, 3-17.
Matsuoka, T. (2015). 'Seinenki no jikokan ni kansuru kenkyu' ('A study on sense of self in adolescence'). Heisei 26 graduation thesis of Kyoto University Faculty of Education. Unpub. ms.
Roesler, C. (2018). 'Dream content corresponds with dreamer's psychological problems and personality structure and with improvement in psychotherapy: a typology of dream patterns in dream series of patients in analytical psychotherapy'. *Dreaming*, 28, 4, 303–21.
Takaishi, K. (2009). 'Some problems of psychological growth in current students and student support required for higher education' (in Japanese). *Kyoto University Researches in Higher Education*, 15, 79-88.

Dreaming under fire: the psyche in times of continuous stress

Tamar Kron
(IIJP) *Jerusalem, Israel*

In a seminar Jung delivered in 1938 exploring the dreams of individuals suffering from 'Shell Shock', he explains how recurring dreams after war trauma indicate an absolute shift in the psychic system. 'They are completely identical repetitions of reality. That is proof of the traumatic effect. The shock can no longer be "psychified"' (Jung 1938/2010, p. 21). Jung continues to elucidate the way in which some traumatic experiences must be altered slowly into symbols, allowing the shock to be absorbed and integrated into the individual's psyche. Although trauma-related dreams were not the focus of Jung's interest, the short comment cited above corresponds to one of the main findings in current research: trauma dreams are concrete rather than symbolic.

Trauma dreams and nightmares have been recognized as a main symptom of PTSD among combat soldiers. On the other hand, although traumatic reactions among civilians living under conditions of persistent terrorism and war have become a subject of vital concern in the helping professions, dreams have not yet become a focus of psychoanalytic and analytical psychology theory and research. Donald Kalsched (1996) and Ursula Wirtz (2014) have contributed much to our understanding of trauma and its impact on the soul from studies based on their clinical work and observations. Research on the dreams of civilians living under conditions of terror and war is needed to complement and enhance our understanding. We are still in the dark about which archetypes and what images are actualized in situations of being 'under fire'. It has been my aim and the aim of my students to understand more about this in our researches on the dreams of Israeli residents of the area bordering the Gaza strip and Palestinians living in the West Bank during times of war and terror.

Participants of the first study in the wake of the Gaza Wars included 44 women, and 18 men, all residents of the area near the Gaza border. They were recruited by chain-referral or the 'snowball' sampling process. We sought participants who were 'just civilians', not patients or clients receiving treatment through a mental health or social work organization, and who had agreed to write down their dreams and share them with us. The youngest participant was 14 years old and the oldest was 65. Our researchers met twice with each participant. The first meeting consisted of an open interview where questions were asked relating mainly to residence in the area and its consequences, feelings and manners of coping. At the end of the first meeting, each participant received a dream diary, a notebook prepared by the researchers, which included an instruction page. Each page began with the same sentence: 'Last night I dreamed that…'. Participants were *not* directed by us to tell specific dreams. Instead they were instructed to write down all their dreams and all associations to them over a period of four weeks. In this manner, a total of 661 dreams were collected during our first study, 525 from women and 136 from men.

Basic content analysis of all dreams in first study

In analysing all the dreams collected in the first study, we looked for recurrent themes related to the ongoing stress. Here from the list of recurrent themes are those which appeared with the greatest frequency.

List of recurrent themes

Fear, helplessness and loss of control (33%).
Active ego (62%): engagement in activities either useful or futile.
Togetherness (68%): the dreamer joins others in the dream situation and/or gets support from others.
Concrete dream (68%): the dream describes the real 'under fire' situation as is.
Symbolic dream (32%): fantastic or metaphorical dreams which describe events that did not or could not happen in reality.
Shadow (29%): appearance of a human figure, animal or other symbol representative of aggression, danger, evil, death.
Personal issues or personal complex unrelated to the traumatic situation (40%).

The method of analysis we used in this first study and our list of themes were the basis for our content analysis of all subsequent research data. Each study was further analysed in accordance with a population-specific research question.

Analysis of the women's dreams in first study

As the majority of our participants in the first study were women here is our analysis of the women's dreams (Kron, Hareven & Goldzweig 2015). We divided the women research population into three age groups:

Adolescent, 14-19 years of age (19 participants; 204 dreams).
Young Adult, 20-44 years of age (17 participants; 222 dreams).
Mature adult, 45-65 years of age (8 participants; 105 dreams).

The occurrence in percentage for each theme out of the total number of dreams was calculated separately for each age group. Though generally the frequency of symbolic dreams was found to be quite low, in accordance with findings from other studies of trauma dreams, *the differences between age groups indicate that adolescents make up the most vulnerable group,* and the frequency of symbolic dreams in their group is lower in comparison with the other two groups.

Frequencies (in percentage) of symbolic dreams

Adol.	Y. Adult	M. Adult
22%	40%	36%

The frequency of shadow images among adolescents is likewise generally low, appearing with the highest frequency in the dreams of the young adults.

Frequencies of shadow images

Adol.	Y. Adult	M. Adult
24%	35%	28%

Does the low frequency of shadow images have anything to do with the fact that rockets are faceless and come 'from above?'. The adolescent age group displays a significantly higher frequency of the 'togetherness' theme than the other two groups. It can be safely hypothesized that the 'togetherness' theme is a compensatory reaction to traumatic events.

Frequencies of togetherness theme

Adol.	Y. Adult	M. Adult
78%	60%	66%

In the dreams of the mature adult group, the personal issues or 'PI' theme occurs with the highest frequency.

Frequencies of personal issue theme

Adol.	Y. Adult	M. Adult
29%	45%	51%

This finding is in keeping with Erich Neumann's principle of 'centroversion' – the movement of the psyche towards integration, a process which involves the ego's shifting from preoccupation with outside reality to the inner world. According to Neumann, this shift usually occurs around midlife (Neumann 1954). The young adults, mainly mothers with small children, were the most preoccupied with active coping, both consciously and unconsciously. We did find a high level of the 'active ego' theme in this group (64.4%). In order to cope with their stressful situations these women required inner work at a deeper level as conveyed by the relatively high frequency of symbolic dreams among them.

Sequence of dreams

In addition to our overall content analysis, we looked at the sequence of dreams as they appeared in the dream diaries. As an example, here following are three dreams from the dream diary of one of our participants. Orit, a 38-year-old married woman with three small children lives on a kibbutz near the Gaza border. From her dream sequence we discerned that she is anxious and distressed and feels guilty towards her children, yet she shows no signs of PTSD.

Dream 1:

I dreamt that I'm in my office, but the office is suddenly in a tall building in Manhattan and then we hear a siren and everyone gets confused, worried about what will happen next and what to do. I tell them 'In Israel we know what to do when the siren goes off, but what do we do here?'. We all run to the window to see what's happened – somebody was murdered in the street below and that was the reason the siren sounded. It was a sad and frightening dream.

This dream is one of many in which Orit finds herself abroad, in flight from the harrowing situation on the kibbutz only to realize in the end that she and the children have not escaped the danger.

Dream 2:

We and other families are out in the kibbutz playground when suddenly everyone starts to run, so I start running too. In the end we're locked up in a building by a group of bad guys with guns. Their leader is Paul McCartney and I say to Paul: 'I never took you for a bad guy'. He's wearing blue jeans and a black belt. He tells me to go stand in the corner along with two women friends and he says: 'I'm going to execute you three first'. I wake up just as he's about to start shooting.

In her dream diary Orit wrote these associations: 'The dream was really scary. I don't understand what Paul McCartney was doing there and why he was a bad guy. Good guys suddenly turn into bad guys; you can never tell where evil looms'.

Dream 3:

    I am near the kibbutz dining room with my younger son and meet my two daughters with another boy and I ask them: 'Where will you run if you hear the warning siren?'. They point at the house of their grandmother where there is a security room. I say 'OK' and start to walk with them in the direction of the house. Suddenly, a huge helicopter flies out of the house and hovers very low in the direction of the dining room. I look at it admiringly and say to one of the kids: 'Look! It's a show!' but suddenly the helicopter bursts open and out jump these characters from *Star Trek* and start shooting. One of them shouts: 'Run for your life' and I take off in the direction of our house with my son.

All the elements of trying to cope with a dangerous situation are in this dream. The dreamer prepares herself and her children for the coming attack, and as kind of compensation the enemy is not real but a fantasy figure. But reality overpowers fantasy, and the dreamer runs for shelter, defending her son.

Analysis of the men's dreams in first study

Eighteen men participated in the study and a total of 136 dreams were collected from them. The main findings of the content analysis are as follows: 42% of the men's dreams were concrete, and 58% were symbolic. Compensatory processes appear in many of the men's dreams. In contrast to their conscious position expressed in interviews of denial or making light of the experience of fear and anxiety, these components appearing in their dreams fill in the partial picture.

The archetype that appears more than any other male archetype in the men's dreams is that of the hero's journey (Kron & Hareven 2011, 2012). The need for symbols of the hero arises when the ego needs strengthening. But the picture of the hero's journey that emerges in the men's dreams is one of a truncated journey in which there is a departure, characterized by the effort to distance oneself and flee from the difficulties of daily life, and an attempt to enlist various helpers. The beginning and end of the journey are almost completely removed from the men's dreams, and none of them is a dream in which the full process is reflected. The 'helpless heroes' do not have a compensatory identification with a hero/warrior archetype. One other main finding is that hardly any anima figures appear in the men's dreams! No eros in times of terror and war. Animus figures do appear in the women's dreams (40%) – they look for help from the masculine!

Dreams of Israelis and Palestinians during war nights

The last research presented here is a study comparing the dreams of Israeli inhabitants of southern Israel and Palestinians on the West Bank during the recent Gaza war. (Kron & Halfon 2015, 2016). Unfortunately, for our study we were denied access to the dreams of the Gazans which would have afforded us a far broader scope. Participants included 38 Palestinian women and 25 Palestinian men, as well as children, living in villages and towns in the West Bank and 18 Israeli women and 10 Israeli men, residents of the Sderot area near the Gaza border. The disproportionately low number of Israeli subjects may have been due to the difficulty of their participation in the midst of the rocket attacks. One hundred and nine dreams were collected from Palestinians and 32 from Israelis. The main findings of the content analysis follows.

Frequencies of concrete and symbolic traumatic dreams[1]

Israelis	Palestinians	
75% (24)	12% (13)	Concrete traumatic dreams
16% (5)	31% (34)	Symbolic traumatic dreams
91% (29)	44% (47)	Total traumatic dreams

Although we did not find significant differences between the two groups in the frequencies of trauma indicators, we did find differences in the themes. The significant difference we found among the groups is a preponderance of symbolic dreams in the Palestinian group as opposed to a preponderance of concrete traumatic dreams in the Israeli group.

Common themes in the dreams of the Palestinian group

Animals and imaginary creatures are a common theme in Palestinian dreams, one that *never appeared* in the dreams of the Israeli group. Most of the animals and creatures were described as dangerous and threatening, bearing death and destruction to the dreamer and causing the dreamer to flee or slay them. The different animals that appeared in the dreams, like mythical serpents and predatory birds, were often wild and fierce. Some dreamers described them as monstrous, ancient beasts, half-human half-animal, endowed with superpowers that made them undefeatable. Here is a symbolic traumatic dream of a 32-year-old Palestinian woman:

---

[1] Frequencies and percentages of concrete and symbolic dreams were calculated from the total of traumatic dreams for each group.

I dreamed there was an earthquake that destroyed the city. Water flooded the roads and damaged them. Mice were nibbling the fingers of little children and people were walking on broken glass. And then different kinds of birds flew by and snatched up the people till none were left. And then the sun rose, there was no more water on the roads and ants started crawling out of the ground.

Common themes in the dreams of the Israeli group

In many of the traumatic concrete dreams within the Israeli group, men see themselves as either fighting or helpless and in flight. Women dreamers express concern for others. There may be several reasons other than geographical proximity to the war zone for the variance in themes, due to various cultural, religious and socioeconomic differences. Researchers of dreams in different cultures have found that dream characteristics vary in accordance with tradition and religious and social ethos. In both groups, however, archetypal symbols of evil like snakes and terrorists emerge from underground, in keeping with the Jungian approach to the collective unconscious. Another parallel is the appearance of archetypal evil swooping down from the sky in the form of predatory birds and rockets. The enemy in both groups is dehumanized and without individual identity, a projection of the shadow which threatens to destroy the collective.

Conclusions

Dreams can help us detect emotional distress, even where no specific symptoms of PTSD are reported, and subjects seem 'ok'. Early detection and treatment can help prevent the severity of delayed PTSD. Working with dreams enhances the ability to cope with continuous stress situations and to recover from emotional distress. Many of our subjects reported that writing down their dreams in the diary was, in the words of a woman from Sderot, 'self-therapy'. Last but not least, dreams, like emotions and feelings, are part of human nature. I believe in the power of dream-telling and hearing to pave the way towards dialogue with the 'other', even when that other is perceived as the enemy.

References

Jung, C.G. (1938/2010). *Children's Dreams: Notes from the Seminar Given in 1936-1940*, eds. M. Meyer-Grass & L. Jung, trans. E. Falzeder & T. Woolfson. Princeton NJ: Princeton University Press.

Kalsched, D. (1996). *The Inner World of Trauma: Archetypal Defenses of the Personal Spirit*. London: Routledge.

Kron, T. & Hareven, O. (2011). 'Helpless heroes: the dreams of men and women in the shadow of continuous life-threatening missile attacks'. *28th Annual Conference of the International Association for the Study of Dreams*, Kerkrade, The Netherlands.

— (2012). 'Dreams in the nights of terror: continuous stress and coping'. In *Montreal 2010. Facing Multiplicity: Psyche, Nature, Culture: Proceedings of the XVIIIth Congress of the International Association for Analytical Psychology*. Einsiedeln: Daimon Pub.

Kron, T., Hareven, O. & Goldzweig, G. (2015). 'Dream dome: do dreams shield the psyche in times of continuous stress?' *Dreaming*, 25, 2, 160-72.

Kron, T. & Halfon, T. (2015). 'The psyche under stress: dreams of Israelis and Palestinians in a time of war'. Third European Conference on Analytical Psychology, 'Analysis at the Cultural Crossroads', Trieste, Italy.

— (2016). 'Dreaming under fire: dreams of Israelis and Palestinians in a time of war'. Prague Conference on 'Civilians at War: Losses, Recovery and the Experience of the Helpers' (organized by the Czech Psychoanalytic Society, October 2016).

Neumann, E. (1954). *The Origins and History of Consciousness*, trans. R. F.C. Hull. Bollingen Series XLII. Princeton NJ: Princeton University Press.

Wirtz, U. (2014). *Trauma and Beyond: The Mystery of Transformation*. Louisiana: Spring Journal and Books.

Integration versus conflict between schools of dream theory and dreamwork: integrating the psychological core qualities of dreams with the contemporary knowledge of the dreaming brain

Ole Vedfelt
(DSAP) *Hillerod, Denmark*

Introduction

In my many years of working with dreams, I have scrutinized the knowledge of the most prominent psychological and psychotherapeutic dream schools, their understanding of dream processes and personality theories, as well as each school's suggestions for dreamwork practices. This includes Freud's psychoanalytic dream theory, C. G. Jung's depth psychology, the dream theories of the successors of Freud and Jung, theories that focus on correlations between dream experiences and waking lifestyles, existential dream interpretation, experiential work with dreams plus Cognitive Therapy and contemporary focus-oriented therapy. Furthermore, I am acquainted with non-therapeutic dreamwork methods, including community-based dream groups, social dream matrix, personal development groups, as well as how dreams are utilized in religious and spiritual traditions (Vedfelt 1994/2002).

The theoretical models of the various schools have been developed through varying research strategies and 'knowledge interests' (Habermas 1968/2007). There are conflicting perceptions of consciousness and unconsciousness, nature and culture, the individual and society, and even of views of humanity. In addition, personal ambitions, career options and marketing issues have often stimulated conflict rather than integration.

By studying the various methods and particularly testing their knowledge in practice, I have however found that they all have something to offer on one level or the other.

My approach to dreaming is based on an understanding of the human psyche as a multi-layered, self-optimizing, complex information system. It functions as a parallel-processing neural network where many subsystems are active, simultaneously accessing differing yet overlapping memory systems that learn through practice. The system is open but swings rhythmically between states more or less in contact with the outer world (Vedfelt 1996/2019 and 2002/2018).

I have delineated ten core qualities of dreams supported by both therapeutic knowledge, as well as natural scientific research. Related to the core qualities I provide short dreamwork vignettes from my own practice and schematic illustrations of imagined brain processes.

My overriding view is that we dream because we are complex beings who need to shift between states of mind that process information in different ways to provide us with differing perspectives on our lives and the world (Vedfelt 2017).

The dreming brain and the fourfold brain

Advances in scanning methods, research in brain chemistry and studies of people with brain injuries have expanded our knowledge of the dreaming brain. Various overall models of the brain anatomy and function have been proposed depending on anatomical structures, knowledge-interest and didactic simplifications.

Since brain anatomy is extremely complex, it is not possible to give a complete graphic illustration in a single picture of the multitude of neural networks that are active while dreaming. In this schematic illustration (Fig. 1), some structures are depicted on the same plane, even though they overlap or even hide each other. I call the model that I present here a fourfold brain and have marked four sections with different colours [see the e-book version of this volume].

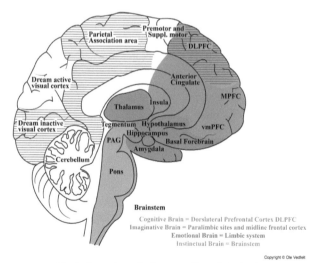

Fig. 1. *A cut through the centerline of the brain*

When we dream, outer sensing, and executive motor mechanisms are almost completely uncoupled. Brain activity, however, is equally intense as when we are awake. This gives a surplus of activity for other tasks. The relatively deactivated areas are shaded on the picture.

The brown is the brainstem, an evolutionary reptilian brain. It elaborates basic instinctual action plans for primitive emotive processes such as exploration, feeding, aggressive behaviour, and sexuality (Panksepp 1998, pp. 1745-67). In the upper brainstem an area called the periaqueductal grey, abbreviated to PAG, has small networks directed towards inner bodily sensations, such as wellbeing or discomfort. Parallel networks in the PAG may translate this as 'background emotions', such as being calm or tense, relaxed or irritable, enthusiastic or depressed, etc. (Damasio 2000, p. 52). The PAG network is included in a 'reticular activation system', which is important for arousal, alertness and awareness in dreams and waking alike (Solms & Turnbull 2002).

The red is called the emotional brain, the limbic system or the old mamalian brain. It adds behavioural and psychological resolution to all of the emotions and specifically mediates behaviours 'such as separation distress/social bonding, playfulness, and maternal nurturance (Panksepp 1998, pp. 1748-49). The amygdala plays a role in a fear system. Information from external stimuli reach the amygdala via a fast route that allows us to act immediately to potential danger and even survival (LeDoux 1998, p. 162ff). The strength of the output from the amygdalae and the rest of the emotional brain is far greater *towards* the 'cognitive brain' than in the opposite direction (Nunn et al. 2008, p. 135). This gives our emotions considerable power over our rational cognitive considerations.

The hypothalamus and pituitary gland distribute hormones and chemicals necessary for vital tasks (Nunn et al. 2008).

Areas indispensable for dreams and their visuospatial imagery are found in a junction between the occipital, temporal and parietal lobes (left side of the picture). With damage to this area you will not be able to dream (Solms & Turnbull 2002, p. 203).

The hippocampus is vital to 'declarative' episodic memory in waking life (Nunn et al. 2008). In dreams, this memory is fragmented. Individual elements of episodes are selected and combined in new ways.

The blue is an intermediary zone I call the imaginative brain. It contains networks of tremendous importance for dreaming, creativity, social intelligence, higher feeling and imagination. They are related to sensing and feeling the inner realms of the mind and body.

In the blue area the anterior cingulate cortex coordinates, regulates and modifies the information flowing between the emotional brain and the neocortex (Ratey 2001, p. 1972). The insula is a fifth brain lobe.

It is important to emotional attunement between people, to the body-mind connection and to the attunement of ego consciousness to the needs of a more global self (Siegel 2007). The medial prefrontal cortex, abbreviated to mPFC, and below that the ventromedial prefrontal cortex, abbreviated vmPFC, are generally larger in the right hemisphere than in the left. They are related to intuitive, imaginative and unconscious information processing. The medial prefrontal cortex is important for self-awareness as well as for the ability to mentalize the intentions and feelings of others (Gusnard 2006). The vmPFC is absolutely necessary for dreaming. If the connections to the vmPFC are damaged, it can lead to serious emotional and social disturbances, including problems with long-term planning in life, all of this coinciding with a total loss of the ability to dream (Solms 1997). These various systems are usually synchronized by the thalamus – in the red area – at 40 hertz oscillations called gamma waves. The thalamus is a crucial relay for circulating information between brain systems (Gold 1999, Ratey 2001).

The purple part of the of the picture is called the Dorsolateral prefrontal cortex (DLPFC). It generates higher cognitive functions, reasoning, and logical thought (Panksepp 1998, pp. 1745-67).

Core quality 1: dreams deal with matters important to us

Research has shown that if deprived of our dreams, we will become dysfunctional in a variety of psychological and social ways. Freud was convinced that 'dreams always contain important material if one takes the trouble to interpret them...' (Freud 1900, pp. 93-97). His successors in psychoanalysis underscore that dreams focus on central, personal conflicts and important emotional relationships (Vedfelt 2002). Jung credited dreams with superior wisdom (Mattoon 1978, p. 103). Calvin Hall, who is famous for introducing statistical content analysis of dreams, concluded that dreams attempt to resolve inner problems of the individual (Hall 1953a, pp. 233-34). His prominent successor, William Domhoff, suggests that dreams reveal the 'intensity of dreamer's overriding concerns' (Domhoff 2010). Fritz Perls considered dreams as expressions of the 'wisdom of the organism' (Perls 1969, p. 37). Aaron Beck, originator of cognitive therapy, viewed dreams as 'core cognitive schemas' (Dowd 2004). Further, it has been demonstrated that indisputable important events, such as severe, acute trauma, are intensely commented on and processed in dreams (Hartmann 1998). This is also true of the dreams of pregnant women whose dreams mirror intense preoccupation with babies, the body, and mothering issues, which are obviously important in this situation (Van de Castle 1994).

In a cybernetic sense 'importance' signifies that the system moves to a higher level of self-organization. Self-organization is a principle introduced by such cybernetic pioneers as Ross Ashby (1962) and Norbert Wiener (1948). In self-organization, some form of principle order emerges out of the interactions between smaller parts. The emergence of traits encompasses the system as a whole, which cannot be reduced to the properties of the constituent parts. This is increasingly deemed valid as an explanation for the spontaneous processes of transformation where multiple variables are involved (Cicchetti et al. 1996). During transitions, this system moves into a destabilizing state between chaos and order. Yet this state can be stabilized through positive feedback from the environment (Nicolis & Rouvas-Nicolis 2007). Thus, positive feedback on resources in dreams is a valuable feature of good dreamwork.

A parallel can be drawn to the ideas of German system theorist Niklas Luhmann, renowned for his writings about self-organization or 'autopoiesis' as he calls it in social systems. Systems can make themselves unstable in order to regain stability on a higher level of organization. When a system begins to turn its own properties inward on itself, it can renew itself without jeopardizing its identity. Thus, it can manage more complex tasks, prepare itself for situational shifts, and even 'learn to learn' (Luhmann 1966). This may be what is happening in the introverted state of dreaming, and even more so in dreamwork (Vedfelt 2017).

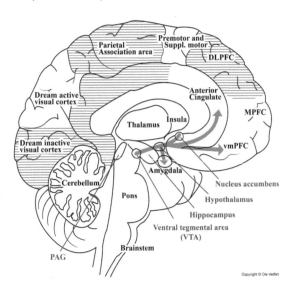

Fig. 2. The seeking system. When we dream, a so-called 'seeking system' moving from the brainstem through the emotional brain (the limbic system), is activated.

On the neuropsychological level, Antonio Damasio, based on groundbreaking research, assumes that our entire system of emotion and feeling (highly active in dreams) is a self-regulating device mostly functioning without our awareness (Damasio 2000). We find a very similar understanding in neuroscientist Allan Schore's theories of the neurobiology of emotional development and the brain. He writes about 'self-organizing systems that use energy to facilitate the co-operativity of simpler subsystem components into a hierarchically structured complex system' (Schore 2000, p. 157).

The seeking system starts in a ventral tegmental area (VTA) in the brainstem. It includes a reward system in the nucleus accumbens, activates amygdala, and hypothalamus, as well as systems in the midline structures of the imaginative brain.

It provides arousal and energy to feelings of curiosity and interest, and expectancy that something good will happen if we explore the environment or interact with objects (Solms & Turnbull 2002, p. 115).

The first task of dreamwork is to connect the dreamer to these motivating powers, facilitating a sense that the work will lead to something vital. Since psychotherapeutic dream schools have primarily focused on problems, they have had a tendency to overlook positive and non-conflictual content in dreams. According to William Domhoff, who proposes a neurocognitive dream theory and totally discards Freud and Jung's theory, 'Emotions like sadness, anger, confusion, and apprehension, taken as a whole, greatly outnumber the expressions of happiness' (Domhoff 2010). However, more recent research in the dream laboratory suggests that the number of positive feelings in dreams equals that of negative feelings (Yu 2015).

My personal experience with thousands of dreams confirms that within any dream there are important needs, which can enable a more harmonic personality

Recognizing this contributes to a never-ending, self-optimizing process. The self-regulating value of pleasant dreams is to make the dreamer aware of important qualities not taken seriously enough. Taking a beneficial bath, for example, can underscore the importance of cleansing oneself of toxic emotions; dreams of a helpful spouse can recall a partner's positive qualities, or even qualities in oneself not adequately appreciated.

If dreams are unpleasant, we can see them as warnings or corrections of attitudes that are not helpful, and we can begin to imagine what could be beneficial. Dreamers often recount 'bad' dreams with a focus on the most emotionally intense parts, thus ignoring less energy-charged positive details. Often, a more detailed clarification of the actual dream can point to resources such as helpers, pleasant places, positive feelings, etc.

If that is not the case, we have to ask ourselves what it is that dreams are trying to regulate. If a dreamer is driving too fast, it may indicate that he, in waking life, is pushing himself too hard. In a pursuit dream, the pursuer may represent undeveloped aspects of our personalities with which we will not find peace until taken seriously. The death of a person may symbolize outlived patterns in one's personality that have to pass away in order to make room for new developments.

Therefore, focusing on the resources in dreams is of primary importance to maintain the dreamer's interest and motivation.

Core quality 2: dreams symbolize

Fig. 3 shows areas related to metaphoric and symbolic mentation. Symbols and metaphors help people create coherent experiences, also called experiential gestalts (Lakoff & Johnson 1980.) For example, the metaphor, a 'warm person', contributes to an overall impression, which enables quick responses without lengthy analytical examinations.

The ability to understand symbolism is related to the imaginative brain networks particularly the mPFC and the vmPFC and their strong connections to the Right Brain. They are related to our intuitive 'feeling of knowing' (Schnyer et al. 2004).

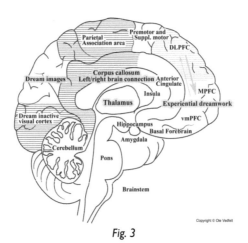

Fig. 3

Symbolization gives items meanings different from the original and literal sense. However, damage to the mPFC and the vmPFC also damage the ability to understand ambiguous knowledge and double meanings (Zald 2010). In dreams, the same brain networks are at work with a surplus of energy. Through their elaborated symbolism they give us much deeper explanation than what intuitively strays the waking 'fringe consciousness'.

Freud explored sexual symbolism and Jung studied archetypes and symbols of individuation. Medard Boss, the leading pioneer of the existential dream school, comprehends dreams as 'poetically condensed images of a person's life situation' (Stern 1977, p. xiii). Their methods in each their way have enriched the understanding of dream symbols.

Dorothy, a woman in her late thirties, had no prior knowledge of dreams and psychotherapy. In a first session she told me a recurrent nightmare where she lost her teeth. The nightmares started in her teenage years. She was very unhappy with her divorced parents at that time and experienced intense feelings of powerlessness with her whole life situation. Variations of the theme of toothlessness also appeared in more recent dreams connected with subjective experiences of powerlessness that prevented her from pursuing important goals.

In another yet positively exciting recurrent dream, Dorothy was in an apartment she knew: *'Suddenly, I discover an extra room. It is a wonderful dream. I explore the place, I fantasize how I can use it'.*

The first appearance of this dream was in connection to a creative idea of a new business. Friends and colleagues discouraged her saying that she could never make a living out of that, but she persisted against all odds and actually succeeded in making a sustainable business. Also with this recurrent dream type, we found meaningful variations referring to different life contexts.

Originally, Dorothy had understood these dreams as maybe urging her to go to a dentist or find a new apartment but during the session, she discovered that they were important and meaningful metaphors about states in her own mind. Thus, metaphoric thinking is a skill that can be learned by working with dreams.

Core quality 3: dreams personify

Personification is a way for the mind to process information that is too extensive for cognitive verbal consciousness. The personified systems are manifestations of an unconscious and practical intelligence. From birth, these systems regulate our behaviour and experience. They create groups of networks that develop through relationships with our closest caregivers and later important relations (Stern 1985). The personified systems are active in everyday waking life and appear clearly in dreams.

Systematic content analysis shows that a dream character's behaviour and experiences are strikingly equal to waking persons. They display facial expressions, emotional gestures and prosody... as complex as in waking life (Nielsen 2012). *'Within* dream scenarios dreamers' thoughts are generally logical and similar to waking cognition, but thinking *about* scenarios is usually unrealistic' (Kahn & Hobson 2005).

Both dream selves and other characters have a 'theory of mind', i.e. an ability to conceptualize what takes place within the minds of other characters (McNamara 2012), surprisingly about three times as much as in reports from waking life (McNamara et al. 2007).

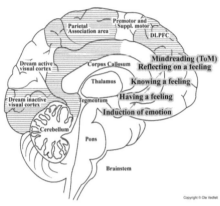

Fig. 4

From the brainstem, to the limbic system and further to the networks in the 'imaginative brain' Damasio distinguishes between having an emotion and feeling that you have an emotion. Knowing that you have a feeling is a higher level. 'Reflection on feeling is yet another step up' (Damasio 2000, p. 284). This applies to all the dream characters. (The above picture shows a schematic representation of the levels of consciousness). The state of mind of the dreaming ego is very much like the state of mind of waking ego (Hall and Nordby 1972) (Dieckmann 1980) (Nielsen 2012). Thus, dreams give us an excellent opportunity to evaluate the ego's level of consciousness.

Lisa, a 20-year-old woman in therapy with me was haunted by nightmares. From 10-12 years she was hospitalized for cancer and treated with chemotherapy. The nightmares were about a dystopic world where she was threatened by monstrous aggressive animals. The level in these dreams was induction of emotion, i. e. without any awareness. After two years of therapy, Lisa dreamt that she *meets a 12-year-old girl who is being haunted by ghosts at night. She consoles the girl. Morning arrives, the light returns and the ghosts disappear.* She visualized and contemplated the meeting with the girl and cried softly and deeply for a long time. She said that it was only now that she could allow herself to fully sense the depth of her loneliness and sorrow, knowing that she could come back to ordinary consciousness again.

The dream as well as the session showed the dramatic process of how having a feeling, knowing a feeling and reflecting on a feeling on the subjective level, coupled with empathy, could personify Lisa's lost-and-found self. Lisa's process is described in detail in my book *A Guide to the World of Dreams* (Vedfelt 2017).

Core quality 4: dreams are trial runs in a safe place

Jung (1938-9) suggested that most dreams are structured like a classical drama, and further that a dream is 'a preliminary unconscious sketch ... of future conscious achievements, ... an anticipatory combination of probabilities' (Jung 1916/1948, para. 493). In addition, many other authors have described dreams as creative and prospective narratives (Horton & Malinowski) (Meltzer 1983) (Vedfelt 2017). Since in dreams we are uncoupled from acting in the outer world, they provide a safe place to make trial runs in narrative form.

From a cybernetic point of view, a parallel distributed network makes 'mental models' that allow actions to be performed on an interior plane and also evaluates the consequences of possible outcomes (Rumelhart et al. 1986, pp. 38-44). It can be compared to the manuscript of a 'stage play with characters portrayed by different actors' (Rumelhart 1980).

The image below suggests some hypothetical negotiations between different brain networks when Graham, a 40-year-old male dreamt the following:

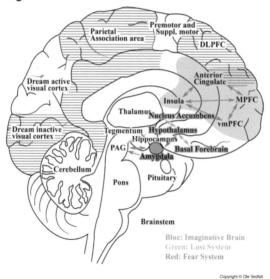

Fig. 5

My wife and her girlfriend are swimming. They are attractive in their bathing suits. A green lust system in the reward network Nucleus

Accumbens goes to the hypothalamus and the basal forebrain. It is related to the PAG, at the top of the brainstem, where it is perceived as pleasurable inner sensations (Solms & Turnbull, p. 120). The dream continues: *I see a crocodile lying in the water. I become frightened.* A fear system, generated in the Amygdala communicates danger (ibid., p. 127). Graham reacts by freezing. With impressive speed however, other sites gets involved in modifying the first induction of the inner action driving emotion. This connects the dream narrative to much grander patterns in a 'global workspace' (Baars 2005). The imaginative brain networks – insula, cingulate, vmPFC and mPFC – play a leading role in this and share information about Graham's more global autobiographical experiences of encounters with women in general and his wife in particular. They orchestrate the activation of a reassuring image from the dream active visual cortex and then Graham *discovers that the crocodile is only an inflatable toy.* Energy and information stream down the PAG and further to the vagus nerve and the parasympathetic nerve system. The dream continues. *I am relieved.*

When clarifying the dream content, it became clear that the appearance of the inflatable toy was not a bizarre transformation of a virtual crocodile, but the result of the dreamer's sharpened awareness and conscious evaluation of the object. This detail, which could have easily been overlooked, points to a relatively high level of feeling consciousness in the dreaming and the waking ego, which is relevant for dreamwork. The dreamwork circled around Graham's marital, intimate, sensual life. Graham recognized that his wife often encouraged him to take a more masculine initiative and that she was more playful than him. The wife's friend was understood on the subjective level as a feminine anima attitude, where a more masculine and also playful attitude was desired. The solution to the dramatic structure was promising.

Core quality 5: dreams are online to unconscious intelligence

For almost a quarter of our waking life, we are not occupied with rational, analytical thinking or with attention directed towards the outer world (Foulkes 1975), (Kripke & Sonnenschein 1978). Phenomenologically, these states may be filled with wishful phantasies or worried ruminations, (Mason 2007), but they also can be regenerating and creative. We can use these states and 'go online' to the unconscious intelligence that creates dreams (Vedfelt 2017).

The altered states of consciousness are related to a so-called 'default network' where the imaginative brain plays a central role. Altered states have been accessed by the dynamic dream schools through the use of free association, drawing, role-play, imagination and bodywork, thereby providing energy, creativity and new information to the dreamwork. Even dreaming by itself increases the ability to resolve conundrums of creativity upon awakening (Lewin & Glaubmann 1975).

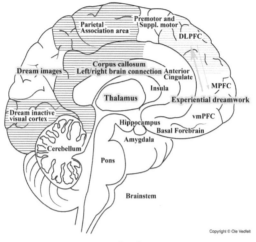

Fig. 6

The highlighted networks on the image (Fig. 6) illustrate the interaction between the cognitive and the imaginative brain in an experiential dreamwork. The thickness of the arrows in the right side of the picture illustrates that more energy moves from the imaginative brain to 'the cognitive brain' (DLPFC) than the other way around.

What I aim to achieve in dreamwork is a creative learning of new attitudes, relational skills and self-insight. In a parallel distributed network 'learning can occur with gradual changes in connection of strength by experience' (Kincaid 2017). It is consistent with a highly acclaimed theory by the Nobel laureate Edelmann that during brain development networks of nerve cells, which are often used together will be strengthened while connections between neurons not used will be weakened (Edelman 1993).

When energy mobilizing experiential methods are used, there must be a balance between energy, meaning and the person's ability to integrate new content. The ability to generate creative ideas in waking life is highest with a balance between brain regions with cognitive control and imaginative processes related to mPFc and vmPFC (Beaty and Benedik 2014).

With Dorothy, Lisa and Graham, we used drawing, free association, active imagination, body-sensing and sometimes role-play. Energy-charged emotion and feeling was balanced with analytical thinking. The overall rationale was to strengthen connections to resourceful issues while self-destructive connections were weakened. I call this a cybernetic reorganization (Vedfelt 2002/2018).

Core quality 6: dreams are pattern recognition

According to the cybernetic network theory, the human personality is an open, context-sensitive system, which utilizes pattern recognition as a fundamental principle of knowing. From birth, this makes the world and our close relationships comprehensible in all their complexity. The 'goodness-of-fit' between the inner pattern and the incoming data can be depicted as a three-dimensional energy landscape. The best matches create sharp peaks in 'the goodness-of-fit-space', while fluid patterns produce softer hills and valleys (Smolensky 1986; McClelland et al. 1986).

In dreamwork, pattern recognition – as opposed to fixed interpretations – is a useful tool, so we match dream patterns with various aspects of dreamer's life context in order to find the best matches in the 'goodness-of-fit-space'.

In the image below, the context is an emotionally significant day residue (Freud, S. (1900/2013) on the fast unconscious route to the amygdala initiating a fearful dream, but there may be many other relevant contexts for a goodness-of-fit.

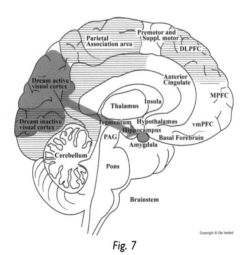

Fig. 7

The various dream schools have emphasized specific aspects of the context: Freud the childhood experiences; Jung the future developmental potentials; Calvin Hall the current behaviour. Thus, in any dream, we can search for events from the past, present and potential future until we find a goodness-of-fit pattern that makes sense in the ongoing life process of the dreamer. In a session, we may start with fluid patterns of recognition and at some point reduce the complexity and connect the interpretation to something the dreamer can handle.

In Graham's as well as Lisa's long-term dreamwork, childhood parental figures, acute or ongoing current issues, as well as future potentials wavered back and forth in the energy landscape fertilizing each other, solving small problems and synthesizing more global changes in their personality.

Core quality 7: dreams are high-level communication

The image below illustrates communication between the imaginative brain and the emotional brain in response to the dreamer's attitude to life. They are proactively communicating far-reaching future developmental possibilities

A caring parent couple was concerned about their 14-year-old daughter, Ida's,

precocious and eccentric lifestyle. She had dismissed several psychologists because they made her feel that there was something fundamentally wrong with her.

In her dreams, *she often had Walt Disney's wacky inventor Gyro Gearloose's Little Helper with his blinking light bulb head as her faithful companion. In another dream she travelled through many strange cities and always found her way by following a red thread.* She associated these cities with artistic activity, in which she had an intense and precocious interest.

I evaluated on the basis of a 'goodness-of-fit', that this dream might stretch far into Ida's future life.

I communicated in various ways that she was quite OK and let her go after few sessions. I encouraged the parents not to worry but rather to support her talent. Since then, I have had the opportunity to follow her 25-year career. She creates original art valuable to society and is a sensible, down-to-earth mother.

Fig. 8 illustrates a rewarding dream responding to an earnest attitude towards life and the totality of the psyche, and a warning dream responding to an inappropriate attitude towards life and a more global inner self. The image shows the imaginative brain as an assembled entity, which receives positive feedback in an encouraging, reassuring dream from the reward system, and negative feedback from the amygdala as corrective to an unhealthy, self-destructive or one-sided attitude.

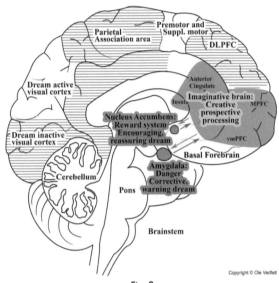

Fig. 8

Dreams close to sessions usually give valuable comments on the process as such, and to hidden transference countertransference issues, positive as well as negative.

After the session with the new-room dream, Dorothy sent me a grateful sms and wrote '... I got wiser, and *I had the most fascinating dream tonight. I was pregnant and the baby in my stomach laughed loudly and we could see it's face through the skin and it's sweet toes and feet. It was a wonderful dream'.*

Negative experiences that activate grand autobiographical patterns in the client may be caused by small mistakes in the therapist's relational attunement. Such dreams provide valuable corrective information. For example, a young physician, Anders, dreamt he is *talking to his boss. While they are talking, a threatening biker guy enters the room. Anders hurries out.* In the dreamwork, it emerged that the aggressive person and Anders's rapid evacuation became associated to the experience of an insensitive remark by me in the previous session. He had repressed the feeling fearing that it could jeopardize my sympathy for him, and I had overlooked it (Vedfelt 2017, p. 120).

Core quality 8: dreams are condensed information

Freud found that dream elements are determined by several latent meanings, and that each dream element is charged with the energy (cathexed) of the associations (Laplanche & Pontalis 1953, p. 82). Jung called this 'contamination' meaning '... a central point, which links together issues and objects not connected in waking life' (Jung 1933-1935, p. 203). Calvin Hall called it a stenographic language providing several bits of information at a time (Hall 1953).

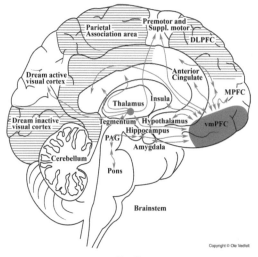

Fig. 9

More recent dream and brain researchers emphasize that the dreaming brain is hyperassociative (Horton & Malinowski 2015), that it supports connectivity (Hartmann 1998) and that particularly the vmPFC is 'privy to signals about virtually any activity taking place in our body and mind' (Damasio1994, p. 181). This is highlighted in Fig. 9.

Arthur Koestler (1964), in his great work on creative processes, introduced the term 'bisociation' to distinguish it from association understood as a more random process. Bisociation means that information from different frames of reference are combined in meaningful ways, creating new levels of understanding. Koestler showed that this is the case with most new inventions.

A basic rule of cybernetics, the law of requisite variety, states that in an encounter between two systems, the one with most possibility of relevant variation potentially can regulate the more narrow system, not the other way around. Thus the multiple meaningful connections in the dreaming brain open more possibilities for grander transformations through dreamwork than rational cognitive counselling.

With all this in mind, I suggest that condensation is a creative synthesis of areas and levels of the personality separated from each other during the routine thinking of everyday life. This process is guided by overall self-regulation and self-organization. This is in accordance with theories of a self-regulating, emotional, feeling and relational brain (Damasio 2000), (Cozolino 2014), (Schore 2009).

That dreams, from the perspective of normal waking consciousness, are condensed information implies that their connectivity must be unfolded in a creative process.

Core quality 9: dreams are experiences of wholeness

From early in childhood, experiential modalities such as visual imagery, bodily sensations, movement, emotion, and thought are employed as meaningful information channels and synthesized to express the wholeness of an experience (Stern 1985). Dreams combine all these modalities.

An ultimate consciousness product occurs from 'numerous brain sites at the same time and not in one site in particular', according to Damasio (2010, pp. 23-25). Baars's 'global workspace' mentioned in connection to Core Quality 2 is a neuronal term. Damasio finds a parallel to this in what he calls the 'image making regions' (ibid., p. 188-91) derived from brain scans of volunteers actively imagining and associating to feelings. For my work with dreams and therapeutic processes, I have introduced the term 'the supramodal space' (Vedfelt 2001).

What I call a supramodal method pays equal attention to all the modalities. An emotion may evoke an image, which elicits an involuntary movement, e.g. facial expression, which is felt as an inner bodily sensation, which connects to thought or unfolds an autobiographical memory. Paying attention to the 'supramodal' flow of the energy, you are engaging in a creative process that circumscribes the dream's entire experiential spectrum. It helps the therapist to facilitate resources and to navigate past defences that should not be provoked (Vedfelt 2017).

The term convergence-divergence zones refers to areas with respectively multimodal perception and experiences on one modality (Lallee 2013).

The images below (Fig. 10) show the vmPFC as a convergence zone (Schore 2000 p.172) and overriding regulator of a somatic marker system, which provide a felt sense or 'gut feeling, to intuitive decisions' (Damasio 1996).

The green areas in the left picture are related to interior sensing of the body. The red areas in the right picture are related to experienced movements in dreams.

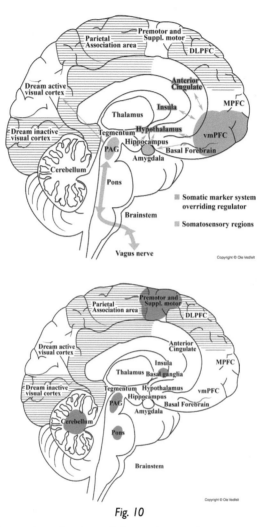

Fig. 10

Dorothy made a drawing of the earliest and most intense of her new-room-dreams, which was related to the creative breakthrough of her life. A staircase led to a long corridor in the attic and further to a large room with a magnificent view. The corridor fascinated her most. We circumambulated the image on all experiential modalities. The visual image of the corridor evoked a feeling of powerlessness. In our systemic relational attunement, she was able to stay with the feeling. Then slowly light streamed in between the tiles of the attic and dust particles gleamed in the air. Her feeling shifted to quiet joy.

She now understood, sensed, felt and imagined her experience as a useful guide to a creative process: to stay with the powerless state until it – not by will – but by inner power transforms, and leads to the room with the wide view.

Core quality 10: dreams are psychological energy landscapes

In every individual's life there are many areas of interest that are important. A competition between the most meaningful themes of our lives takes place in our internal network. What motivates us most at any given moment is not only dependent on rational considerations, but equally so on the intensity of unconscious patterns of experience and behaviour. In a network model, the balance between the patterns that regulate personality can be depicted as 'energy landscapes' with sharp peaks and low hills. Dominating patterns are sharp peaks in the landscape, while flexible patterns are lower hills and valleys (Rumelhart et al. 1986). In dominating patterns, information is packed tightly together. If such a pattern is activated, it has a tendency to siphon energy from all other patterns. In flexible patterns, the bonds between the individual parts are weaker so associations can
flow more freely within the network.

Network function is explained on the basis of a 'harmony theory', so-called because the interpreting schemas activated seek out that which is most 'harmonious', i.e. the most likely states in the surroundings with which to harmonize. In dreams, the self-organizing system properties search for optimal harmony within high-level personality dynamics under the given circumstances (Vedfelt 2017, p. 142).

Particularly intense energy and information can be attributed to so called 'Big Dreams' related to important life transitions (Jung1928, paras. 276-77 and Jung 1945/1948, paras. 554-55). Systematic research has described features to identify such dreams (Kluger 1955), (Bulkeley 2006).

Dorothy's dream of the undiscovered rooms was a peak in her psychological energy landscape. Also, her dream of the happy foetus pointed to the possibility of a totally new start in her life. Lisa's dream of the girl haunted by ghosts lifted her personality to a totally new level of dealing with her trauma. Likewise, the teenager Ida's red thread dream had far-reaching consequences.

Peaks can also be connected to single dream elements. In Dorothy's dream it was the dusty corridor with the gleaming light. In Lisa's dreamwork it was the feeling of a connection to her own 12-year-old lost-and-found self.

A peak experience dream can emerge after having worked on a general theme from many different angles. A peak in Graham's dream landscape of masculinity was the following: *He participated in an* accomplished men's choir where he sang the bass voice, and all the voices were in perfect harmony.

Before and after such peak-experience dreams there will be many soft hill dreams, which are the necessary preparation and follow-up to the peak dreams as Fig. 11 shows.

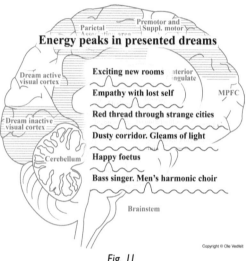

Fig. 11

Conclusion

It has been my privilege to work with and supervise a great variety of settings for dreamwork. Instead of letting this be a cause of conflict, I have found it inspiring on various levels of complexity adjusted to different needs and treatment resources. This experience is in accordance with the overriding integrative theory of cybernetic theory of complex neural network dynamics that I have presented.

When a complex system like the human personality is exposed to disturbances, it can find its way to more harmonic states via many paths' – cybernetically called 'equifinality' (Cicchetti et al.1996).

Asby's law of requisite variety that the more complex system potentially can regulate the less complex system and not the other way around (see Core quality 8) must be observed and practiced. This implies in-depth understanding of the principles of emergence and self-organization (See Core Quality 1) as well as of connectivity as a fundamental creative principle in complex dynamic networks (See Core Quality 8).

The integrative view finds support in contemporary systematic research in psychotherapy-effect, which indicates that the most experienced, flexible and method-integrating therapists have the best results (Von Wyl 2016), (Tschuschke et al. 2015).

Global perspectives

Good dreamwork creates harmony between subsystems in our psychological energy landscapes. A better balance in the ecological systems of our inner world will likely lead to more balance in both our relational environment and with the ecological systems of the world at large. Our dreams are an enormous resource. Globally, humankind dreams for a total of 15 billion hours every night. Dreamwork can contribute to humankind growing out of self-destructive conflicts and allow our potential to create a better world to unfold.

10 core qualities of dreams in rhymed verses by Ole Vedfelt

1) Dreams Deal with important Matters:
   We dream of important matters
   And never of trivial chatters
   Dreams know our motivations
   And most intimate relations.

2) Dreams Symbolize:
   The language of dreams is symbols
   And more than verbal talk
   They unfold a world of meanings
   That night after night us stalk.

3) Dreams Personify:
   The People in your dream-life
   Are portions of Your Self
   Negotiating through your strife
   To keep you off the shelf.

4) Dreams are Trial Runs in a Safe Place:
   The dreaming state is a safe place
   A playground for the mind
   Where new ideas can be tested
   Until you the best of them find.

5) Dreams are Online to Unconscious Intelligence:
   At night your dreams are online
   To unconscious intelligence
   The full spectrum of dreamwork
   Will allow for its emergence.

6) Dreams are Pattern Recognition:
   The dreams are dealing with patterns
   And searching a good-ness of fit
   You must match it with the context
   And use your poetic wit.

7) Dreams are High-Level Communication:
   The dreams have resources to offer
   So the wholeness of life doesn't suffer
   They are the psyches United Nations
   With high level communications.

8) Dreams are Condensed Information:
   The dreams make new connections
   They synthesize separations
   What looks as condensations
   Are natural creations.

9) Dreams are Experiences of Wholeness:
   Experiencing Wholeness
   Is hallmark of any dream
   A supramodal fullness
   In one assembled Stream.

10) Dreams are Psychological Energy Landscapes:
    A dream is a narrative landscape
    That measures the energy
    In any of our motives
    Striving for harmony.

References

Ashby, R. (1956/1961). *An Introduction to Cybernetics*. London: Chapman and Hall.

Baars, B.J. (2005). 'Global workspace theory of consciousness: toward a cognitive neuroscience of human experience'. *Progress in Brain Research*, 150, 45-73.

Bulkeley, K. (2006). 'Revision of the Good Fortune Scale: a new tool for the study of "Big Dreams"'. *Dreaming*, 16, 1, 11-21.

Cicchetti, D. & Rogosch, F.A. (1996). 'Equifinality and multifinality in developmental psychopathology'. *Development and Psychopathology*, 8, 4, 597-600.

Damasio, A. (1994). *Descarte's Error: Emotion, Reason and the Human Brain*. New York: Penguin Books.

— 'The somatic marker hypothesis and the possible functions of the prefrontal cortex'. *Phil. Trans. R. Soc. Lond.* B 351, 1413-20.

— (2000). *The Feeling of What Happens*. London: Vintage.

— (2010). *Self Comes to Mind: Constructing the Conscious Brain*. London: William Heineman. Kindle Edition.

Cozolino, L. (2010). *The Neuroscience of Psychotherapy: Healing the Social Brain (2nd Ed.)*. New York: W.W. Norton & Co. Kindle edition.
Dieckmann, H. (1984). *Träume als Sprache der Seele*. Stüttgart, Germany: Bonz.
Beaty, R.E., Benedek, M., Wilkins, R.W., Jauk, E., Fink, A., Silvia, P.J., Hodges, D.A., Koschutnig K. & Neubauer, A.C. (2014). 'Creativity and the default network. A functional connectivity analysis of the creative brain at rest'. *Neuropsychologia*, 64, (Nov.), 92-98.
Domhoff, G.W. (2010). 'The case for a cognitive theory of dreams'. Available online at: dreamresearch.net/Library/domhoff_2010.html (retrieved October 2015).
Dowd, T.E. (2004). 'Foreword' in *Cognitive Therapy and Dreams*, eds. R.I. Rosner, W.J. Lyddon & A. Freeman. New York: Springer Publishing.
Edelman, G.M. (1993). 'Neural Darwinism: selection and reentrant signaling in higher brain function'. *Neuron*, 10, 115-25.
Foulkes, D. & Fleischer, S. (1975). 'Mental activity in relaxed wakefulness'. *The Journal of Abnormal Psychology*, 84, 66-77.
Freud, S. (1900/2013). *The Interpretation of Dreams*. Sunderland, UK: Dead Dodo Vintage. Kindle edition.
Gusnard, D. (2006). 'Neural substrates of self-awareness'. In *Social Neuroscience: People Thinking about Thinking People*, eds. J.T. Cacioppo, P.S. Visser & C.L. Pickett. Cambridge, MA: MIT Press.
Habermas, J. (1968/2007). *Knowledge and Human Interest*. Cambridge: Polity Press.
Hall, C. (1953). 'A cognitive theory of dream symbolism'. *Journal of General Psychology*, 48, 169-86.
Hall, C.S. (1953). *The Meaning of Dreams*. New York: McGraw Hill.
Hall, C.S. & Nordby, V.J. (1972). *The Individual and His Dreams*. New York: New American Library.
Hartmann, E. (1998). *Dreams and Nightmares*. New York: Plenum.
Horton C.L. & Malinowski, J. (2015). 'Autobiographical memory and hyperassociativity in the dreaming brain: implications for memory consolidation in sleep'. *Frontiers in Psychology*, 6, 874.
Jung C.G. (1916). 'General aspects of dream psychology'. *CW* 8.
— (1928). 'The relations between the ego and the unconscious'. *CW* 7.
— (1933–5). 'Modern Psychology I-II'. Zürich: Eidgenossische Technische Hochschule.
— (1938–9). 'Kinderträume I og II'. Zürich: Eidgenossische Hochschule.
— (1945/1948). 'On the nature of dreams'. *CW* 8.
Kahn, D. & Hobson, A. (2005). 'State dependent thinking: A comparison of waking and dreaming thought'. *Consciousness and Cognition*, 14, 429-38.
Kluger, H.Y. (1955). 'Archetypal dreams and "everyday" dreams'. *Israel's Annals of Psychiatry and Related Disciplines*, 13, 6-47.
Koestler, A. (1964). *The Act of Creation*. London: Hutchinson & Co.
Kincaid, M. (2017). 'Parallel distributed processing models' in The University of Alberta's Cognitive Science Dictionary. penta.ufrgs.br/edu/telelab/3/paralled.htm Parallel Distributed Processing Models.

Kripke, D. & Sonnenschein, F. (1978). 'A biological rhythm in waking fantasy'. In *The Stream of Consciousness*, eds. J. Pope & K. Singer. New York: Plenum Press.
Lakoff, G. & Johnson, M. (1980/2008). *Metaphors We Live By*. Chicago, IL: University of Chicago Press. Kindle edition.
Laplanche, J. & Pontalis, J. (1967/2012). *The Language of Psychoanalysis*. London: Karnac Books. Kindle edition.
Lallee, S. & Dominey, P.F. (2013). 'Multi-modal convergence maps: from body schema and self representation to mental imagery'. *Adaptive Behavior*, 21, 4, 274-85.
Lewin, I. & Glaubmann, H. (1975). 'The effect of REM-deprivation. Is it detrimental, beneficial or neutral?', *Psychophysiology* 12, 349-353.
LeDoux, J. (1998). *The Emotional Brain*. London: Phoenix Paperback.
Luhmann, N. (1966). 'Reflexive mechanism'. *Soziale Welt*, 17, 1-23.
Mason, M.F., Norton, M.I., van Horn, J.D., Wegner, D.M., Grafton, S.T. & Macrae C.N. (2007). 'Wandering minds. The default network and stimulus independent thought'. *Science*, 315, (Jan.), 393-95.
Mattoon, M.A. (1978). *Applied Dream Analysis*. London: John Wiley.
Nunn, K., Hanstock. T & Lask, B. (2008). *Who's Who of the Brain*. London: Jessica Kingsley Publishers.
McClelland, J.L. & Rumelhart, D. (1986). 'A distributed model and human learning and memory'. In *Parallel Distributed Processing*, eds. J.L. McClelland & D. Rumelhart. Cambridge, MA: The MIT Press.
McNamara, P. (2012).'Philosophy of mind and dream characters'. In *Encyclopedia of Sleep and Dreams*, eds. D. Barrett & P. McNamara. Santa Barbara, CA: Greenwood Publishing, Kindle edition, 4976–5010.
Meltzer, D. (1983). *Dream – Life – A Re-examination of the Psychoanalytical Theory and Technique*. Strathclyde, UK: Clunie Press.
Nicolis, G. & Rouvas-Nicolis, C. (2007). 'Complex systems'. *Scholarpedia*, 2, 11, 1473.
Nielsen, T. (2012). 'Characters in dreams'. In *Encyclopedia of Sleep and Dreams*, eds. D. Barrett & P. McNamara. Santa Barbara, CA: Greenwood Publishing, Kindle edition, 3202-94.
Panksepp, J. (1998). *Affective Neuroscience: The Foundations of Human and Animal Emotions*. Oxford: Oxford University Press. Kindle Edition, Kindle edition,1745-67.
Perls, F. (1969/2013). *Gestalt Therapy Verbatim*. Gouldsboro, ME: The Gestalt Journal Press. Kindle edition.
Ratey J. (2001). *A User's Guide to the Brain: Perception, Attention, and the Four Theatres of the Brain*. New York: Knopf Doubleday Publishing Group. Kindle edition.
Rumelhart, D. (1980). 'Schemata: the building blocks of cognition'. In *Theoretical Issues in Reading Comprehension*, eds. R.J. Spiro, B.C. Bruce & W.F. Brewer. Hillsdale, NJ: Lawrence Erlbaum Associates.
Rumelhart, D., Smolensky, P., McClelland, J.L. & Hinton, G.E. (1986). 'Schemata and sequential thought processes in PDP models'. In *Parallel Distributed Processing: Explorations in the Microstructure of Cognition, Vol 2: Psychological and Biological Models*, eds. J.L. McClelland & D. Rumelhart. Cambridge, MA: The MIT Press.

Schore, A. (2000). 'Neurobiology of emotional development'. In *Emotion, Development and Self-Organization*, eds. M. Lewis and I. Granic. Cambridge: Cambridge University Press.

— (2009). 'Relational trauma and the developing right brain. An interface of psychoanalytic self'. *Annals of the New York Academy of Sciences*, 1159, 189-203.

Schnyer, D.M., Verfaellie, M., Alexander, M.P., LaFleche, G., Nicholls, L. & Kaszniak, A.W. (2004). 'A role for right medial prefrontal cortex in accurate feeling-of-knowing judgments: evidence from patients with lesions to frontal cortex'. *Neuropsychologia*, 42,7, 957-66.

Solms M. (1997). *The Neuropsychology of Dreams*. Mahwah, NJ: Lawrence Erlbaum.

Solms, M. & Turnbull, O. (2002). *The Brain and the Inner World*. New York: Other Press.

Stern, D.N. (1985). *The Interpersonal World of the Infant: A View from Psychoanalysis and Developmental Psychology*. London: Karnac Books. Kindle edition.

Stern, P. (1977). 'Foreword' in *I Dreamt Last Night*, ed. M. Boss. New York: Gardner Press Inc.

Tschuschke, V., Crameri, A., Koehler, M., Berglar, J., Muth, K., Staczan, P., Von Wyl, A., Schulthess, P. & Koemeda-Lutz, M. (2015). 'The role of therapists' treatment adherence, professional experience, therapeutic alliance, and clients' severity of psychological problems: Prediction of treatment outcome in eight different psychotherapy approaches. Preliminary results of a naturalistic study'. *Psychotherapy Research*, 25, 4, 420-34.

Van de Castle, R. (1994). *Our Dreaming Mind*. New York: Ballantine Books.

Vedfelt, O. (1994, 2002). The Dimensions of Dreams. The Nature Function and Interpretation of Dreams. London: Jessica Kingsley Publishers.

— (1996/2019). *Consciousness – Psychotherapeutic, Creative and Meditative Forms of Consciousness*. Amazon. Kindle.

— (2001), 'The supramodal space – a missing link between body, soul and spirit'. Conference paper. Institute for Biosynthesis. Zürich.

— (2002 /2018). *Unconscious Intelligence. You Know More Than You Think*. Amazon. Kindle.

— (2009). 'Cultivating feelings through working with dreams'. *Jung Journal: Culture & Psyche*, 3, 4, 88-102.

— (2017). 'Psychosis as a means to individuation – a case of severe psychosis healed through working with dreams, active imagination and transference'. *Proceedings of the 20th Congress of the International Association for Analytical Psychology, Kyoto*. Einsiedeln, Switzerland: Daimon Verlag.

— (2017). *A Guide to the World of Dreams – An Integrative Approach to Dreamwork*. London: Routledge.

Von Wyl, A., Tschuschke, V., Crameri, A., Koemeda-Lutz, M. & Schulthess, P. (eds.). (2016). '*Was wirkt in der Psychotherapie? Ergebnisse der Praxisstudie Ambulante Psychotherapie zu 10 unterschiedlichen Verfahren*'. Giessen: Psychosozial-Verlag.

Wiener, N. (1948/1962). *Cybernetics, or Control and Communication in the Animal and the Machine*. Cambridge, MA: The MIT Press.

Yu, C. (2015). 'The vicissitudes of the affective valence of dream emotions across the night. A high-density electroencephalographic study'. *Dreaming*, 25, 4, 274-90.

Zald D.H. & Andreotti, C. (2010). 'Neuropsychological assessment of the orbital and ventromedial prefrontal cortex'. *Neuropsychologia*, 48, 12, 3377-91.

Wednesday, 28 August 2019

Freud and Jung on Freud and Jung

Ernst Falzeder
Salzburg

with the collaboration of

Jörg Rasche
(DGAP) Berlin

In 1932, Jungian analyst E.A. Bennet was received by Freud in his home, after having met with Adler and Stekel a day or two earlier. 'I asked him,' writes Bennet, 'Why was it that he and the other pioneers in psychological medicine were on such bad terms with one another?' 'Adler's departure was not a loss,' Freud answered, and 'separation from [Stekel] was unavoidable because of personal characteristics in Stekel himself.' Regarding 'the rupture with Jung[,] Freud, after a pause, said very quietly, "Jung was a great loss." No more was said' (Bennet 1961, p. 58). On the other side, when Freudian analyst Kurt Eissler interviewed Jung in 1953 about his relationship and breakup with Freud, he, Eissler, said: 'This encounter between you and Freud was really something unique in history,' and Jung agreed: 'Yes, in that you are certainly right.' But then Jung spoke about what he called Freud's neurotic element: 'If only he had succeeded in getting over himself! ... If he could have overcome *that*, well ... It would have been crazy, wouldn't it, ever to want anything else than to work together with him!' (Freud Archives, Library of Congress).

I find it incontestable that this was a crucial encounter for both protagonists, although there is also one caveat I would like to mention. Important as their relationship was, we should be careful not to view it from a purely Freudocentric or Jungocentric standpoint. Neither was Jung's theory primarily 'an offshoot from psychoanalysis,' which would represent a 'mislocation' of Jung and complex psychology in the intellectual history of the twentieth century' (Shamdasani 2003, pp. 12-13), nor was Freud's thinking primarily influenced by Jung, although I have found that, rather surprisingly, Freud seems to have taken over more from Jung's ideas, or further investigated them, than vice versa (cf. Falzeder 2012). On the other hand, I find it incontestable that this was a crucial encounter for both of the protagonists.

The challenge for the intellectual historian, as I see it, is to investigate this encounter not from a partisan viewpoint, trying to show that one was right and the other wrong, as has been done in much of the secondary literature, but rather to see it as a sometimes volatile hotbed of emerging ideas and conflicts that had a great impact for decades to come, and can even today still generate heated discussions. Another complication arises from the fact that perhaps nowhere else in science are the so-called personal equation and affect-laden relationships, be they intimate or professional or both, so closely linked to the generation of theory. As a consequence, a history of ideas in this field cannot discard the personal background of the persons who conceived them, and of the web of relationships in which this took place. And finally, what Freud wrote about the psychoanalyst, holds also true for the historian: 'every unresolved repression in him constitutes what has been aptly described ... as a "blind spot" in his analytic perception' (1912e, p. 116). We must always be careful not to read something into the material that is not there, but exists only in our own heads and hearts.[1]

In April 1906, Jung sent Freud his recently published *Diagnostic Association Studies*, a collection of six studies by Jung and some colleagues at the Burghölzli Hospital in Zürich. These studies had already earned Jung an international reputation in psychiatry, and Freud wrote back that in his 'impatience' he had already bought the book and found that Jung's experiments confirmed 'that everything I have said about the hitherto unexplored field of our discipline is true' (p. 3[2]). He responded by sending Jung his own collection of *Short Papers on the Theory of the Neuroses* (1906). Subsequently, there developed, in very short time, an intimate and intense relationship between the two men, even with erotic undertones, as both later acknowledged. From the beginning, however, Jung made it clear that he did not agree with important parts of Freud's theory, in particular about the sexual aetiology of neuroses, whereas Freud wrote to him repeatedly that he, Freud, was absolutely confident that Jung would eventually come around to his viewpoint:

> Freud: 'I venture to hope that in the course of the years you will come much closer to me than you now think possible' (p. 5).

---

1 This problem has been variously addressed in the literature under the heading of the researcher's 'countertransference,' which word has become a kind of umbrella term for anything personal that interferes with the investigator's unbiased perception. However, since I am not aware that either Freud or Jung ever 'transferred' anything onto me, to which my countertransference would then be a reaction, I would suggest to see this, if we stay with this terminology, as simply the historian's transference. All this, I suggest, also holds true for the Freud/Jung relationship and the truly astonishing wealth of ideas that were developed – be it in close collaboration, or in an effort to prove the other wrong – by the two protagonists, arguably the most powerful tandem in the history of psychology.
2 Simple page numbers refer to the Freud/Jung letters (1974, ed. William McGuire).

Jung: 'Perhaps ... I have misunderstood you and would be entirely of your opinion. Even so, however, one feels alarmed by the positivism of your presentation' (p. 7).

F: '... the "transference," the chief proof that the drive underlying the whole process is sexual in nature, seems to have become very clear to you' (p. 8).

J: 'I am only beginning to understand many of your formulations and several of them are still beyond me, ... [but] I have gradually learnt to be cautious even in disbelief' (pp. 10-11).

F: '... your last letter has given me great pleasure, without qualification or auxiliary hypothesis' (trans. mod.[3]; pp. 11-12).

J: '... we do not see eye to eye on certain points' (p. 14). 'But you should not imagine that I am frenetically set on differentiating myself from you by the greatest possible divergence of opinion. I speak of things as I understand them and as I believe is right' (p. 15).

F: 'I beg of you, ... don't deviate too far from me when you are really so close to me, for if you do, we may one day be played off against one another' (p. 18). 'May we continue to work together and allow no misunderstanding to arise between us' (p. 19).

J: 'I am still young and now and then one has one's quirks in the matter of recognition and scientific standing. ... But ... you may rest assured: I shall never abandon any portion of your theory that is essential *to me*' (p. 20; my ital.).

When Jung wrote those words, he had already finished his next important book, *The Psychology of Dementia Praecox*,[4] or schizophrenia (published in 1907). It should be borne in mind that when the two men started their personal relationship and scientific collaboration, Jung was in fact already an internationally highly reputed scientist, regarded by many as a rising star in psychiatry. Freud, on the other hand, had won a reputation as a highly controversial figure. After he had started out as a promising young neurologist, and even after the publication, with Josef Breuer, of the *Studies in Hysteria* (1895), which met with mixed, but overall fairly positive reactions, his subsequent development of psychoanalysis proper and his stress on sexuality, be it in phantasy or in real life, made many of his colleagues view him as someone having gone astray.

After the publication of *The Interpretation of Dreams* (1900a), and the cooling-off and eventual break of his relationship with Wilhelm

---

[3] ... *daß ich mich über Ihren letzten Brief ohne Einschränkung und Hilfshypothese gefreut habe.*
[4] The foreword is dated July 1906.

Fliess, Freud was at a crossroad. He was nearing his 50th year, and looked back at a series of dead-end streets and failures. Practically all his relationships with potential supporters or followers (e.g., Josef Breuer, Emma Eckstein, Wilhelm Fließ, Felix Gattel, Heinrich Gomperz, Hermann Swoboda) had ended, or were about to end in separation. The personal friends who remained (Emanuel Löwy or Oscar Rie, for example) had nothing to do with psychoanalysis. His academic career, too, had come to a stalemate. This was partly due to a hostile or at least not welcoming attitude of the powers that be, but it is equally clear that Freud had not pursued a straightforward career. He had speculated about, or tried and given up, careers as a philosopher, as a zoologist, as a politician, as a paediatrician, as a psychopharmacologist, and as a neurologist. Although he had twice come very close to fame, in one instance he had missed the chance to make an important discovery, and in the second instance had wrongly claimed he had in fact made such a discovery. It was not Freud, but his friend Carl Koller who discovered the medical use of cocaine, while Freud remained mainly known as the one who had imprudently and indiscriminately recommended the use of this drug, e.g. for curing morphinism, with disastrous results. And shortly after declaring his so-called seduction theory the discovery of a '*caput Nili*' (Freud 1896c, p. 203; Freud 1985, p. 184), he had to retract it, if only privately.

With the publication of his *Three Essays on the Theory of Sexuality* (1905d) and the *Fragment of an Analysis of a Case of Hysteria* (1905e), both in 1905, in which he set forth his theory of the sexual aetiology of neuroses, the vast majority of his colleagues in academia, psychiatry, and psychology took their distance. Although his name was widely known in German speaking countries, it was little more than a party joke in many circles. As a matter of fact, by associating himself with Freud, Jung had much more to lose than Freud himself, for whom the possible support from Jung, Eugen Bleuler, and other renowned researchers at the Burghölzli clinic and the University of Zürich was like a win-win situation.

Jung himself explicitly stated later:

> I did not start from Freud, but from Eugen Bleuler and Pierre Janet, who were my immediate teachers. When I took up the cudgels for Freud in public, I already had a scientific position that was widely known on account of my association experiments, conducted independently of Freud, and the theory of complexes based upon them. My collaboration was qualified by an objection in principle to the sexual theory, and it lasted up to the time when Freud identified in principle his sexual theory with his method.
>
> (Jung 1934, footnote to § 1034)

In the honeymoon of their relationship, however, Freud seems to have made such an impression on Jung that for some time Jung seemed to be completely won over to Freud's viewpoint. This must also have been the time when, according to Abraham Brill, who also worked at the Burghölzli, Jung 'gave the impression that he was fully convinced of everything (Freudian),' and that one 'could not express any doubt about Freud's views without arousing his ire' (in Glover 1950, p. 45). After his first visit to Freud in Vienna, in early March 1907, Jung praised Freud in enthusiastic terms, and Freud revelled in the other's admiration and had high-flying plans for him.

J: 'I am no longer plagued by doubts as to the rightness of your theory. ... my stay in Vienna ... was an event of the first importance. ... I hope my work for your cause will show you the depths of my gratitude and veneration' (p. 26).

F: '... you have inspired me with confidence for the future ... I now realize that I am as replaceable as everyone else and that I could hope for no one better than yourself ... to continue and complete my work' (p. 27).

J: '... it seems to me that one can never quite understand your science unless one knows you in the flesh. ... Hence my visit in Vienna was a genuine confirmation' (p. 30). 'The identification with you will later prove to be very flattering; now it is *honor cum onere*' (p. 36).

F: 'Don't take the burden of representing me too hard. ... Perhaps you will incur the onus but not the odium of our cause, and in later years you will reap the full reward of your labours' (pp. 42-43).

J: 'I think one would have to be struck by the gods with sevenfold blindness not to see things now as they really are.... before the reformation of my psychological thinking ... [m]y thinking ... seems to me not only intellectually wrong and defective but, what is worse, morally inferior, since it now looks like an immense dishonesty towards myself' (p. 49).

F: '... don't worry, everything will work out all right. You will live to see the day, though I may not' (p. 43). 'I become more convinced than ever that we are in possession of a great idea' (p. 55).

J: 'Anyone who knows your science has veritably *eaten of the tree of paradise and become clairvoyant*' (p. 56; my ital.). 'I rejoice every day in your riches and live from the crumbs that fall from the rich man's table' (p. 56).

F: 'I am very much surprised to hear that I am the rich man from whose table you glean a few crumbs.... If only I were!' (p. 58). 'I can give no more, but I am *very* willing to receive more' (p. 62; ital. in orig.).

When we have a look at Jung the man and scientist during his correspondence with Freud, from April 1906 to January 1913, that is, over a period of seven years, we find that he underwent an astonishing development. He was nearing his 31st birthday when the correspondence started, and 37 when their personal relationship ended (Freud was 49 and 56 respectively.) This is Jung in a state of flux and great changes. This is Jung from the association experiments to the *Psychology of Dementia Praecox* (1907), from a completely Freudian analysis of his own daughter to the Fordham lectures, the two parts of 'Transformations and symbols of the libido' (1911/12), and the beginnings of *The Red Book* (2009). This is a searching and sometimes very insecure Jung, prone to mood swings and changing opinions, sometimes oscillating between extremes, including his attitude towards Freud.

Enter another figure, Eugen Bleuler, head of the Burghölzli and Jung's direct superior. Bleuler had already authored a positive review of the *Studies on Hysteria* (Breuer & Freud 1895), declaring the book to be 'one of the most important recent publications in the field of normal and pathological psychology' that would offer 'a new insight into the psychic mechanism' (Bleuler 1896, p. 525; also in Kiell 1988, p. 74). When *The Interpretation of Dreams* (Freud 1900a) came out, Bleuler was greatly impressed, and 'realised its correctness after the first reading' (Freud & Bleuler 2012, p. 74). As a matter of fact, it had been Bleuler, not Jung, who had introduced psychoanalysis at his clinic. He quickly recruited a staff open to dynamic psychiatry in general, and to this new discipline in particular. 'It was me, after all, who called Jung's attention to [psychoanalysis],' as Bleuler himself later pointed out to Freud (ibid., p. 189).

Bleuler had handpicked Jung to join the staff and had offered him a position as an assistant physician even before the latter had finished his studies (15 July 1900, ETH Archives). At Bleuler's instigation, Jung conducted his experiments on word associations, a brilliant combination of two cutting-edge approaches of the time, which he used for his *Habilitation* (the thesis necessary to apply for tenure). In his report, Bleuler particularly stressed, and endorsed, Jung's finding that the reaction time was influenced by strong affects which 'need not be conscious,' thus allowing for a 'unique insight into unconscious psychical processes.' Bleuler added that Jung's interpretations had proven valid 'in a great number of cases' and that his method had given 'insights into the genesis of hysterical and particularly of catatonic symptoms, insights one could not even have thought of before' (5

January 1905, ETH Archives). This went beyond the usual support for a young collaborator – it is evidence that Bleuler had approved of the notion of unconscious affects and their role in symptom formation, and that he was prepared to defend it against his colleagues on the faculty. In 1904, he published another defence of Freud's views: 'Freud ... has shown us part of a new world' (Bleuler, 1904, p. 718). For Freud, it must have been the wish-fulfilment of a dream.

One could say that Bleuler was really the greatest 'catch' Freud ever made: a world-renowned university professor and head of a leading psychiatric clinic, and also a Gentile. Bleuler recognized Freud's greatness at once and defended his views against the practically unanimous hostility in his own psychiatric circles, but he criticized Freud's more sweeping generalizations, asked for more hard evidence for some of the theories, and in particular objected to the increasing sectarian character of the so-called psychoanalytic 'movement.' Added to this came the experiment of having his dreams analysed by Freud by correspondence, which did not convince him. Freud made great efforts to win Bleuler over, but eventually did not succeed. Bleuler distanced himself more and more from Freud's theories and the 'movement,' although he never became openly hostile, and remained on respectful terms with Freud personally. This distancing had the consequence, however, that, at least in Europe, psychoanalysis lost the foothold it had had with him in academia and in psychiatry, with far-reaching consequences for many decades to come.

As to Jung's position in this triangle, for some time he seemed to side completely with Freud against Bleuler and his increasing reservations. Moreover, his personal relationship with Bleuler had always been complicated and sometimes became strained to breaking point. When Freud visited Jung in the Burghölzli, Jung persuaded Freud *not* to pay his respects to Bleuler who lived just one floor below Jung's apartment in the clinic, in fact to studiously *avoid* him, a terrible affront to Bleuler. A comparable thing happened at Christmas 1911, when Freud met both Bleuler and Jung in Munich, but separately and one after the other, so that the two men would not meet. In fact, Bleuler must have been under the impression that Freud had come exclusively to talk with him, because Freud did not tell him about his other meeting with Jung.

Jung continued to praise Freud, albeit often with interspersed doubts and reservations vis-à-vis the latter's theories and generalizations, while Freud kept stressing that he was absolutely confident that with increasing experience Jung would eventually come to see the absolute correctness of Freud's theories.

> J: 'The most difficult feat of all is to leach out the wealth of your ideas, boil down the essence, and finally bring off the

master-wizard's trick of producing something homogeneous. ... Often I want to give up in sheer despair' (p. 76).

F: 'What you call the hysterical element in your personality ... will come into its own ... And when you have injected your own personal leaven into the fermenting mass of my ideas in still more generous measure, there will be no further difference between your achievement and mine' (p. 77).

J: 'I would now like to ask you for an explanation: Do you regard sexuality as the mother of all feelings? Isn't sexuality for you merely one component of the personality ...?' (p. 79).

F: '*I should be very sorry if you imagined for one moment that I really doubted you in any way*' (p. 79; my ital.). 'As for your question, ... I do not believe that anyone is justified in saying that sexuality is the mother of all feelings.... I regard ... the role of sexual complexes ... merely as a theoretical necessity.... Proof, I believe, is not yet possible' (p. 80).

J: 'I am very grateful to you for formulating your view of the role of sexuality; it is much what I expected' (p. 81).

F: 'I take comfort by telling myself that ... *you as the other, the second*, will be spared at least a part of the opposition that would have been in store for me.... I wish I were with you, ... telling you about my long years of honourable but painful solitude ... about the terrifying moments when I myself thought I had gone astray and was wondering how I might still make my misled life useful to my family ... and about the serene certainty which finally took possession of me and bade me wait until a voice from the unknown multitude should answer mine. That voice was yours' (p. 82; my ital.).

J: '... it did me good to feel that I was fighting not only for an important discovery but for a great and honourable man as well' (p. 84). 'I would dearly like to have a photograph of you ... I would be ever so grateful because again and again I feel the want of your picture' (p. 86).

F: 'But please, don't make too much of me. I am too human to deserve it. Your desire to have a picture of me encourages me to make a similar request' (p. 88).

J: '[I have] *sentiments d'incomplétude* compensated by sentimental posing.... I am an odd mixture of fear and courage, both of them extreme and off-balance' (p. 114). 'I have a sin to confess: I have had your photograph enlarged. It looks marvellous' (p. 115).

F: 'You are joking about your *sentiments!*... too bad I haven't got you here to shake your hand; I'd shake it more than once. Spirit of my spirit, I can say with pride, but at the same time something artistic and soft, lofty and serene, something ingratiating that I could never have produced ... I approve exceedingly of what you are doing' (p. 115).

And shortly afterwards, Freud started to address Jung no longer as 'Dear colleague,' but as 'Dear friend.'

With hardly any exaggeration, one could say that Jung had a crush on Freud, a crush that was to him 'disgusting and ridiculous because of its undeniable erotic undertone.' '*I therefore fear your confidence*' (p. 95) he wrote and underlined it. But it also had *religious* overtones. It was *faith* that made him believe in Freud: 'Where so much still remains dark to us outsiders only faith can help; but the best and most effective faith is knowledge of your personality' (p. 30), he wrote, and that he had 'veritably eaten of the tree of paradise and become clairvoyant' (p. 56). At times Jung was subservient, submissive, seductive, vulnerable, and completely loyal. When he wrote to Freud that 'My old religiosity had secretly found in you a compensating factor' (p. 97), Freud answered drily, however: 'a transference on a religious basis would strike me as most disastrous; it could end only in apostasy' (p. 98).

One could say that Jung very much felt the 'erotic undertone' which he himself had at least co-introduced into their relationship, but fought against situations that would bring this out more openly, and in general fought against sexualization – both in their relationship and in theory. Indeed, what he did was to *accuse the other*, Freud, of sexualizing, and of having a deeply neurotic attitude towards sexuality in general.

In the course of their relationship as mirrored in their letters, *both* gradually became more and more vulnerable by opening themselves up, while simultaneously getting more and more weapons against the other at their disposal – weapons furnished by psychoanalysis. A nice example would be the game – a favourite game among psychoanalysts at the time – to catch someone making a Freudian slip and then to rub the other's nose in it. Jung wrote, for instance: 'I must point out with diabolical glee your slip of the pen [when writing about the Americans]: you wrote "your prudishness" instead of "their prudishness"' (p. 198). At the time, they could still take it with humour, and they tried to contain their differences by stressing how well they got along with each other.

J: 'Your line of thought on the paranoia question seems to be very different from mine, so I have great difficulty in following you' (p. 133). 'I am eager to hear of my errors, and hope to learn from them' (p. 139).

F: 'I am not at all angry with you' (p. 140). 'After all, it has never been my habit to reproach you with your partial disagreements, but rather to be pleased with your share of agreement. I know it will take you time to catch up with my experience of the past fifteen years' (p. 140).

J: 'Don't take any notice of my moodiness. If not too much is expected of me personally, I am usually at the top of my form' (p. 142).

With hindsight, Freud did expect too much of Jung. Three events stand out in particular: Jung's appointment as managing editor of the *Yearbook*, their joint trip to America, and Jung's installation as the first president of the newly founded International Psychoanalytical Association (IPA).

The first international meeting of analysts, in April 1908 in Salzburg/Austria, initiated and organized by Jung, strengthened the bond with Zurich. 'Bleuler was very, very celebrated,' one participant observed. 'I remember the pleasure of Freud that Bleuler came. Everybody was introduced to Bleuler, and Bleuler was the center of the Congress' (Klemperer interview; Freud Archives, Library of Congress). Bleuler also became co-editor, with Freud, of the first psychoanalytic periodical, the *Jahrbuch für psychoanalytische und psychopathologische Forschungen* [*Yearbook for Psychoanalytical and Psychopathological Research*], and Jung was tasked with the actual editorial work as a managing editor. Its first half-volume (March 1909) contained, besides Freud's case history of Little Hans, only works by authors linked with the Burghölzli: Abraham, Maeder, Jung, and Binswanger. Freud was pleased about this 'preponderance of the Zürich school' (Freud & Abraham 2002, p. 89).

Before the meeting, Freud had already had some doubts about Jung's loyalty to himself and The Cause, but reassured him afterwards:

> I wasn't worried [about you] ... At one time, yes, before our last meeting. But just seeing you in Salzburg ... I knew that our views would soon be reconciled, that you had not, as I had feared, been alienated from me by some inner development deriving from the relationship with your father and the beliefs of the Church (p. 158)

Still, scientific differences persisted, above all about the aetiology of schizophrenia and paranoia:

> J: 'Probably ... I am angry that you see my efforts to solve the D(ementia). pr.(aecox) problem in a different light' (pp. 160-61).

> F: 'Why shouldn't we get together to discuss a matter of such importance to both of us? The only question is ... whether I should go to see you or you come to see me' (p. 161). 'I need

you, ... the cause cannot do without you' (pp. 164-65). 'My selfish purpose, which I frankly confess, is to persuade you to continue and complete my work by applying to psychoses what I have begun with neuroses.... you seem better fitted than anyone else I know to carry out this mission. Besides, I'm fond of you [ich habe Sie lieb]' (p. 168; my ital.).

They did resolve to settle their differences for the time being. However, Freud sometimes had to wait for a long time for Jung to answer his letters. Jung became increasingly immersed in the study of mythology, which took up more and more of his time. At first, Freud made light of this:

> F: 'You know how much pleasure your letters give me, but I am far from wishing to burden you with the obligation of a formal correspondence ... Still, I hope you will not be surprised to hear from me as often as my own need prompts me to write' (p. 222).

Soon, however, he was clearly irritated:

> F: 'It probably isn't nice of you to keep me waiting 25 days ... for an answer ... I can't help responding to my own rhythm, and the only compromise-action I am capable of is not to post the letter I am now writing until Sunday' (p. 259).

> J: 'Pater, peccavi – it is indeed a scandal to have kept you waiting 25 days for an answer' (p. 262).

A second important event was the journey that Freud, Jung, and Ferenczi undertook together to America in 1909. Much has been written about this already, and I won't go into much detail here. But let me please point out that the three men spent practically all their time together, be it on the ship to and from America, be it during their stay there. They spent much of their time analysing each other's dreams, and I sometimes wish I could have been a little bird listening to their conversations.

There is one episode that has gained some notoriety. Edward A. Bennet recounts what Jung later told him (1961, p. 43): '[W]hen their boat was approaching New York with its famous sky-line, Jung saw Freud gazing – as he thought – at the view and spoke to him. He was surprised when Freud said, "Won't they get a surprise when they hear what we have to say to them" – referring to the coming lectures. "How ambitious you are!" exclaimed Jung. "Me?" said Freud. "I'm the most humble of men, and the only man who isn't ambitious." Jung replied: "That's a big thing – to be the only one."'

There is another version of this episode that has gained some notoriety and is often quoted in the literature, although most often without giving a reliable source for it, according to which Freud actually said: 'Don't they know that we're bringing them the plague?' (e.g., Noll 1994, p. 47). According to Elisabeth Roudinesco (1993, p. 398), this anecdote goes back to what Jacques Lacan claimed Jung had told him. Lacan had visited Jung in 1954 to ask him about his relationship with Freud. In a seminar given in Vienna the following year, in German (!), Lacan then declared publicly that Jung had allegedly told him about that statement of Freud's. Roudinesco notes that Lacan's word is the only evidence we have that this might actually have happened. All other sources I consulted (Jones, Schur, Ellenberger, Brome, Oberndorf, Roazen, Hale, Gay, or the above quoted Bennet) only report that Freud said something like: 'They will be quite surprised at what we will have to say to them!' In his interview with Eissler, Jung has the following to say: 'When we entered the harbor of New York, we were standing on the bridge, and Freud said to me: "If they only knew what we are bringing them!" I thought: Well, we will soon see what the Americans will do, won't we?! (laughs)' (Library of Congress, Freud Archives).

In New York City there also occurred one scene, which Jung later described as a turning point in his relationship with Freud. There exists one short reference to it in Ferenczi's *Clinical Diary* (1985), and two more detailed accounts of it, the latter both going back to Jung himself. One is an interview he gave to Saul Rosenzweig in 1951, who then wrote about it in his book on the psychoanalysts' expedition to America (1992). The other is the account Jung gave Kurt Eissler, when the latter interviewed him for the Freud Archives in 1953.[5]

Ferenczi – obviously an eyewitness – simply mentions Freud's 'hysterical symptom' of 'incontinence on Riverside Drive', a 'weakness, which he could not hide from us and himself' (1985, p. 184). Rosenzweig tells the story as follows:

> [In the interview, Jung] described one aspect of the American journey in detail. ... [T]here was a visit ... to the Columbia University Psychiatric Clinic ... While looking at the Palisades[6] Freud suffered a personal mishap. He accidentally urinated in his trousers and Jung helped him out of this embarrassment. ... Freud entertained a fear of similar accidents during the time of the lectures at Clark University. So Jung offered to help Freud

---

5 Jung also alluded to this incident in a talk with E.A. Bennet: 'In New York Freud spoke to Jung of personal difficulties – Jung did not talk of these – and asked his help in clearing them up' (1961, p. 42).
6 Rosenzweig comments that this reference to the Palisades was at first puzzling to him, but he then concluded that the mishap must have happened 'on the occasion of the group's visit to Columbia University ... The group were on Riverside Drive ... and could see the distant Palisades on the other side of the Hudson river' (1992, p. 292). Rosenzweig's conclusion that this happened on Riverside Drive is substantiated by Ferenczi's remark quoted above (first published seven years before Rosenzweig's book, but obviously overlooked by the latter).

overcome this fear if Freud would consent to some analytic intervention. Freud agreed and Jung began the 'treatment.'

(Rosenzweig 1992, pp. 64-65)

It was then that the following famous incident occurred: Jung asked Freud to give him some intimate personal details, and Freud refused on the grounds that he could not 'risk his authority.' It was precisely at that moment, as Jung later said and wrote various times, that Freud lost his authority altogether (e.g., Jung 1962, p. 182).

In his interview with Eissler, Jung also mentions that there was no public toilet in the vicinity and that Freud was suddenly afraid he wouldn't be able to hold his water, upon which he promptly wet his pants, and they had to get a cab to go back to the hotel. Freud was extremely embarrassed, but also feared that this was a sign of approaching senility, a symptom of a paralysis, to which Jung replied, nonsense, that would simply be a neurotic symptom. But of what?, Freud said. Everybody can see that you are extremely ambitious, Jung retorted, which Freud vehemently denied.[7] Still, he told Jung, that he would be immensely relieved if this were 'only' a neurotic symptom. So Jung offered to analyse him and asked him to tell him some dreams. He analysed them up to the point, at which – and here Jung again tells the story quoted above – Freud refused to give him further details of a very intimate nature. When pressed by Eissler, Jung then hinted at family affairs, with a thinly

veiled reference to Martha Freud and Minna Bernays. Still, Jung maintained, the little analytic work they had done was enough to make Freud's symptom disappear for the duration of their trip.

If this scene and Freud's refusal were so important to Jung, and robbed Freud of his authority, it is surprising that no trace of this can be found after their trip in their correspondence. On the contrary:

> J: 'I feel in top form and have become much more reasonable than you might suppose.... On the journey back to Switzerland I never stopped analysing dreams and discovered some priceless jokes' (p. 247).
>
> F: 'The day after we separated an incredible number of people looked amazingly like you; wherever I went in Hamburg, your light hat with the dark band kept turning up. And the same in Berlin' (p. 248). '[Thanks to] your companionship during the trip ... I never felt that I was among strangers' (p. 250).

---

7 Psychoanalytic theory linked enuresis to excessive (repressed) ambitiousness. On Freud's denial of being ambitious, see also above.

J: 'Occasionally a spasm of homesickness for you comes over me, but only occasionally ... The analysis on the voyage home has done me a lot of good' (p. 250).

Still, the reverberations of this extremely intense encounter over a period of 40 days, including analyses with each other, probably mostly of dreams and probably in the presence of the third member of the party, must have been immense. Let us not forget that both Jung and Ferenczi could have realistic hopes to succeed Freud as the leader of the psychoanalytic movement.

After the trip to America, Jung wrote even more to Freud about the 'coy new love,' as he called it, which had him in its grip, and which should preoccupy him to the end of his life: mythology. At first, this met with the complete approval of Freud, who obviously hoped and thought that Jung would apply Freud's theories, especially of the so-called nuclear complex, the Oedipus complex, to the vast field of mythology, and thus show that it was not only the *primum movens* in neuroses, as Freud himself had shown, or in psychoses, where Jung and Bleuler had already demonstrated that the symptomatology of the illness followed what Bleuler called 'Freudian mechanisms' (1906/07). Jung even encouraged Freud to join him in this interest and write himself about it.

J: '... mythology has got me in its grip, it's a mine of marvellous material. Won't you cast a beam of light in that direction, at least a kind of spectrum analysis *par distance*?' (pp. 251-52).

F: 'I am glad you share my belief that we must conquer the whole field of mythology' (p. 255).

J: 'I was immersed every evening in the history of symbols, i.e., in mythology and archaeology' (p. 258).

F: 'I was delighted to learn that you are going into mythology. A little less loneliness. I can't wait to hear of your discoveries.... I hope you will soon come to agree with me that in all likelihood mythology centres on the same nuclear complex as the neuroses' (p. 260).

J: 'For me there is no longer any doubt what the oldest and most natural myths are trying to say. They speak quite 'naturally' of the nuclear complex of neurosis' (p. 263).

F: 'I am delighted with your mythological studies.... These things cry out for understanding, and as long as the specialists won't help us, we shall have to do it ourselves' (p. 265).

J: 'I often wish I had you near me. So many things to ask you. For instance, I should like to pump you sometime for a definition of libido' (p. 270). 'The question of the original sexual constitution seems to me particularly difficult. Would it not be simplest, for the time being, to start with sensitivity as the general foundation of neurosis?' (p. 276)

F: 'I believe ... that the younger men will demolish everything in my heritage that is not absolutely solid as fast as they can.... Since you are likely to play a prominent part in this work of liquidation, I shall try to place certain of my endangered ideas in your safekeeping' (p. 277).

J: 'I have the most marvellous visions, glimpses of far-ranging interconnections which I am at present incapable of grasping' (p. 279). 'It is a hard lot to have to work alongside the father creator' (p. 279). 'I note that my difficulties regarding the question of libido and also of sadism are obviously due to the fact that I ... still haven't understood properly what you wrote me.... I would really have to question you on every sentence in your letter' (p. 280).

F: 'I am delighted that you yourself take this interest so seriously ... I could have dreamed of nothing better ... I know *the other*[8] has an easier time of it if one does not interfere with him' (p. 282; my ital. and trans.).

J: 'Mythology certainly has me in its grip.... I have no idea what will come out.... I ... am very unsure of myself as I'm oppressed by the feeling that I am just starting to learn.... my coy new love, mythology ... will set me many a test of courage' (p. 285).

F: 'Your deepened view of symbolism has all my sympathy.... it ... is ... in a direction where I too am searching, namely, *archaic regression*, which I hope to master through mythology and the *development of language*' (p. 291; ital. in orig.).

But Freud had also other plans for Jung. Fritz Wittels, Freud's first biographer, speculates that it was on the journey to America that the three men decided to found the IPA, and possibly discussed Jung's role in it: 'Naturally I do not know what the three gentlemen – Freud, Jung, and Ferenczi – talked about on their journey back across the ocean, but I have reasons to assume that they discussed the necessity of a tight organization of psychoanalysis' (1924, p. 121). As a matter of fact, the prehistory of the IPA's foundation is still quite mysterious. In my research, for instance, I found no written or other evidence when and how Jung learned that he was to become its first president. There is no mention of this in the Freud/Jung or Freud/Ferenczi or any other letters, instead Freud was still speculating shortly before

---

8 *der andere.*

the congress that the psychoanalysts could join other, already existing organizations, such as a rather obscure 'Order for Ethics and Culture,' or an association of psychotherapists founded by Auguste Forel, or, as Freud wrote to Alfred Adler, 'to join a certain party in practical life' (in Falzeder & Handlbauer 1992).

When the Nuremberg Congress began, on March 30, 1910, Jung arrived only at the last minute, probably at five o'clock in the morning, coming back from Chicago where he had gone for a consultation about his former patient Joseph Medill McCormick. At the end of the first day, it fell to Ferenczi, Jung's rival, to propose the foundation of a new international society and to nominate Jung as its president. As a matter of fact, Ferenczi acted as a proxy for Freud, who wrote afterwards: 'I had conceived of a project which with the help of my friend Ferenczi I carried out.... What I had in mind was to organize the psychoanalytic movement, to transfer its centre to Zürich and to give it a chief who would look after its future career.... This man could only be C. G. Jung ... I feared the abuses to which psycho-analysis would be subjected.... There should be some headquarters whose business it would be to declare: "All this nonsense is nothing to do with analysis; this is not psycho-analysis"' (1914d, pp. 42-43).

When Ferenczi revealed Freud's plans this came as a complete, indeed shocking surprise to nearly all the approximately 60 participants, particularly to the Viennese: Zürich was to become the new centre, and Jung was to become the lifetime president, with an extraordinary range of power: 'all papers written or addresses delivered by any psychoanalyst [were] to be first submitted for approval to the President' (Jones 1955, p. 69). Wittels – who was present – even writes that Jung should have had 'the absolute power to appoint or depose analysts' (1924, p. 122). After a revolt by the Viennese analysts, a compromise was reached: Jung was indeed elected president, but his term of office was limited to two years, and his power was significantly curtailed. To appease the Viennese, Adler was to replace Freud as the president of the Viennese society, and a new journal was founded to counterbalance Jung's editorship of the *Yearbook*, the *Zentralblatt*, edited by Adler and Stekel.

We may ask why Freud installed Jung, of all persons, as the president of the IPA and wanted to invest him with extraordinary powers to boot. Why not Ferenczi or Abraham, for instance? Or Alfred Adler? Sure, many factors spoke in Jung's favour: young, brilliant, Gentile, original, independent position, full of energy, and already author of important contributions to psychoanalysis. But surely the most important question for Freud had to be whether the new president would toe the line and act as his spokesperson, as it were, as someone who could indeed say with Freud's full approval: 'This is psychoanalysis, and this is not.' From the beginning of their acquaintance, Jung had made it very clear, however, and not once but repeatedly and also in print, that he did not subscribe to Freud's theories lock, stock and barrel, but that he had great reservations against their cornerstone, the alleged unique role sexuality played in the development of humans in general, and in the aetiology of neuroses in particular. And the second question is of course why Jung accepted this role.

As to Freud, I would suggest that, in addition to all the positive qualities Jung represented, exactly those reservations he voiced were a contributing factor. In fact, I think one can discern a pattern in Freud that whenever a brilliant and promising follower threatened to become lost to the cause, Freud tried to avert this by offering him a promotion in the movement, so to speak, a position of responsibility in which, as Freud thought and also sometimes wrote, he would then be more or less forced to represented the common cause. He also seemed to count on their personal loyalty to himself. This happened when he offered Bleuler the co-editorship of the *Yearbook*, and Jung its managing editorship, or Adler the presidency of the Viennese Society, Stekel, with Adler, the editorship of the *Zentralblatt*, Ferenczi the presidency of the IPA, Rank the presidency of the Viennese Society, and so on. As to Jung's motives, we can only speculate why he accepted to represent a man who in his own words had lost all authority to him only months earlier, and a theory with which he could not fully agree and was in fact on the verge of altering significantly.

For Jung, the years from 1908 to 1910 were crucial in his personal and scientific development. In general terms one could say that they contained landmarks, on the one hand, in his public career to more international prestige and recognition, and on the other hand, in his personal development to more independence and to finding his own way, his own 'myth.'

Seen from the perspective of his relationship with Freud and his role in the psychoanalytic community, these years saw his near-meteoric rise from an outsider, from one of quite a number of people who had positively commented on Freud in print, while simultaneously voicing criticisms against parts of his theories, to an insider. Jung initiated the first international meeting of analysts, which was the starting point for an international network, and he became the *de facto* editor of the first analytic journal, which also marked a decisive point in history. For the first time, analysts no longer depended on the goodwill of publishers or editors of other journals, and no longer needed to tailor their texts to the expectations of an uninformed or critical audience. As Freud wrote to Jung, with the *Yearbook*, 'the printing press has been invented so to speak for our benefit' (p. 282). This also brought about a significant change in the 'discussion culture' among psychoanalysts. Instead of oral discussions, which by the way were often surprisingly controversial and critical (see the *Minutes of the Vienna Psychoanalytic Society*; Nunberg & Federn 1962, 1967, 1974, 1975), and instead of articles that were scattered in the most various journals, psychoanalysts now had a forum of their own and could basically write what they wanted, although now they had to reckon with criticism in print from within their own ranks. Freud to Jung: 'I suggest that you and I share the work on this critical section, you will rap the Viennese on the knuckles and I the Zürich people ... this is an attempt at literary dictatorship, but our people are unreliable and need discipline' (pp. 259-60). And Jung was in charge of the journal in which all this was going to take place.

In March 1909, Jung visited Freud for the second time in Vienna, at which occasion Freud, as he wrote him, 'formally adopted you as eldest son and anointed you – *in partibus infidelium* – as my successor and crown prince' (p. 218). This visit coincided with Jung's resignation from his post at the Burghölzli, and also with the move of the Jung family into the new house he had built on Seestrasse 228 in Küsnacht, where he set up in private practice. Through his wedding with Emma Rauschenbach in 1903 he had also become a wealthy man and was no longer dependent on a regular income.

1909 was also the year, as we have seen, that he received an invitation to speak at Clark University. This invitation, it should be noted, was independent from that of Freud, although it was known of course that he was close to him. At the time 'he was only 34 years old' and thus 'the youngest of all the invited lecturers' (Rosenzweig 1992, p. 34), and it was a great honour to be invited to present there, together and in the midst of some of the leading and most respected researchers of the time. There were in all 29 distinguished lecturers there, all of whom received honorary degrees, among them two Nobel laureates, and the entire gamut of the sciences was represented (cf. ibid.; Burnham 2012).

Coming back to 1910 and the Nuremberg Congress, at which Jung arrived just in time, back from a visit to his celebrity patient McCormick, this represented another milestone in his career. He became in fact the head of a new and increasingly influential international movement and the way was clear, as it seemed at the time, that he would eventually succeed Freud and make it his own.

Instead of tightening his ties with Freud and the movement, however, Jung now went increasingly his own way. He did not take his duties as president as seriously as Freud wished, and also his secretary, Franz Riklin, neglected his editorship of the newly founded news bulletin, the *Korrespondenzblatt*, with news from each branch society. Second, their scientific differences became more and more pronounced and Jung more and more followed his own 'myth,' as he called it. And third, more and more personal misunderstandings cropped up, of which the infamous 'gesture of Kreuzlingen' is only one example. But for some time, the difficulties could still be contained.

F: '... we must stand firmly together, and now and then you must listen to me, your older friend, even when you are disinclined to.... You know how jealous they all are – here and elsewhere – over your privileged position with me' (p. 330). (And, after having read a paper of Jung's:) 'This sentence, "Sexuality destroys itself," provokes a vigorous shaking of the head. Such profundity is perhaps not clear enough for mythological thinking' (p. 334).

J: 'With regard to the sentence, "Sexuality destroys itself," I would remark that this is an extremely paradoxical formulation which I do not regard as in any way valid or viable' (p. 335). 'What it boils down to is a *conflict at the heart of sexuality itself*' (p. 336; ital. in orig.).

F: 'I believe that such far-reaching interpretations cannot be stated so succinctly but must be accompanied by ample proof, which, I am sure, you will now add' (p. 338).

J: 'I have been gadding about again like mad. For a fortnight I have pottered around Lake Constance ... with my sail-boat' (p. 341).

F: 'I believe I went ahead too fast.... the first months of your reign, my dear son and successor, have not turned out brilliantly. Sometimes I have the impression that you yourself have not taken your functions seriously enough' (p. 343).

J: 'I realize now that my debut as regent has turned out less than brilliantly' (p. 344). 'I heartily agree that we went ahead too fast.... there are far too many who haven't the faintest idea of what ΨA is really about' (p. 345). 'ΨA is too great a truth to be publicly acknowledged as yet' (p. 346).

F: '... we can't really expect to control the course of events by deliberate effort, but must observe with interest how they are shaped by the dark powers. We have let ourselves in for something bigger than ourselves. That calls for modesty' (p. 347). 'We understand each other' (p. 348).

J: 'Motto for ΨA: ... "Give what thou hast, then shalt thou receive"' (p. 350).

F: 'I send you my kind regards and an expression of my certainty that nothing can befall our cause as long as the understanding between you and me remains unclouded' (p. 355).

·J: 'I am working like a horse and am at present immersed in Iranian archaeology' (p. 355). 'I wallow in wonders' (p. 356).

F: 'I see that you go about working in the same way as I do; rather than take the obvious path that leads straight ahead, you keep your eye peeled for one that strikes your fancy. This is the best way, I think; afterwards one is amazed at the logical sequence in all these digressions' (p. 358).

We could say, with hindsight, that we are no longer 'amazed at the logical sequence' in Jung's digressions. It is my impression that what Jung must have perceived as Freud's pressure to represent and be the figurehead for his, Freud's, 'cause' proved too much. Although doubtlessly very much flattered and honoured by Freud's personal friendship and trust, he didn't want to go down in history as Freud's 'bulldog,' like Thomas Henry Huxley was known as 'Darwin's bulldog.'

We all know how it ended. To conclude, I won't summarize all the details of the following estrangement and rapprochement dance of Freud and Jung, and of the painful final rupture, which can be followed in their correspondence. From today's perspective, the parting of ways was inevitable. Still, for Freud Jung remained a great loss, and for Jung, as he said, it would have been crazy ever to want anything else than to work together with Freud. Today we have to live with the legacy of the friendship and rupture of two such great and outstanding psychologists. They both tried to light a candle in a sea of darkness, even if it was in different places.

References

Bennet, E.A. (1961[2006]). *C.G. Jung*. Wilmette, IL: Chiron, 2006.
Bleuler, E. (1896). 'Breuer und Freud: "Studien über Hysterie".' *Münchener Medizinische Wochenschrift*, 43, 524-25.
— (1904). 'Löwenfeld: "Die psychischen Zwangserscheinungen".' *Münchener Medizinische Wochenschrift*, 51, 718.
— (1906/07). 'Freud'sche Mechanismen in der Symptomatologie von Psychosen'. *Psychiatrisch-Neurologische Wochenschrift*, 8, 316-18.
Breuer, J. & Freud, S. (1895). *Studies on Hysteria*. SE 2.
Burnham, J. (ed.). (2012). *After Freud Left. A Century of Psychoanalysis in America*. Chicago, IL: Chicago University Press.
Falzeder, E. (2012). 'Freud and Jung, Freudians and Jungians'. *Jung Journal, Culture & Psyche*, 6, 24-43.
Falzeder, E. & Handlbauer, B. (1992). 'Freud, Adler et d'autres psychanalystes. Des débuts de la psychanalyse organisée à la fondation de l'Association Psychanalytique Internationale'. *Psychothérapies*, 12, 219-32.
Ferenczi, S. (1985). *Journal Clinique (Janvier-Octobre 1932)*, ed. Judith Dupont. Paris: Payot. *The Clinical Diary of Sándor Ferenczi*, (1932), ed. Judith Dupont, trans. M. Balint and N.Z. Jackson. Cambridge, MA: Harvard University Press, 1988.

Freud, S. (1896c). 'The aetiology of hysteria'. SE 3, 191-221.
— (1900a). The Interpretation of Dreams. SE 4 and 5.
— (1905d). Three Essays on the Theory of Sexuality. SE 7, 135-243.
— (1905e). 'Fragment of an analysis of a case of hysteria'. SE 7, 7-122.
— (1906). Sammlung Kleiner Schriften zur Neurosenlehre aus den Jahren 1893 bis 1906. Leipzig, Vienna: Franz Deuticke.
— (1912e). 'Recommendations to physicians practising psycho-analysis.' SE 12, 111-20.
— (1914d). 'On the history of the psycho-analytic movement'. SE 14, 7-66.
— (1985c [1887-1904]). The Complete Letters of Sigmund Freud to Wilhelm Fließ 1887-1904, ed. Jeffrey M. Masson. Cambridge, MA: The Belknap Press of Harvard University Press.
Freud, S. & Abraham, K. (2002). The Complete Correspondence of Sigmund Freud and Karl Abraham, 1907-1925: Completed Edition, ed. Ernst Falzeder. London: Karnac.
Freud, S. & Bleuler, E. (2012). "Ich bin zuversichtlich, wir erobern bald die Psychiatrie." Briefwechsel 1904-1937, ed. Michael Schröter. Basel: Schwabe.
Freud, S. & Jung, C.G. (1974). The Freud/Jung Letters. The Correspondence Between Sigmund Freud and C.G. Jung, ed. William McGuire. Cambridge, MA: Harvard University Press.
Glover, E. (1950). Freud or Jung. New York: W.W. Norton. Reprint Evanston: Northwestern University Press, 1991.
Jones, E. (1955). The Life and Work of Sigmund Freud. Volume 2: Years of Maturity, 1901-1919. New York: Basic Books.
Jung, C.G. (1907). 'The psychology of dementia praecox'. CW 3.
— (1911/12). 'Wandlungen und Symbole der Libido. Beiträge zur Entwicklungsgeschichte des Denkens.' Jahrbuch für psychoanalytische und psychopathologische Forschungen, 1911, 3, 120-227; 1912, 4, 162-464.
— (1934). 'Letter to Neue Zürcher Zeitung'. CW 10, p. 544.
— (1962). Memories, Dreams, Reflections. Recorded and edited by Aniela Jaffé. New York: Pantheon, 1973.
— (2009). The Red Book: Liber Novus, ed. Sonu Shamdasani. New York: W.W. Norton.
Jung, C.G. et al. (1906). Diagnostische Assoziationsstudien. Beiträge zur experimentellen Psychopathologie. Band I. Leipzig: Ambrosius Barth.
Kiell, Norman (ed.) (1988). Freud Without Hindsight: Reviews of His Work (1893-1939). Guilford, CT: International Universities Press.
Noll, R. (1994). The Jung Cult: Origins of a Charismatic Movement. New York: Free Press, second ed. 1997.
Nunberg, H. & Federn, E. (eds.) (1962, 1967, 1974, 1975). Minutes of the Vienna Psychoanalytic Society. Volume 1: 1906-1908. Volume 2: 1908-1910. Volume 3: 1910-1911. Volume 4: 1912-1918. New York: International Universities Press.
Roudinesco, E. (1993). Jacques Lacan: Esquisse d'une vie, histoire d'un système de pensée. Paris: Librairie Arthème Fayard.
Rosenzweig, S. (1992). Freud, Jung, and Hall the King-Maker: The Historic Expedition to America (1909), with G. Stanley Hall as Host and William James as Guest. Seattle: Hogrefe and Huber.
Shamdasani, S. (2003). Jung and the Making of Modern Psychology: The Dream of a Science. Cambridge: Cambridge University Press.

Wittels, F. (1924). *Sigmund Freud: His Personality, His Teaching, and His School.* London: Allen & Unwin.

Opening the closed heart: affect-focused clinical work with the victims of early trauma

Donald E. Kalsched
(IRSJA, NMSJA) *Santa Fe, New Mexico*

Introduction

For the last several decades I have been writing about a group of patients who have suffered early developmental trauma. These patients have been injured in their earliest years – sometimes as far back as infancy – to the point of requiring dissociative defenses to survive. In previous work I have described such defenses as a 'Self-Care-System' (Kalsched, 1996, 2013) and I have tried to illustrate the various parts of this system and to explore their dynamic interaction and how they function to protect (while also persecuting) a vulnerable and vital core of the self often imaged as an inner 'child.'[1]

In the present paper I want to explore a different question, namely what is it that these powerful, dissociative defenses are defending *against*? Recent literature in the field of affective neuroscience points us toward an answer to this question. It suggests that the central problem for these patients is the issue of their overwhelming affects and the struggle to regulate these affects – a struggle that only dissociative defenses can win for them. In order to survive, they have had to cut off connections with their feelings and with their bodies in which feelings are housed. Their brave efforts at self-control and self-healing

---

1 To illustrate the various parts of what I call the 'Self-Care System', I have utilized William Blakes' illustration of the 'Good and Evil Angels Fighting for Possession of a Child', which is in the Tate gallery in London. The interested reader can find this image on the cover of my most recent book and also on the Internet. It shows a dark angel on the left, chained to the hellish flames of material reality, groping with blank, unfeeling eyes towards a terrified child who is fleeing into the arms of a 'bright angel' on the right. I have interpreted the two 'angels' in this image as violence on the one hand and illusion on the other – two sides of a protector/persecutor defense. Meanwhile, the 'child' in the system might be thought of as the wounded child, carrying the injuries of early trauma in its small body (implicit memory) – early unbearable feelings trapped in a system of archetypal defenses – prevented from becoming conscious to the ego. The child also carries the imperishable spirit of the personality – pre-traumatic innocence – what Jung identified in his own active imagination as a spark of the divine, imaged as a 'divine child.' So the angels have a double reason for protecting the 'child.' They don't want its impossible emotion to be made conscious and they don't want to endanger the vulnerable core – the ineffable mystery it carries. This spark is hidden in the pain ... 'in stecore' (the shit) as the alchemists put it ... in the dark, rejected *prima materia* of traumatic memory.

have left them heroic survivors but affectively impoverished. While often highly successful in the outer world, they are defended against emotional experience. They can't feel their feelings very well and they often feel like strangers in their own bodies. Winnicott (1949) reminds us that the good-enough mother is constantly introducing and re-introducing the baby's mind and body to each other. The result is what he calls 'psychosomatic indwelling' (1964, p. 113). For these patients, psycho-somatic indwelling has not taken place, or taken place only partially. *We might say that their hearts have been broken before they had hearts to break.*

So I want to put affect and the body in the foreground of my presentation today. My inspiration to do so came from some remarks made by the late psychoanalyst Paul Russell who said, very succinctly, that *'trauma is an injury to the capacity to feel'* (Russell 1999, p. 24). He went on to say that this injury constitutes a tragedy in the life of the trauma survivor, because 'feelings are the window to life' (ibid., p. 45). Hence when the capacity to feel is injured, a person's very core of aliveness and vitality is compromised. Intuitively I knew Russell was right about this, but then the question remained, 'how does the capacity to feel get injured?' and 'how can it be addressed therapeutically?' How can the window to life be re-opened?

Russell starts us on a path towards an answer to this question by pointing out that injuries to our capacity to feel always occur in the context of our earliest attachment relationships. Recent research by Allan Schore (2019) and others in the attachment field, confirms this fact. Trauma originates in our earliest relationships because that is where affect in the body and images or words in the mind get connected through the dyadic attunement, empathy and emotional playback between mother and infant. If attunement is optimal, the positive affects of joy, curiosity, and interest take root and a centre of aliveness and vitality consolidates. On the other hand, if dyadic interactions between the mother and her infant are chronically mis-attuned then what Pierre Janet (1889 in van der Kolk, 1989) called the *'vehement emotions'* – i.e., life-threatening, intensely negative stressful affects take over. The mis-attuned mother is not able to help her infant or young child process these vehement emotions, or help to regulate the overwhelming bodily states that go with them. Hence, the traumatized child learns that he must process and contain these emotions and bodily states *all by himself.*

Of course he cannot do this *all by himself.* He is too small, vulnerable, and overwhelmed. So dissociative defenses do it for him. These defenses then cause an injury in the capacity to feel. They shut down healthy instincts for attachment outwardly and they shut down the connections between the body and the mind inwardly – a process Bion (1969) called 'attacks against linking'. What Jung (1916) called the 'transcendent function' is foreclosed and rendered inoperative by dissociative defenses. The important point here is that the outer traumatic event is not what injures the capacity to feel. It is the psyche's *defensive response* to the vehement emotions caused by trauma that injures it. Because this is true, we have a chance to intervene. We can't change history but we can change the psyche's *response* to history.[2] This means doing our best to help soften defenses while encouraging a relational field in which the patient can feel safe in our presence – all with the goal of touching that core of vitality and aliveness referred to in recent neuro-psychological literature as the 'implicit self' (see Schore, 2011).

A final facet of Paul Russell's ideas about trauma is this: When patients with a history of early trauma come into psychotherapy and a new attachment relationship starts, the original longings for attachment, the painful memories of mis-attunement, the resulting vehement emotions, and the defenses against them, will all be triggered and *repeated in the transference*. In these patients there is always both a powerful urge toward life and an equally powerful 'force' against life – a 'killing' energy stalking the inner world. Freud called this the 'repetition compulsion'. It's a destructive pattern for the patients who are caught in it, but it also gives us therapists an opportunity to participate in the original injury in the transference, and to work directly with the healthy longings for attachment and the murderous defenses preventing it, at the same time.

So, Russell's statement that 'trauma is an injury to the capacity to feel' seemed to me a good summary for a new affect-centred exploration of early trauma and its treatment. It was also consistent with the approach of some of the best psychotherapists I have known and studied with over the years. Two in particular stand out – Dr. Manny Hammer in New York, whose book *Reaching the Affect* (1990) was important to me in my training. He pointed out that our major challenge is how to reach out and touch the patient with words, rather than literally or concretely. And for this he said we need the vitalizing words of poetry and great literature – not the dried-up language of theory and interpretation. We must use whatever is needed, he said – metaphor, poetry, psychodrama, dreams, music, movement, sandplay – to help re-establish the link between affect in the body and imagery in the mind that was severed in the patient's early life. Quoting Frieda

---

2 It might be worth underscoring the therapeutic implications of this point. The outer traumatic event is not what injures the capacity to feel. Therefore, in therapy, commiserating with the patient's often-repetitive victim/perpetrator story about what happened to him in the outer world is not effective trauma therapy. (Regretfully, I have spent a lot of time doing this.) Eventually I realized that this incessant, victim-perpetrator narrative is one of the ways the patient's defensive system kept me distracted from the underlying pain, grief, and orphaned vulnerability.

Fromm-Reichman, Dr. Hammer used to say 'the patient is in need of an experience, not an explanation!' (Hammer 1990, p. 19).

The second mentor was Dr. Elvin Semrad, who once said in a seminar, and without apology, 'Ladies and gentlemen, we are in the feeling business!' We must, he said, 'go right through the defenses and pursue what the patient feels and cannot feel by himself' (Rako & Mazer 2003, p.103). We must 'help him to acknowledge what he cannot bear himself, and stay with him until he can stand it' (ibid., p. 105). 'And if we can't wait until he feels it in his own body, we're in the wrong business' (ibid., p. 107).

Semrad and others remind us that the powerful emotions that inevitably accompany trauma – when they remain unprocessed – get encoded in the body's musculature, posture and various psychosomatic states where they stay alive as concrete physical symptoms and tension-states, while their deeper symbolic and feeling-significance remains 'implicit' and invisible – buried in what we would call the 'somatic unconscious'. Reaching the affect lying underneath these concrete bodily manifestations means that the therapist must be able to move fluidly back and forth between the somatic and psychological poles of experience, while working with her patient.

This means experientially focused therapy and is not something that most of us Jungian analysts were trained to do. I confess that with sensation as my inferior function, I'm still struggling to learn how to include the body in my work.[3] But contemporary research on trauma shows that the body is as much the 'royal road' to unconscious emotion as dreams. I have found that simply asking the patient to pay attention to an unconscious bodily gesture or posture, or asking where a feeling is felt in the body, or taking a patient through a simple exercise in progressive relaxation (a body-scan), pays great dividends in accessing unconscious emotion – and helping to heal the injury to the capacity to feel.[4]

Finally, Russell's statement, with its focus on feeling, encouraged me

---

3 Others in the Jungian tradition have made important contributions to body-sensitive ways of working, especially Marion Woodman's 'Body-Soul Rhythms', the longstanding work of Joan Chodorow in California and Anita Greene in New York, the 'authentic movement' work of Tina Stromsted and most recently the creative contribution of Marian Dunlea to what she calls 'Body Dreaming'. Outside the Jungian area, Peter Levine's work has been widely recognized as well as Pat Ogden's articulation of a 'sensorimotor approach' to psychotherapy and Diane Fosha's well-known AEDP approach.

4 Paying attention to the embodied 'field' with the patient also helps us to notice when dissociative defenses are operating in the moment-to-moment processing of experience. Being able to 'spot' a moment where the patient dis-connects and moves out of relationship and back into the Self Care System allows us to inquire about the feeling that immediately preceded the dissociation. Becoming aware of these 'triggering' situations and witnessing the defense that follows can be a constructive lesson in affect-regulation. An example of such a moment follows in the case example of 'Beth.'

to explore some nagging questions I had about the seemingly minimal role of feelings in Jung's understanding of how therapy works. Describing the healing moments in his analytic practice, Jung frequently emphasized the experience of the numinous, or the revelatory meaning that can come from understanding archetypal parallels to personal dream images. These are all left-brain interventions connected to meaning. He rarely talked about the recovery of feelings or feeling-capacity as a change-agent in psychotherapy. This always puzzled me because of the otherwise central role Jung gives to affect. 'The essential basis of our personality is affectivity', he wrote (Jung 1907, para. 78). Plus Jung's personal struggle with his own vehement emotion was central to all the discoveries he made, during the night-sea-journey later recorded in *The Red Book*. He would have drowned in his emotions, he said, (Jung, 1963a) if he had not found ways of holding them until they transformed into images and fantasies. And the archetypes, in Jung's understanding were *affect-images*. The affect from the body gave them their dynamic charge and the image, from the mind, gave them their meaning. So affect-images, linking body and mind, spirit and matter in a dynamic symbol, became, for him, the basic building blocks of our dreams, our complexes and the imagination itself.

So what happened to affect in the development of Jungian thought? That's my first nagging question. Is there not a tendency in our psychology to get carried away with the image, leaving the affect aside? 'Image is psyche' (Jung 1929, para. 75), said Jung. 'Stick with the image', said Hillman (1975, pp. 114, 222). Are we perhaps inclined to forget that it's not just the image that's psyche but the affect-image that's psyche? In my experience, 'sticking with the image' is important because it will lead us to the affect – and vice versa.

And where do *feelings* fit into this equation? That's my second nagging question. Jung makes clear that archetypal affects are not yet feelings, because they are unconscious. Feeling, on the other hand, is a function of consciousness, and, as John Perry puts it: 'to the degree to which feeling is differentiated – it has the quality of choice and intentionality in its judgments of value' (Perry 1970, p. 2). This understanding leads naturally to Jung's choice of feeling as one of the major orienting function-types of consciousness, along with sensation, intuition, and thinking. Here's my point. If feeling is limited to one of the four functions of consciousness, and placed inside a typology, its central role in the dynamics of psychological life *across all typologies* may get neglected or overlooked, and with it, the role of defenses against feeling. Let me give you an example from my own analysis that might help clarify some of these concerns.

Personal example

One of the most important and memorable moments that occurred in my training analysis was the following: My second analyst was a very feeling man – which is why I chose him in the first place, and he helped me a great deal. During that time in my life, in my early 30s, I was trying to assimilate and process the emotional impact of my decision to leave a seven-year marriage and my two small children, ages two and four, in order to be free to explore a new relationship. This meant completely undoing the life I had created. And I had gone ahead with this. The feelings underneath were more than I could bear to feel consciously, and as a result, I was depressed. I wasn't dreaming. And my inner life was a desert. Somewhere underneath, I was in deep pain, saturated with guilt and shame over this decision and what it would mean for my children and my relationship with them, but I wasn't feeling it, and my analyst said to me 'you know it's really important that you carry this grief consciously'.

He said this with obvious feeling in his voice and concern for my psychological well-being. And I think there was wisdom in his statement, which is probably why I remember it almost 50 years later … and why I'm talking about it today. But what a peculiar way of saying it! I want to say what a peculiarly 'Jungian' way of saying it. 'It's really important that you carry your grief consciously'. I guess the message was 'don't let your grief fall into the unconscious (which it already had!) because it will make you psychologically ill' (which I already was). I knew instinctively that he was right. I just didn't know how to do it. *I needed an experience instead of an explanation.*

So let's imagine, with the benefit of hindsight (and 45 years of clinical experience) that I could re-do this moment with a perfect ideal analyst … and of course, with me as a perfect ideal patient. Indulge me for a moment … this is a thought experiment. My analyst might have interrupted my obsessive worried talk about myself – the incessant self-punishing thoughts that were cutting off my feelings, and said something like this: 'look, let's just slow down for a moment – close your eyes, and let yourself sink into your body – just relax, follow your breath and pay attention to any sensations, images or feelings that come up. Just notice the felt-sense of what you're experiencing'. Had something painful emerged, he might have asked me where I felt it in my body, and he would have asked me to stay with it – not move back into my head, as I was so wont to do. He might have handed me paper and crayons and had me draw my feelings. He might have helped me with a guided imagination instead of sending me home to do active imagination by myself with an imagination that had already dried up. He might have read me a poem – like Mary Oliver's (2017)

'Wild Geese' (a poem I know by heart and hold in mind for moments like this with patients).[5]

These kinds of interventions by my ideal analyst *might* have jump-started the dead battery of my imagination at that time, helping me get to the underlying affect sealed off under my over-active defenses. I desperately needed – somehow! – to let my heart break right there in the room with him – and *fully occupy this tragedy that I was living* – a tragedy that I couldn't bear to bring into full awareness.

Fortunately, I didn't stay in this dried-up, dissociated condition forever. Eventually I began to gain access to my underlying affects. And the way this happened for me was that *I started dreaming*. And this is often the way it is – as we all know. For those of us fortunate enough to have had a more or less adequate attachment relationship at the beginning, the imagination usually arrives to help the frozen psyche thaw itself out.

One of the points I'm trying to make with this example is that consciousness comes about by making unconscious emotion conscious – as feelings. It's not just a mental or left-brain thing but involves bi-lateral information-processing requiring both right and left hemispheres. And it happens in relationship. We can talk all we want about the 'contents of the unconscious' about 'incompatible tendencies', about the 'opposites' about the 'transcendent function', about the 'analytic third' but *consciousness comes about through emotional transformation*. It's about recovering feelings from the deadening grip of defenses that have all but 'killed' our access to them. Jung (1954, pp. 96-99) puts it this way in a statement I've always appreciated:

> The stirring up of conflict is a Luciferian virtue in the true sense of the word. Conflict engenders fire, the fire of affects and emotions, and like every other fire, it has two aspects, that of combustion and that of creating light ... *for emotion is the chief source of consciousness*. There is no change from darkness to light or from inertia to movement without emotion (italics mine)
>
> (Jung 1954, para. 179)

---

5 Jung once helped a patient out of psychological paralysis by singing a song. His young female patient was so anxious she couldn't sleep, so frozen with fear that she couldn't relax in his presence. Aniela Jaffé (1989; 122) tells how Jung had the courage to use his own feeling imagination while sitting with this highly defended patient. Attending to his inner world, Jung suddenly heard his mother's voice singing a lullaby to his little sister when he was only eight or nine – a song about a little girl in a little boat on the Rhine with tiny fishes. He found himself singing this same lullaby to his young patient to help her relax and feel safe in his presence. Jaffé tells us that this completely opened her up and her sleepless symptoms vanished. Here Jung was taking on the transcendent function for his patient whose own symbolic function wasn't working – any more than mine was in the above example. Her defenses relaxed and her feelings came forward and as Jung reported, she was 'enchanted'.

> A complex can be really overcome only if it is lived out to the full. In other words, if we are to develop further, we have to draw to us and drink down to the very dregs what, because of our complexes, we have held at a distance
>
> (ibid., para. 184)

In the second part of this quote Jung is saying, in effect, that we have to feel things fully – and that our complexes have prevented this. He sees the defenses that cause the injury to the capacity to feel entirely through the lens of the complexes. I'm not sure this is an adequate model when it comes to severe early trauma or the pockets of trauma and dissociation such as I was struggling with in the above example. In my experience, the primitive defenses I've described in my writing do more than 'hold feelings at a distance'. They put the symbolic process out of commission altogether, stopping the flow of the imagination. They sever head from heart so that conscious feeling is not possible. There was a great sadness that lived in my body, but it was frozen there and unavailable. And, there was no defined 'complex' to be worked with. There was no 'divorce complex'. There was the general problem of my *unconscious suffering* – and it was a big one – of my underlying emotion and my defenses against it. There was the injury to my capacity to feel and the fact that I couldn't heal this injury all by myself.

A clinical example of reaching the underlying affect

Now I'd like to describe a clinical vignette with a patient who suffered (like I did) from an injury to the capacity to feel and how this was partially restored by attending carefully to the embodied relational connections with the patient in the moment.

'Beth', (as I will call this patient) was a pediatric physician in her mid-50's who consulted me because the breakup of a relationship had left her depressed, withdrawn, and unable to work – dead inside. She told me she had many years of prior therapy and analysis, but nothing lasted, adding to her sense of failure.

She was very depressed when I first saw her, constricted in her body, frozen in her posture, thin and disheveled like a waif or an orphan. Like many patients with survival defenses, she was functioning but not living. 'I want my Spirit back', she said, with a great sense of longing in her voice. Her life reminded me of the I-Ching phrase, 'Difficulty at the Beginning'. Born in poverty to Eastern European Jewish parents who were both Holocaust survivors, she spent much of her early life as a refugee and immigrant as the family tried desperately to leave a communist-dominated Eastern European country. At nine months of age, she was near death with a smallpox infection and had to be quarantined in a big-city hospital far from her parents – kept in isolation for a whole month before she had even been weaned. Beth had no memory of this early trauma but later in life, any hint of abandonment could send her into a panic.

Then, when she was only three years old, her family made plans for their final escape. With soldiers prowling all the check-points, and children not allowed over the border, she had been sedated, tied-up, gagged and thrown across her father's back in a potato sack for concealment. Here, after the sedative wore off, she had kicked and screamed and vomited in her bindings for the rest of the long march through the snow. She was left exhausted, traumatized and near death once again. Serious pneumonia followed and with it, another threat of being left behind in another hospital. Beth screamed herself into a fever until they took her along. Finally, after another year of chaotic travel as immigrants, the family arrived in New York City where Beth entered school without knowing a word of English. Needless to say, further trauma and humiliation followed.

'I have severe abandonment issues', Beth said in an early session. 'I can feel really tiny and vulnerable – very condensed inside ... a fear of reaching out and getting hit or hurt. When I'm depressed, it's all consuming. I'll go into a dissociated place ... daydream a lot .... consoling myself that I'm practicing my own death.... I can't live so well but I know how to "die" – that's what I say to myself – so it won't be so bad later'.

The week prior to our first session, while Beth was anxiously (and excitedly) anticipating the hour, she had a dream that gave us a picture of her inner world and its major players. It did not exactly make her want to come to therapy. Here's the dream:

'I'm watching a therapy situation in a house by the ocean. The therapist is a young man. The patient, also a male, is lying on the couch. The therapist is trying to hide his sexuality... he has a hard-on. Something ominous is about to happen. I go into my 'observer' mode and can see this as if it's in the future. The patient wants to bring his child to the therapist. There's a cabinet in the office which looks like a child-cabinet full of toys and playthings (it even has a label – 'Child' on it) but I can 'see' that inside are knives and ropes and the implements of torture. The therapist is really a serial killer. If his patient brings his child here, the child will be sexually violated, then murdered. I want to help the man and his child ... to warn them about what lies ahead'.

Beth knew instinctively that this dream and its inner figures showed us something of her psyche's fears about therapy, and she told me the dream in our first session. 'Being a patient is difficult', she said....

'I'm so self-sufficient ... you can't help me ... that's my operational assumption. I marvel at anyone who gets in'.

There's a tension in this dream between attachment longings, vehement emotion and defenses against this emotion that allows us to 'see' what's going on. This tension is between the 'child', and the serial killer representing the defense against feeling. We could think of this 'child' as representing both the healthy longing for attachment and the early, un-remembered psychic pain from Beth's childhood. Threatening this child, is the serial killer/therapist – what I call the 'protector/persecutor' figure in the Self-Care System. I have found such violent imagery to be common in the dissociated psyche. When we get such images of murderers or killers in dreams I have come to realize that they are almost always defenses against underlying affect and against consciousness of this affect. So the killer is a killer of consciousness.[6] His 'vocation' (if we can call it that) is an *opus contra*

---

6 Jung found a similar dark and violent figure in his own inner world. At perhaps the most depressed moment of his life – when he had lost his relationship with Freud, when his own creative ideas had yet to be born – when he was terrified of 'doing a psychosis' as he told Mircea Eliade – he had an encounter with a similar inner killer of emotion. For 28 days, he sat in his study listening every night to the voices of mockery, telling him he was a fraud, that his ideas were worthless – that he was going mad…. He couldn't feel anything … he wasn't dreaming … he was empty … he had lost his soul. Looking back on that terrible time later, and advising his readers what they should do in similar circumstances, Jung said:

> *You are sterile because, without your knowledge, something like an evil spirit has stopped up the source of your fantasy, the fountain of your soul.* If you will contemplate your lack of fantasy, inspiration and inner aliveness, which you feel as sheer stagnation and a barren wilderness, and impregnate it with interest born of alarm at your inner death, then something can take shape in you, for your inner emptiness conceals just as great a fullness if only you will allow … your longing for fulfillment [to] quicken the sterile wilderness of your soul as rain quickens the dry earth.
> (1963a, para 190-91)

We all know the end of that story and the gesture that Jung described as turning his life around…. 'I let myself drop' he says … and suddenly his imagination was alive again. Unfortunately, reading Jung's heroic description of this moment, without the relational context of his life at the time, may cause us to miss the fact that his healing did not occur in a state of isolation. It was not just his lonely heroic individuation process. He didn't defeat his demon and open up his unconscious all by himself. He had Toni Wolf. And he had Tony Wolf's body! We don't know the details of how she helped him (and there was of course Emma and perhaps others) but if we have any imagination for the dramatic repair in Jung's capacity to feel that occurred between 1912 and 1916, it would start with what he calls his 'longing for fulfillment' and beyond that, we would have to imagine lots of deep pain and lots of tears. It is possible to imagine that *maybe* for the first time in Jung's life, he experienced *relational containment* in the arms of someone who could (literally and figuratively) hold his heartbreak.

It is significant that when Jung truly 'fell apart' and cried out in his journals 'Meine Seele, Meine Seele, wo bist du?' (Jung, 2009, p. 232) 'my soul, my soul, where are you?' – one of the first inner figures to greet him was a child and a maiden. In the Black books, written before *The Red Book*, Jung says of this maiden 'And I found you again only through the soul of the woman' (ibid., p.233 n49). This woman is almost surely Toni Wolf. And this child was a duality – partly the orphaned, injured child carrying the unbearably painful feelings Jung could not let himself feel and partly *conscientia*, a work against consciousness. Jung never identified such a figure in his taxonomy of unconscious representations. Instead, he found this killing energy in the systemic undertow of unconscious darkness itself i.e., the world of 'The Mothers' against which the heroic ego must always struggle. This understanding is apt for a conflict psychology, but is not adequate for a dissociative psychology where archetypal defenses can take over the inner world becoming violent anti-life forces. My own work is an effort to fill this gap in how we understand the 'inner world of trauma'.

The first several months of Beth's and my work together were spent getting to know one another, gathering history and exploring current issues that made life difficult. I liked her enormously, and was personally moved by her story, her resilience, and her heroic struggle. But not surprisingly, her tendency to isolate and withdraw began to appear in the therapy relationship itself. Another way to say this is that her serial killer entered the space between us and tried to prevent genuine emotional contact. Often during these periods she would come in with no dreams and seemingly little to talk about. Life seemed difficult enough without dredging up more suffering in the hour. She would start to feel the old familiar vacuum filling the spaces inside and between us. During these moments, I became just another 'objective' helper ... no-one really involved with her life. I was well-meaning – she knew that – but it was her life. She had to take responsibility ... no-one was 'out there ... really out there for her'.

During one of our sessions about a year into the work, while telling me of yet another tragic failure of her courage in a social situation, I noticed Beth avert her gaze as the negative, life-killing thoughts set in. I could feel her starting to dissociate ... and so I asked 'what just happened then?' 'Did you notice you were slipping away?' 'Yes', she said, and looked down. Silence. 'Can you tell me what you were feeling just before you disconnected?' I asked. She shook her head. More silence. 'I don't think I can do this', she said, and I could feel the gap between us growing wider. She was shutting down. 'Are you feeling afraid right now?' I asked her. Beth nodded. 'That's understandable'. I said. 'There's no reason you shouldn't be afraid. You're sitting with a strange man who you have no reason yet to trust. You have many memories that warn you against risking feelings in this moment. It's important that you feel safe here before that vulnerable 'child' in you can join us'. (Here I was talking to Beth's ego but also to her inner protector/persecutor and it was 'he' who needed to know she was safe before he would release any genuine feeling).

At some point, sensing that Beth was still struggling, I moved my chair closer to her and said, 'Beth please, just look at me!' Slowly her

---

something ineffable, numinous – a 'divine child'. Because of the ineffable qualities of this 'child', Jung recognized it as his returning soul.

gaze met mine. 'Listen', I said, 'this is no longer just your problem ... or just your lonely struggle ... because my eyes have seen it too. I'm in this with you now, and I'm invested in what happens. It's our story now, and we're in it together. If we're going to get that child in you some help we'll have to do it together – so come back to me'. I extended my hand to her and slowly, she reached over and took it. Now her eyes were rimmed with tears and then she began to cry, muffled and choked-off at first, but then, encouraged by me to stay with her feelings, more fully, sobbing for the first time in my presence – bringing her 'child' to therapy. During the time of her crying, I simply made encouraging sounds to keep her in the field with me and keep her inner critic from interrupting her feelings and closing her down.

When she did speak Beth said she was suddenly aware of the tragedy that this moment highlighted – the life she was missing – even with me right there in the room – about how easy it was for her to slip away and how much she discounted her own suffering and took it all back inside, sharing nothing. This made her incredibly sad and made her aware of her deep longing for connection and aliveness. She left the session with a renewed sense of energy and hope.

That night she had a vivid dream:

> I'm at work preparing to see a patient. A large family enters the office. They have no money and are carrying an infant who I can see is sick. I take this little girl into the office. There is distortion of her limbs on one side of her body and the leg on that side is hanging disjointed. There are sores all over her body and they are oozing pus and infection. Holding her, I realize I'm repulsed by her. I can see the family is incapable of caring for this infant. 'Whose child is this?' I ask. They point to a 15-year-old girl. She averts her gaze. She is ashamed. Then I see my own mother in this girl's face. I say 'I will treat the child for no charge until she recovers'. Meanwhile I tell them very clearly that they must tie a red ribbon on the right side of her body and a green one on the left side. This will help stop the lopsided distortion of one side, and heal the sores. I seem very confident in the dream about my treatment. I know exactly what to do.

Beth and I were both deeply moved by this dream, which seemed to both of us to be her psyche's response to our previous session. The sick child in Beth's dream is 'dis-jointed' and 'one-sided' just as Beth herself had been forced to develop one side of herself to the neglect of her vulnerable, feminine feeling life. And the treatment for this one-sidedness is red and green ribbons – both colours of life. The child (who in keeping with her earlier dream image has now been 'brought to therapy') is full of sores and pustules – just like she was as a nine-month-old in quarantine. So apparently the work we did in the previous hour evoked an early un-remembered trauma together with its affects of life-threatening fear, repulsion and shame. However, while she is 'repulsed' by this child, Beth also agrees now to care for it. This represented a huge shift in attitude towards her inner childhood self away from the shame she sees in the young mother's face where she also finds the face of her own mother. This led to further memories of how her mother – herself a beautiful woman – complained that Beth was ugly and was dark and swarthy like her father. Beth never felt that her mother really wanted her.

There was a lot of explicit feeling in this dream, so I encouraged us to stay with its imagery and especially with any affects that were part of the dream text – for example the feeling of repulsion towards the baby. Associating to this feeling, Beth wondered if it might be her *mother's* repulsion for Beth herself. She asked to draw the baby and as she did the repulsion came up again. Then, she asked if I could create a baby out of something for her to hold in the session. I found an old towel in my closet, wrapped it up and made a baby out of it, handing it to her, and she held the baby for a moment. Then she felt the repulsion again and aggressively dropped the baby on the floor in disgust. She picked it up and threw it down again. This spontaneous gesture brought tears … and recognition.[7] Suddenly she remembered a part of her childhood history that she had totally forgotten.

The memory was from eight years of age. That had been a terrible year, both at home and at school. She remembered how she had hated her mother that year, wishing she would never come home from the hospital where she had gone for a gall bladder operation. She also recalled with great vividness an obsessive ritual she had performed with her doll during that year: she would run up to the top of their 5th floor tenement and throw her doll down the five flights of stairs – then run down to see if it had broken. 'Each time', she said, 'I dreaded my success, but I kept doing it. I couldn't stop'.

The recovery of this memory brought more feeling and more shame, rage and guilt for us to work through – but also more clarity and more aliveness. I recalled with Beth, Harry Guntrip's (1969) insight that if a child hates her mother, she simultaneously ends up hating her *need* for the mother, and in this way the hate-filled mother insinuates herself into the inner world as self-hatred. We agreed that this might be part of how Beth's inner 'serial killer' had taken up residence inside her and why 'he' was activated whenever she reached out for help.

In Beth's gesture of throwing the baby on the floor, she embodied

---

7 Robin van Loben Sels, in her new book *Shamanic Dimensions of Psychotherapy* (Routledge, in press), explores the ways in which seven shamanic 'attributes' (including posture and gesture) operate within the unconscious 'field' of the shaman complex – activated between partners in the analytic adventure. Awareness of these attributes, she demonstrates, can sensitize us to the 'implicit' aspects of unconscious memory operating beneath words.

an angry impulse that she couldn't previously permit herself to know or feel – and the tears that followed were a recognition of this fact. Defenses against vulnerability and her un-remembered self-repulsion were softened in this embodied psycho-dramatic enactment and Beth emerged more consciously for having suffered these affects from archetypal depths – now rendered through the imagination, into conscious feelings she could bear.

Final thoughts

Jung said that his own personal myth was the creation of consciousness. In this paper, I have tried to articulate my own understanding of how I share in this myth and how I find myself re-shaping it in certain ways to include the experiential transformation of highly defended archetypal emotion into feelings. I have tried to suggest that the transcendent function and the creative imagination which expresses it, is not something we can take for granted in all patients that come to us for help. These otherwise foundational realities of our psychological life can sometimes be put out of commission altogether by dissociative defenses. In some cases of early traumatic injury there is relational work to be done with embodied emotion, connecting psyche and soma, and opening the imagination, before conventional analytic work can be initiated.

In these cases, to carry something consciously is not just a matter of adjusting our mental attitudes or of insight alone. We need what Bruno Bettleheim (1979) called 'an informed heart'. The great *coniunctio* that we're after with these patients – and that Jung discussed in reference to the dis-embodied 'opposites' – cannot happen without the body and its unredeemed, unknown, un-remembered, and frozen affects. In trying to heal our capacity to feel we're pursuing a consciousness of the heart. That, for me, is the numinous *mysterium* in what Jung (1963a) called the *Mysterium Coniunctionis*. The heart is the hidden third. And recovering a heart that can break is how we help ourselves and our patients recover the capacity to feel.

References

Bettelheim, B. (1979). *The Informed Heart*. New York: Avon Books.
Bion, W. (1959). 'Attacks on linking'. In (1967) *Second Thoughts*. New York: Jason Aronson.
Guntrip, H. (1969). *Schizoid Phenomena Object-Relations and the Self*. New York: International Universities Press.
Hammer, E. (1990). *Reaching the Affect*. New Jersey: Jason Aronson Inc.
Hillman, J. (1975). *Re-visioning Psychology*. New York: Harper & Row.

Jaffé, A. (1989, 2014). *The Life and Work of C.G. Jung*. Einsiedeln: Daimon Verlag,
Jung, C.G. (1953-79). *The Collected Works* (Bollingen Series XX), trans. R. F.C. Hull: eds. H. Read, M. Fordham & G. Adler. Princeton, N.J.: Princeton University Press, 20 vols.
— (1907). 'The psychology of dementia praecox'. *CW* 3.
— (1916). 'The transcendent function'. *CW* 8.
— (1929). 'Commentary on *The Secret of the Golden Flower*'. *CW* 13
— (1954). 'Psychological aspects of the mother archetype'. *CW* 9 (1)
— (1963a). *Mysterium Coniunctionis*. *CW* 14.
— (1963b). *Memories Dreams Reflections*, ed. A. Jaffé. New York: Vintage Books, Random House.
— (2009). *The Red Book: Liber Novus*, ed. Sonu Shamdasani. New York & London: W.W. Norton.
Kalsched, D. (1996). *The Inner World of Trauma: Archetypal Defenses of the Personal Spirit*. London: Routledge.
— (2013). *Trauma and the Soul: A Psycho-Spiritual Approach to Human Development and its Interruption*. London: Routledge.
Oliver, M. (2017). *Devotions: The Selected Poems of Mary Oliver*. New York: Penguin Books.
Perry, J.W. (1970). 'Emotions and object relations'. *Journal of Analytical Psychology*, 15, 1, 1-12.
Rako, S. & Mazer, H. (eds.). (1980, 2003). *Semrad, the Heart of a Therapist*. Authors Guild Backinprint.com Edition.
Russell, P. (1999). 'Trauma and the cognitive function of affects'. In *Trauma, Repetition, & Affect Regulation: The Work of Paul Russell*. Teicholz, J.G. & Kriegman, D. (eds). London: Rebus Press.
Schore, A.N. (2011). 'The right brain implicit self lies at the core of psychoanalysis'. *Psychoanalytic Dialogues*, 21, 1, 75-100.
— (2019). *Right Brain Psychotherapy*. New York: W.W. Norton & Co.
Van der Kolk, B.A., Brown, P., & van der Hart, O. 'Pierre Janet on post-traumatic stress'. *Journal of Traumatic Stress*, 2, 4, 368.
Winnicott, D.W. (1949). 'Mind and its relation to the psyche-soma'. In *Through Paediatrics to Psycho-Analysis*. New York: Basic Books.
— (1964). 'Psycho-somatic illness in its positive and negative aspects'. In *Psychoanalytic Explorations*, eds. C. Winnicott, R. Shepherd, & M. Davis. Cambridge, MA: Harvard University Press.

Thursday, 29 August 2019

The other between fear and desire – countertransference fantasy as a bridge between me and the other

Daniela Eulert-Fuchs
(ÖGAP) Vienna, Austria

Introduction: Fear and Desire.
The chasm between the experienced and the hoped-for

In this paper I will explore the challenges that I experience when working with people whose implicit expectations of primary relationships were badly disappointed in the preverbal stage.

What is it that makes this work such a challenge?

Infant research has shown that the human being is disposed for relationships from the start.

The early experience of being in the world and with the other is implicitly stored in procedural memory, without (secondary) symbolic representation (cf. Roussillion, 1999, p. 237). This does not make it any less powerful: as a trace of memory that is stored in physical and actional memory it may be regarded as the background music that, as a melody of life, fatefully spins the yarn. My focus in this paper will be particularly on constellations in which those early experiences are not represented.

How does this happen?

Green describes how intrusion or massive neglect in the primary relationship mobilize a form of defence that consists of withdrawing cathexis from the primary object, which generates a negative of this experience and leads to a state of emptiness and non-being (cf. Green, 1975, pp. 516-17). In this context, Lesmeister speaks of the nihilistic self (Lesmeister, 2009, pp. 65-66).

How does this affect the analytic space?

Kalsched shows that specific defence mechanisms are constructed, which he calls self-care systems (Kalsched 1996, 2013). Our analysands' apprehension that the trauma will once again be repeated in the analytic relationship mainly makes itself felt as distrust.

But this isn't the whole truth. I suggest that what is hidden behind this distrust is hope. A hope that seems to be present from the beginning, but has been buried by the trauma.

How can we understand this buried hope?

Stein Bråten says that the infant psyche is structured dialogically; that the other does not initially form through social interaction, but that it is already there from the beginning, an *a priori* disposition (Bråten, 1992, pp. 77-97). Trevarthen also states that an infant is born with a rough conception of a helpful and friendly companion who cooperatively communicates shared experiences (Aitken and Trevarthen 1997, p. 672). This concept may be understood as an archetypal disposition (cf. Jung, 1939/1954, § 155; Knox, 2004, p. 66).

I will call this archetypal hope. This archetypal hope for a good other seems to be inviting, like the distant song of angels. Like unquenched hunger, it is rekindled again and again. Caught between this archetypal hope on the one hand, and the unconscious personal horizon of expectation on the other hand, a seemingly unbridgeable chasm yawns. Our work starts in and with this chasm.

I will now sketch, with two vignettes, those aspects of analytical treatments in which unconscious processes of exchange cause the analyst to experience non-representation, and explore how she is gradually able to experience and understand it and how this understanding finally – without it first becoming explicit – becomes effective in the analytic space.

Theoretical preliminary note: the absent representation in the analytic space

What is it we have to imagine when representations are lacking? When the meaningful other, while absent, cannot be kept alive within? When the early sensory experience of being-with-the-other cannot be connected to inner images and integrated into contexts of meaning?

An absence of the ability to form complex, linked, affectively significant object representations is necessarily accompanied by an impaired ability to form self-representations. This also means that there can be no secure representation of the relationship, of being with each other, of the 'in-between'. This has massive implications for psychological development and confronts the analyst with unknown challenges.

In my work I came to realize that the late-maturing of this development required an inter-subjective component that necessitates a special readiness to accept and move into a state of 'regression' on the part of the analyst, and a readiness to enter the inner space – the early sensory experience – of the clients. What do we mean by that? Individuals in whom representations aren't formed often appear to be standing behind a glass wall.

Because the limited symbolic processing leads to a lack of a vivid contact with their inner as well as the external world, they have to build a barrier against overwhelming impressions from within and from outside, and limit contact *per se*, or at least steer it into well-controlled channels. In this context, Bovensiepen speaks of life in a bubble (2009).

Even when the person's cognitive abilities are excellent, it becomes clear that they have no access to emotional experience. It also becomes clear that these individuals either do not dream at all, or that their dreams mean nothing to them, and, if the clients are children, they cannot play. It is as though they were standing behind a glass wall, as though their early fate had to repeat itself and they were forced to look on, unable to do anything.

In most cases, this barrier also forms itself in contact. It seems to the therapist as though we failed to make a connection, as though our words did not reach them, as though the glass was soundproof. We therefore cannot just remain in front of the glass wall and call to the other to come out. We have to be prepared to enter the space behind and together venture to find the way out. How can this succeed?

In their book, *The Work of Psychic Figurability*, César and Sara Botella (2005) provided an important contribution to working with unrepresented mental states. They describe how the analyst makes him/herself available and how unrepresented elements become figurable. They understand counter-transference phantasies as a resonance to the negative of the patient's trauma (p. 48). According to the Botellas, provided the analyst gives in to a formal regression of thought, working as a double, the travail *en double* will emerge (p. 71). This regression seems to be the essential step. It leads behind the glass wall. It is here that the work of the analytic pair begins.

I compare the fabric of relationship, which has to be woven by both – analyst and analysand – together, with a carpet which, in the case of non-representation, comes with holes and blank spaces. The symbols, phantasies, and experiences emerging in the intermediary space are the material with which to weave threads and patch holes. In this, the reverie, the dreamlike intuition of the analyst, is understood as a bridge: it connects the analytic pair. However, the reverie also creates the transition between that which was not – the absent representation – and that which wants to emerge. It thus bridges the personal unconscious (implicit expectation) and the archetypal (the archetypal hope).

The function of symbols in coping with loss (cf. Segal, 1957, p. 211) is, I would suggest, represented intersubjectively. In this way, the chasm I mentioned can be bridged, on condition that the holes are not filled prematurely.

Clinical examples

Anna

Anna's conviction that she was not loveable was left unsaid, but dominated the room. Anna, in her early forties, had a very successful career and was single, and came to see me because of a serious psychosomatic condition. 'This therapy really gets on my nerves, the only thing it does is consume time,' Anna says. 'It won't get me anywhere, anyway.' Also, there was nothing to report. In her childhood, she claims, there have been no unusual incidents, everything was normal.

Why, despite this, Anna and I still end up agreeing on a frequency of two sessions a week remains unclear. This continues: for weeks, Anna is either very late or even arrives at a different time from that agreed. When I end the hour on time anyway, or 'put her off' until the agreed date, she reacts with impatience.

Even though under normal circumstances, I am cautious with interpretation, I had the feeling that this enactment forced me to address the conflict. I tell Anna that I had asked myself if that was how she expressed her ambivalence about wanting to meet me but at the same time not wanting to meet me. And whether it could be that this was her way of letting me know that no-one is ever there for her when she needs them. Anna pauses for a moment, then hisses between her teeth: 'What you are saying is completely irrelevant. Talking only makes things worse, and people are never any help.' For months, Anna sits silently on the edge of the chair and stares at me with a fixed gaze.

In these periods of cold and distrustful silence I can feel how my body tenses and my breathing becomes shallow. It is getting more and more difficult for me to find thoughts and words that express my understanding of what is happening here and now between us. Whatever I say, it is nothing that Anna doesn't already know, or that would be helpful in any other way. It is obvious that I cannot find the right words, that I am failing Anna and that Anna cannot use interpretations. James Astor writes about his work with K.: 'K did not want to be translated, he wanted to be received' (Astor 2007, p. 191). Anna, too, made it clear that she wanted to be welcomed, felt, included, 'received'.

I observe that I am drifting away, that I stop thinking about Anna and me, that I lose myself in an emotional no-man's-land. I understand my thought disorder as an expression of my defence and turn inside. Images emerge. I can see a baby, left alone and lonely in its cot. Full of anxiety and panic. More and more often, I have phantasies of baby Anna by herself; nobody reacts to her crying.

Anna is an only child. Only later I learn that her parents had been very busy with their careers and travelled a lot, and that she had grown up with a succession of *au pairs*. Anna reports that she has been at the top of her class at school. She has completed two graduate courses in minimum time, and works for a well-regarded business. She is quickly entrusted with management tasks that she fulfils to everybody's complete satisfaction. Anna is trustworthy and always there. No sick leave, no vacations – until the time 'when this stupid illness upset everything'.

When Anna rings the bell for the 189th session after a pause of one week and I see her in the camera of the intercom, I am surprised. Of course, I knew it was Anna's appointment. But suddenly – exactly at this moment – I recognize, as though on another plane, that for all the time of her absence, she had not been on my mind. It was more than 'not thinking of her', more than forgetting, rather it was an unnoticed gliding from consciousness, as though she had never been there. The self-evident knowledge of her existence had been lost; as though effaced ... I was startled.

And suddenly, she was there. There again? In between: nothing. An unbridgeable chasm. And an extremely disconcerting moment. Only when I become aware of the absence of my thoughts do I understand Anna's early trauma, her desolation, which occupies the space of a natural blank space ... without becoming conscious. An apparent normality.... To become aware of this triggers a sudden and deep sadness in me, and the wish to win her back, or to find her anew, and to lift her from this unconscious 'non-being', which nevertheless is.

This experience opens a new space in the understanding of her inner exile.

As a stand-in for Anna, I had experienced that I had lost the representation of her in myself. I had experienced how it feels to be unable to keep something mentally present that was not in my field of perception. Anna had ceased to exist. I was surprised to see her again, and was shocked about that. Had I regressed? In this case, I had no image, no phantasy, but rather the negative, the unrepresented experience, which is represented in me as an experience of a gap.

Following the Botellas (2005, p. 71-81), I call this memory gap a 'hallucinatory state', or, as Civitarese puts it, a hallucinosis that mutates into a sensory reverie (2018, pp. 787-88). Now I can understand, in an immediate manner, that Anna was unable to form the representation of a caring other due to an overlong absence. Now I am able to better understand my images of baby Anna – because of my direct experience of dead absence – and link these with my experience of deep isolation in being with Anna.

In the following week, one appointment was cancelled due to a professional commitment. While, in the following hour, I am thinking about how to put my understanding of Anna's deep isolation into words, I think of Anne Alvarez when she says, 'I am not suggesting [...] that we need not use words to convey our understanding, only that when we stay in touch with the deepest feelings the patient has evoked in us, we may manage to get the words and the tone and the tact right' (Alvarez 2010, p. 862).

In German, tact has two meanings: on the one hand, tact is a character trait, a virtue, as Plessner has it (1981, p. 109); on the other hand, it also is a concept from music and signifies its basic temporal structure.

In being with Anna, it was important to find a rhythm and a tact in accordance with her early sensory experience, in order to create a common melody to form the basis for developing words and symbolic understanding.

Anna interrupts my contemplation and says: 'This time, I missed you for the first time. I mean, I was able to feel it. Before, when I wasn't here, you didn't exist for me, rather like you were dead. Though I'm afraid of these feelings, I am happy to have them'. This was the first step.

Anna had not only got in touch with her repressed affects, but also with those parts that had never had the possibility to become conscious before. To become aware of desolation enabled her to grieve. The dead repetition, constructed as a bastion against the fear of loneliness, gave way to a painful confrontation with the latter. This sequence in our common work marked a turning point.

The appalling experience of the gap, as well as the subsequent distancing – the 'awakening from hallucinosis', was the condition for a real understanding of Anna. But in particular stepping out of this participation, the awakening – and this is my main hypothesis – allowed Anna to experience that you can be separate but still connected. In this separate and connected space, an emotional thinking space develops, an autonomous inner space is formed (cf. Winnicott 1958, p. 243-44).

Anna and I became closer. The phases of talking and silence had a different rhythm, a different tact. A completely new inter-rhythmicity developed. Anna began to dream, and to link the dream images with her experience. Anna says: 'I am not quite sure what is happening. But I do know something is happening. Somehow it feels right'.

We were able to start working through the early desolation, with it appearing in many meandering formations as presence and absence without ever completely disappearing again. We had gained a point of reference, initiated an understanding, named the blank space and opened a space of hope.

Unconscious communication

The exploration into the phenomena of unconscious communication goes back to the earliest period of psychoanalysis. Jung had already elaborated it in detail in 'The psychology of the transference' (Jung 1946). But Freud, too, writes that the analyst should catch the drift of the patient's unconscious with his own unconscious (1923, p. 3916). He (the physician) should turn his own unconscious toward the giving unconscious of the patient as a receiving organ, to adjust to the analyzed like the telephone receiver is adjusted to the transmitting microphone (1912, 2470). Ferenczi describes these dynamics when he says that the two unconsciouses were in a dialogue 'without the remotest conception of this on the part of the consciousness of either' (Ferenczi 1994/1915, p. 109). Paula Heimann thinks that the unconscious relationship is essential, and that the unconscious perception of the analyst is 'more acute and in advance' of his or her conscious conception of the situation (Heimann 1950, p. 82).

Here I can only touch upon new contributions, such as from infant research, that have much enhanced our understanding in this field (Stern 1985; Beebe & Lachmann 2004).

The Boston Change Process Study Group, compare the regulatory processes of the early dyad with the analytic relationship. They describe research that suggests that many therapies do not fail because of incorrect interpretations, but because the moments when a significant connection between the two participants could have been made were allowed to pass unused (Stern et al., 1998 p. 904). These moments of meeting that happen in the shared, implicit relationship affect and change this relationship. The Boston Change Group see the decisive factor for therapeutic processes as the transformation of this implicit relational knowledge, and that this shows demonstrable effects (cf. BCPSG 2013). I will now trace these processes in my work with Paul.

Paul

When I meet Paul, he is just over three years old. His parents are at their wits' end. Because Paul had been a screaming baby, their paediatrician had already recommended me more than two years earlier, but at the time they hadn't been ready to come. 'But now we just can't manage any more', the parents say. 'Paul drives us crazy with his stubbornness. He says 'no' to every- and any thing, from morning to night he gives us hell with his violent tantrums. For the most innocent reasons, he throws a fit of rage that doesn't abate for hours'.

Even apart from that, everything had been difficult from the beginning: he had cried a lot and hardly allowed himself to be comforted. He hadn't wanted any physical contact, had 'yelled at the breast' and refused to be breast-fed. He had also been a poor and very picky eater. He slept badly and woke the parents often with his night terrors. From the beginning, things had been very difficult with him. 'When, eventually, his sister was born, with whom everything was easy from the start, the situation deteriorated even more. Paul was aggressive towards his little sister and other children. He didn't tolerate separation any more and refused to go to kindergarten. And on top of everything, he has now started to hold stool, with all his might'.

I am waiting for Paul. Today I am going to meet him. Outside it is snowing. Thick white snowflakes. Voices from afar, bells. My stomach feels fluttery and nervous. Then Paul is at the door, straw blond, in a blue duffle coat, small hand in large hand. E.E. Cummings comes to my mind – 'Who are you little I ...'

As though unnoticed he glides past me. Looks around. 'Ah yes. Yes, I know this ...', he says in an offhand manner. With a look towards the shelves, Paul remarks: 'I am really very good at playing with dinosaurs. I can do that very well by myself. You can sit over there'.

Paul takes the lead. Does he have to, I am asking myself. I have to remind myself that he is only three years old. He seems much older to me, he looks around the consulting room like a small adult and then matter-of-factly starts taking trees, plants, stones and dinosaurs from the shelf. But Paul doesn't play, he cannot play. He places things besides each other in a repetitive and mechanical manner. He explains his constructions in detail, and his explanations on dinosaurs sound like a scientific treatise.

I shiver. I am cold. I turn up the thermostat. What is he telling me? Don't come too close. Keep your distance. He makes it clear that he has learned to cope by himself. This is probably also a clue to his bonding experience, but he may also be telling me that contact with others confuses and scares him so much that he has erected a protective barrier around him that I need to respect. 'It's ok,' I tell him, 'I am here watching you'.

Paul shows me how much his playing and creativity are blocked.

The longing for a relationship, and its refusal, the whole ambivalence is bound up in the symptom. Paul is lonely. So am I. I am thinking of Ms C's (Paul's mother's) message: that she cannot cope with her situation. That her affects keep surfacing violently. That she completely loses control. Later, Ms C also told me of her rejection of Paul, of her phantasies of giving Paul away, or of simply leaving him somewhere. Quite unreservedly, Ms C tells me that she doesn't only have difficulties in controlling her emotions with Paul, but in general. That she also has violent tantrums in extremely inappropriate situations. And that it was particularly hard with Paul.

It may be surmised that this causes Paul extreme anxiety. But it probably goes deeper than that. I suspect that it is also unconscious communication, that the opening and mutual penetration of both minds did not help Paul to find and recognize himself in his mother. Paul, who desperately needs his mother, is in an irresolvable dilemma. He has probably not experienced her as a transformational object (Bollas 1979, p. 14) that can hold and helpfully regulate his self-experience.

I am now experiencing this implicit expectation in contact with him. When his mother wants to pick him up, he is unable to end the game. He has to place all the dinosaurs in the landscape. Following through with the plan has an inner urgency that alarms me. It is a must. Anything else is a disaster. I understand Paul and let him be.

In the second hour, Paul decides to do sandplay with his mother: Paul addresses her by her first name. In a slightly pedantic manner, he asks her: 'What's this, Claudia?' 'This is a tank,' his mother dutifully answers.

'No, Claudia, this is a drill.' An awkward silence. 'A drilling tank,' he concedes.

I can see how much Paul attempts to establish a connection. But they do not come together.

It also seems as though the roles were reversed, as though Ms C was perplexed, nearly helpless, and Paul felt responsible for her.

What becomes clear is that the issue is an inability to cope, but also power and domination, which fits his (anal) symptoms. I also understand a little better why he had to grow up so fast. What I mean is, I can experience it, not just theoretically understand.

In the following sessions Paul no longer wants to enter the therapy room, he refuses to take off his coat and remains rooted to the spot in the hall. Or he crouches in the corner beside the door and lowers his gaze while his mother helplessly stands next to him and tries to persuade him. Then he covers his ears and closes his eyes.

I wonder how I might understand Paul's withdrawal and refusal. What had happened? Is his behaviour the expression of a family dynamic? It remains unclear. Intersubjectively, I understand Paul's refusal as a question of how I will deal with this situation: whether I could absorb his unconscious messages? Whether I would allow myself to feel excluded, confused, irritated, helpless, and still preserve the hope of understanding at some point?

My attempts to establish contact with Paul at this time consist of me playfully-dreamily fantasizing about what Paul wants to say by means of hand puppets. Probably because there is a little pressure involved, because I can feel the mother's patience dwindling, the hedgehog tells the teddy bear: 'Well, I think it doesn't make any sense for Paul to play here. Everybody wants him to do something, and he probably thinks we also want him to do this or that, to be good, and to use the toilet. I can understand he doesn't want to let go of his poo-poo, and so I also understand that he thinks all this is kind of stupid.

We are met with his questioning glance. It is as though he emerges from his inner cave. Is he surprised I am thinking about him? The atmosphere changes. While I am still talking to his mother, Paul starts to play. Takes possession of the consulting room and me. I am looking forward to him. Little man in a big coat.

He is strained. Works hard. Builds tunnels and roads with his drill and road maker. He groans. Fills animals, houses, trucks and cars with sand and empties them again. He puts large and small elephants very closely beside each other, and separates them again. Designs forests and landscapes for wild animals, dinosaurs, and spiders. Then exhaustedly collapses on the sofa, gets his 'drinking stuff' from his little kindergarten rucksack, and belches. I hear myself saying, as I would to a baby, 'there, there, a burp' ... his eyes half open, Paul looks at me for a long time with glassy dreaming eyes that aren't with me. I have fantasies of holding him in my arms, of cradling him for a long time.... Suddenly he seems to be a baby again.

Paul is fighting to show his inner world to me. He has grown up early. When his sister was born, the structure that had already been fragile before came apart at the seams. My often bizarre fragments of thought form the following hypothesis: His defence was twofold ... in identification with his mother, he has the baby in his belly, and it has to be held back. And: he has to stop time, to return to the time before ...

But Paul was also angry. He wasn't 'keen' at all to give his mother, who so badly lets him down, a gift. For this is what faeces are in this early period, a gift for the mother – and in many phantasmatic transformations much more: penis, child, symbol of separation (cf. Freud, A., 1965, 72-3).

After some months, it strikes me that Paul is looking forward to his mother. He is waiting for her and joyfully shows her his pictures. Ms C. tells me with tears in her eyes that at home, he is looking for physical contact, he wants to cuddle with her and cannot get enough. He even calls her mama sometimes. She says she is very happy about this. I am pleased, too, but also surprised. I ask myself whether, and how, it is that Paul and his mother experience what I fantasize with him during the sessions, what I carry in me, are linked. So, I am asking myself whether my fantasy, and the new reality for Paul and his mother, are connected with each other. How is nonverbal communication communicated? How deeply do we touch each other and where are the limits? Colman says that analysis is what remains when the interpretations are forgotten, that what came from the analyst's self is more important, that this was what the patient unconsciously felt (cf. Colman 2003, p. 352).

Discussion of the case studies

This discussion has two parts:

Relationship/development:

Both Paul and Anna initially expressed their fear of contact by preventing or denying any meeting. This defence evokes Green's concept of the 'desobjectalising function' (Green, 2001). It develops because of intrusion and/or neglect by the primary object, which in turn results in cathexis being withdrawn from the objects. They become meaningless. This means that that which characterizes an object, namely being irreplaceable, is negated.

Typically, the desobjectalising function is linked to serious disorders; however, parts of the personality remain perfectly functional (cf. Levine 2012, p. 610). With Paul and Anna, this concerns cognition. Both are very talented, but their talents lack affective connection. The mental functions take over the organizing and structuring function in the mind, but turn out to be completely insufficient in addressing the early trauma. Both Paul and Anna expressed their experience through action and their physical symptoms.

Change: The Bridge. The analytic pair – and the dynamic function of the self

So how do we facilitate the next step? Levine says 'analysts must expect to find themselves unconsciously participating in dialogical and interactive processes, which have the effect of offering patients – or helping them to create or appropriate – something that may not yet have achieved sufficient 'presence' in a figured form' (Levine 2012, p. 612). To achieve this – all authors are unanimous – a receptive attitude helps. I believe this attitude corresponds to the Jungian approach.

In his commentary on the *coniunctio* in the *Rosarium*, Jung speaks about a union in unconscious identity, of *participation mystique*, which however 'by nature never [is] an initial state: it is always the product of a process or the goal of endeavour' (Jung 1946, § 462).

My understanding of the symbolic meaning of the image is that the analyst first allows the unconscious contents of the analysand to 'intrude'. She allows herself to be used. Through regression and entering the experiential space of the client, she reaches an initial understanding.

If the analyst contributes these 'threads of understanding' for the gaps in the carpet, these are threads she generates from herself: threads that emerge from the connection with the unconscious, which always also involves one's own wound. This is probably also where the resistance is located that has to be overcome (cf. Botella & Botella 2005, pp. 70-71; Symington, 1983, p. 287; Maier 2014, p. 361).

Rumi says: Don't stop looking at the bandaged place, don't avert your eyes, from there, the light will enter you.... Thus, the analyst is in contact with herself on the one hand, and understands herself – as Bollas (1987, p. 212) suggests – as the other patient. The thoughts, emotions, images and reveries that arise in her can thus be understood as a creative expression of the self-regulatory capacity of the mind.

On the other hand, the self-observing function remains active, aiming to observe the tightrope walk – and thus to avoid either falling into trauma, or to erecting defences against it. Paul's unconscious hope reaches the analyst and becomes apparent in the reverie and the countertransference fantasies of early processes of exchange. These inner images form the opposite pole to the infinite loop of the trauma re-staging itself again and again. The reverie can thus be understood as a link to the *a priori* existing archetypal hope.

Anna, too, has a space in the analyst's psyche, when her early defence against desolation presents itself as an experience of obliteration and finally triggers change. The reverie thus operates as a bridge between the analyst's internal psychic space and the inner space of Paul and Anna. The intersubjective component turns the dead space of repetition into a space of hope and possibility. This demonstrates the final dimension of transference, its sense and purpose, as Jung writes (Jung 1951, § 239).

Conclusion

Countering the powerful expectation of repeated disappointment with a principle of hope is the task facing the analytic pair. Reverie and countertransference fantasy form the connection, the bridge, between implicit expectation and archetypal hope. These fantasies are not only individually relevant, but also connected to the collective unconscious. An archetypal dynamic is activated. This dynamic, an expression of the self, is experienced by the analytic pair. A door opens. In enduring repetition, something new is tested and inscribed. The pair slowly proceeds under the continual surveillance of the distrustful eye of past experience. The individual and the archetypal work hand in hand in this process.

I suggest that the essential issue in this process is that the analyst allows herself to be touched, that she doesn't shy away from stepping behind the glass wall, from regression, from identification, from 'hallucinosis' in the secure knowledge that it is possible to wake from it.

In her movement from identification into reflection, she creates a difference in herself, which – according to my hypothesis – transforms the analytical space by way of unconscious communication.

The question of a good enough other may therefore be answered – with all due caution and in the awareness of human limits and limitations – insofar as the fear of the other can become bearable and the desire for the other can be experienced not only as a space of hope, but also as a space of possibility. It is the secret, implicit commission and the contract both have agreed.

In the best scenario, and in Neumann's sense (1963/1980, pp. 91-92), this experience provides the world factor that helps bridge the chasm between the experienced and the hoped-for. In many essential areas of psychotherapy, Jung proved to be remarkably far-sighted:

in discerning the extraordinary relevance of the affective (Jung 1935, § 318), the inextricable link between body and soul (Jung 1935, § 136), and, last but not least, those dimensions that transcend but also pervade psychotherapy that are reflected in our attitude.

References

Aitken, K.J. & Trevarthen, C. (1997). 'Self/other organization in human psychological development'. *Development and Psychopathology*, 9, 653–77.

Alvarez, A. (2010). 'Levels of analytic work and levels of pathology: the work of calibration'. *The International Journal of Psychoanalysis*. 91, 4, 859-78.

Astor, J. (2007). 'Fordham, feeling, and countertransference: reflections on defences of the self'. *Journal of Analytical Psychology*, 52, 2, 185-205.

Beebe, B. & Lachmann, F.M. (2004). *Säuglingsforschung und die Psychotherapie Erwachsener*. Stuttgart: Klett-Cotta.

Bohleber, W. (2014). 'Psyche'. *Zeitschrift für Psychoanalyse und ihre Anwendungen*, 68, 9, 776-86.

Bollas, C. (1987). 'The transformational object'. In: *The Shadow of the Object: Psychoanalysis of the Unthought Known*. London, New York: Routledge.

Botella, C. & Botella, S. (2005). *The Work of Psychic Figurability: Mental States without Representation*. Hove, London, New York: Routledge.

Bovensiepen, G. (2009). 'Vom Leben in der Seifenblase. Entwicklungszusammenbruch und Verteidigung des Selbst in der Postadoleszenz'. *Analytische Psychologie* 156, 2, 134-51.

Bråten, S. (1992). 'The virtual other in infants' minds and social feelings'. In *The Dialogical Alternative. Towards a Theory of Language and Mind*, ed. A. Wold. Oslo: Scandinavian University Press, 77-97.
Civitarese, G. (2015). 'Transformations in hallucinosis and the receptivity of the analyst'. *International Journal of Psychoanalysis*, 96, 4, 1091-1116.
— (2018). 'Halluzinationen, Traum und Spiel'. *Psyche. Zeitschrift für Psychoanalyse und ihre Anwendungen*,72, 9,785-810.
Colman, W. (2003). 'Interpretation and relationship: ends or means?' In *Controversies in Analytical Psychology*, ed. Robert Withers. London, New York: Routledge.
Dammann, G. (2014). 'Desobjektalisierung: Theorie und Klinik eines Konzepts von André Green'. *Psyche. Zeitschrift für Psychoanalyse und ihre Anwendungen*,68, 886-921.
Ferenczi, S. (1994/1915). 'Psychogenic anomalies of voice production'. In idem.: *Further Contributions to the Theory and Technique of Psycho-analysis*. London: Karnac.
Freud, S. (1923). 'Two Encyclopaedia Articles'. *SE* 13, 3912-34.
— (1912). 'Recommendations to Physicians Practising Psycho-Analysis', *S.E.8*, 2467-74.
Freud, A. (1965). *Normality and Pathology in Childhood*. London: Karnac.
Green, A. (1975). 'The analyst, symbolization and absence in the analytic setting'. *International Journal of Psychoanalysis*, 56, 1, 1-22.
— (2001 [1993]). Todestrieb, negativer Narzissmus, Desobjektalisierungsfunktion. *Psyche. Zeitschrift für Psychoanalyse und ihre Anwendungen*,55, 869–77.
Heimann, P. (1950). 'On counter-transference'. *International Journal of Psycho-Analysis* 31, 81-84.
Jung, C.G. (1935). 'On the theory and practice of analytical psychology'. The Tavistock Lectures. *CW* 18.
— (1939/1954). 'Psychological aspects of the mother archetype'. *CW* 9 (1).
— (1946). 'The psychology of transference'. *CW* 16.
— (1951). 'The fundamental questions of psychotherapy'. *CW* 16.
Kalsched, D. (1996). *The Inner World of Trauma. Archetypal Defenses of the Personal Spirit*. Hove: Routledge.
— (2013). *Trauma and the Soul. A psycho-spiritual approach to human development and its interruption*. Hove: Routledge.
Knox, J. (2004). *Archetype, Attachment, Analysis*. London: Brunner Routledge.
— (2011). 'Die analytische Beziehung: eine Zusammenführung jungianischer, bindungstheoretischer und entwicklungspsychologischer Perspektiven'. *Analytische Psychologie*, 166, 402-27.
Lesmeister, R., (2009). *Selbst und Individuation. Facetten von Subjektivität und Intersubjektivität in der Psychoanalyse*. Frankfurt/M.: Brandes und Apsel.
Levine, H. (2012). 'The colourless canvas. Representation, therapeutic action, and the creation of mind'. *The International Journal of Psychoanalysis*, 93, 3, 607-29.
Maier, C. (2014). 'Über die intersubjektive Entwicklung von Bedeutung im analytischen Prozess'. *Analytische Psychologie*, 178, 4, 356-377.

Neumann, E. (1963/1980). *Das Kind, Struktur und Dynamik der werdenden Persönlichkeit*. Frankfurt/M: Fischer Taschenbuch Verlag, Juni 1999.
Plessner, H. (1981). *Grenzen der Gemeinschaft. Eine Kritik des sozialen Radikalismus*. Ges. Schriften Bd. V. Frankfurt a.M.: Suhrkamp.
Roussillon, R. (1999). *Agonie, Clivage et Symbolisation*. Paris: PUF.
Segal, H. (1957). Bemerkungen zur Symbolbildung. In *Melanie Klein heute*, ed. E. Bott-Spillius. Stuttgart: Klett-Cotta.
Stern, D. (2004). *Der Gegenwartsmoment*. Frankfurt/M.: Brandes und Apsel Verlag.
— (1985). *The Interpersonal World of the Infant*. London, New York: Routledge.
Stern, D. & The Boston Change Process Study Group (1998). 'Non-interpretive mechanisms in psychoanalytic therapy: the 'something more' than interpretation'. *The International Journal of Psychoanalysis*, 79, 903-21.
Symington, N. (1983). 'The analyst´s act of freedom as agent of therapeutic change'. *International Review of Psycho-Analysis*, 283-91.
The Boston Change Process Study Group (2013). 'Enactment and the emergence of new relational organization'. *Journal of the American Psychoanalytic Association*, 61, 4, 727-49.
Winnicott, D. (1958). 'Mind and its relation to the psyche-soma'. In *Through Paediatrics to Psychoanalysis: Collected Papers*. London, New York: Routledge.

Self, Other and Individuation: resolving narcissism through the lunar and solar paths of the Rosarium

Marcus West
(SAP) Findon, UK

In this paper I will describe how narcissism constitutes our infant-like form of behaviour that is wholly appropriate and necessary, and which necessarily persists within us throughout life. I am defining narcissism at this point simply as the sensitivity of the self, in the ordinary sense of the word self: our vigilance about what will happen to us and the ways we protect ourselves. These forms of protection can become problematic, as I will describe, but it is only too easy for us to reject and pathologize this behaviour as unacceptable and destructive, and thus to set ourselves fundamentally at odds with ourselves, or to project our own narcissism onto others.

I will be suggesting that this narcissism can be 'resolved' if recognized, appreciated, accommodated and worked through in particular ways, and will be outlining how this resolution is described in the full 20 woodcuts of the 16th century alchemical treatise, 'The Rosarium of the Philosophers'. I hope to show that this throws new light on the longstanding conundrum of the ego in relation to the process of individuation, as well as on the process of individuation itself.

In parallel, I suggest that this process is equivalent to our lifelong struggle to engage in the world and to manifest our genuine, spontaneous selves – our souls; that is, to incarnate, and by this I mean an embodied-relational-social-spiritual form of incarnation; and this entails precisely negotiating the narcissistic defences we construct against being wounded.

And when we talk about manifesting ourselves in the world, we are necessarily talking about doing this in relationship with an other, and the balance between self and other – who fits in with who – is one of the central aspects that I will be addressing.

Finally, the narcissistic level most closely corresponds to the political level as, like the infant, we are embedded in, and subject to, the cultural and political forces that surround us; and I will be making a few comments on that level.

The early relational roots of narcissism

From my work with adult patients I have come to understand that there are three interlocking characteristics of narcissism:

- First, is the attempt to avoid or evacuate pain, suffering, discomfort and distress;
- Second, is the attempt to exert control;
- Third, is the attempt to distance oneself from relationship in one form or another in so far as it causes distress, and/or to distance oneself from one's reactions of hurt and anger at the distress.

For the infant, it is absolutely natural and necessary to do this. They must not only limit their distress to manageable levels, but signal it to their caregivers – evacuate it – in order to elicit help. They *need* to exercise control, to try to avoid pain and seek out safety, comfort and engagement with their caregivers; to attach and fit in. When the caregiver becomes a source of threat, they have to limit that engagement, as reflected in different patterns of attachment.

A benevolent cycle

Let us start with a picture of an interaction between self and other when things are going well (Figure 1). Imagine the infant in this picture making a gesture to which the mother responds with pleasure; the infant then responds to the mother's response and smiles, or makes a noise, to which the mother in turn responds. This warm interaction continues for a while until it either breaks down, or one or other of them has had enough and looks away.

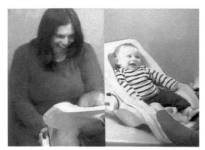

Figure 1: Mother and Baby (from Beebe, Cohen & Lachmann, 2016)

So here we do not just have an infant's self-expression and a passive mother/other, but we have a mother who welcomes, responds to and fosters the expression of the infant's self; this accommodating, welcoming, responding (m)other is then, in turn, received and enjoyed by the infant, enhancing the (m)other's self-expression (Benjamin would describe this in terms of mutual recognition [2018, p. 4], and Fordham [1969] in terms of the deintegration and reintegration of parts of the infant's Self.) This is a benevolent, dynamic interaction of enjoyment and inter-play between self and other.

However, such (benevolent) interactions are not sustained, nor even uniform. As Ed Tronick describes, in every interaction there is a process of mismatching, rupture and repair. When there is a mismatch – perhaps the mother is insufficiently attentive or responsive – the infant instinctively tries to repair the mismatch, attempting to regain the mother's attention by, for example, cooing, gesturing, or expressing distress.

If the mother then responds, the infant has a sense of self-agency and effectiveness, they develop what Tronick and Gianino (1986) call a positive emotional core. They internalize a sense that the other *will* respond and they take this into other relationships as what Bowlby (1969) calls their internal working model(s).

It is one of the infant's primary tasks, as Beebe & Lachmann describe in detail (2013, ch. 1), to develop 'expectancies', to anticipate and accommodate to their early relational environment. The infant therefore needs to be vigilant toward the other, to monitor the other and modify their own behaviour, to balance self and other.

I suggest that this vigilance underlies the Freudian concept of the superego, which ensures we fit in with others, and further suggest that, duly developed and transformed in ways I will describe, it forms the knowing, orienting and guiding aspect of the Self, in Jung's use of the term.

When things go wrong – narcissistic wounding

However, as Tronick and Gianino also describe, if the infant is repeatedly unsuccessful in repairing these mismatches, they come to feel helpless, they focus their behaviour on self-regulation, limit their engagement with their social environment and, rather than developing a positive sense of self, they 'establish a negative affective core' – they feel bad, and feel bad about themselves (1986, p. 156). The 'other' here does not function as an other who allows and enhances the expression of the self, but rather inhibits, suppresses or even kills it off; and shame is the affect that inhibits self-expression.

Looking ahead to what I will be saying about the *Rosarium*, the full 20 woodcuts describe two discrete cycles of interaction, a lunar and a solar cycle. I will be suggesting that the solar cycle relates to self-expression, whilst the lunar cycle represents receptivity of/to the other. In the benevolent interaction I just described, the couple are each engaging in both solar self-expression and lunar receptivity.

When there has been significant narcissistic wounding, there is either an *inhibition* or a *reinforcement* of self-expression or receptivity to the other, and sometimes both together. I believe that the *Rosarium* shows how such relational trauma can be repaired and our natural 'narcissistic' tendencies developed to their fullest potential.

Example

Regarding early relational trauma, the Boston Change Process Study Group describe an observation of a young depressed mother and her 18-month-old toddler. I will condense their description: the mother is smoking on the couch while her son is finishing his bottle and then starts bouncing up and down and flopping over onto his mother's lap, at which point 'she jerks her head toward him and barks, "I told you not to jump on the couch!"' They point out that this clearly has little to do with the toddler's bouncing but rather it relates to his making playful physical contact with her. They add, 'on the same videotape we see her son walk up to her and reach out his hand toward her knee, only to pull it away suddenly before actually touching her'. They comment:

> His mother's aversion to affectionate touch appears to have led him to inhibit his own initiatives around seeking physical contact with his mother. As this pattern is repeated over time, it is being preserved as part of his implicit relational knowing [internal working models] and is likely to color later interactions with others.
>
> (BCPSG 2007, p. 146)

If this occurs repeatedly it is narcissistically wounding for the child and it inhibits his 'solar' self-expression; it is traumatic; Philip Bromberg, defines trauma as occurring when, in relationship with another, self-invalidation or self-annihilation is inescapable (2011, p. 4 ff.). In my clinical experience, the more the individual experiences the threat of annihilation, the more their counter-response will be murderous and annihilatory, as their need to limit and escape from the other's dysregulating power and their 'regime' is imperative.

In Jung's terms (1934a), an autonomous traumatic complex is formed; the child's need for affection is not, then, integrated with his ego – it does not become a fluent part of his personality – and he will likely have powerful affective-somatic reactions related to affection. He is likely to withdraw from relationship to some extent, in a form of disorganized attachment pattern where the individual moves both toward and away from someone at the same time. This occurs when the parent toward whom you would normally turn for comfort is, at the same time, a source of threat.

Mammalian defensive systems and Porges' Polyvagal theory

From very early in life we have different responses to threat, depending on its nature, severity and duration, related to the primitive, fight, flight, freeze and collapse responses, which are common to all mammals. Stephen Porges (2011) describes how there is a hierarchy to these responses, which are all governed by different branches of the vagal nerve (Figure 2).

The Polyvagal Theory - Stephen Porges

		Evolved in humans	System
1st	🙂	Recently Neo-mammalian brain	**Safety** Social engagement
			Facial - heart - lungs system Slows heart rate, supports calmness - inhibits fight-flight ('vagal brake') Myelinated ventral branch of the vagal nerve
2nd	😠	Long Ago Mammalian brain	**Moderate to extreme danger** Fight / flight Mobilisation
			Sympathetic nervous system Ventral vagal system dampened or withdrawn - defence systems activated
3rd	😐	Very Long Ago Reptilian brain	**Life Threatening** Freeze / collapse / feign death Immobilisation
			Parasympathetic nervous system Non-myelinated dorsal branch of the vagal nerve Regulate organs beneath the diaphragm

Figure 2: Information from Porges (2011, 2018)

Our first response relates to *social engagement*, perhaps reasoning with the threatening person; for example, a child saying: "I'm sorry Dad, I was tired, it won't happen again".

If this doesn't work, the more primitive defences, associated with the activation of the sympathetic nervous system, cut in – fight or flight – a shouting match perhaps or, like the boy described with his depressed mother, an avoidance through inhibiting the natural expression of self.

However, if this doesn't work, or if the threat is more severe and more prolonged, the most primitive response is triggered – that of shut down: freezing, fainting, submission and collapse – archetypally, this is the response of the antelope just before it is struck by the lion … or the child who is being abused.

Beebe & Lachmann observed infants at four months old who demonstrated these reactions: jerking their body away as the mother smiled incongruously in response to the infant's distress (a fight/flight response); doing nothing more than blink as the mother poked the infant, trying to elicit a response (a freeze response); or collapsing like a rag-doll after multiple maternal intrusions (2013, p. 63).

In my previous work, I have linked these reactions with the different personality organizations long explored by psychoanalysis – narcissistic, schizoid, borderline and hysteric; with the obsessional responses following from control and hyper-vigilance. I have suggested that these are all different forms of narcissistic defence which protect the core of the self from further wounding, with the narcissistic personality organization being the 'pure form' of narcissism, whilst, on a broad definition of narcissism, the other forms are also narcissistic in their different ways (see West 2007 & 2016).

The controlling (homunculus) ego

Before I give some clinical vignettes to illustrate these patterns, I would like to say more about the controlling, defensive aspects of the ego and draw your attention to the homunculus as depicted in the *Rosarium* (Figure 3). This is the little humanoid figure that ascends into the clouds as part of the process of transformation (and there is a male and female form).

Figure 3: from Fabricius (1976, p. 230)

It is often suggested that the ego needs to be relinquished in some way in the process of individuation; yet it is clear that the process of individuation requires a great deal of understanding, restraint, discipline and forbearance – qualities and functions of the ego. From long pondering on this subject (viz. West 2008), I suggest that it is precisely the controlling, narcissistically defensive aspects of the ego which need, ultimately, to be relinquished.

It is the *early* ego's task to *try* to exert some control, to *try* to avoid pain, to *try* to direct the individual beneficially and develop a working understanding of the world around. However, I suggest that the process of maturation, and of individuation, requires the individual to relinquish this control if they are to come to a more realistic view of the self in relation to others, and to trust in, and cede control to, the Self[1].

I link this control to the idea of the homunculus as the little person who controls the larger organism. As examples of these homunculi, there is the 'somatic homunculi' of neurobiology, which correspond to the motor and sensory functions in the brain; the homunculi shown in the Disney film *Inside Out* or, in a much-loved comic from my childhood, *The Numskulls* who appeared in *The Beano*, all of whom tried, with varying degrees of success and failure, to control the person in whom they dwelt; there is also McGilchrist's metaphor of the Master and his emissary, which he links to the two hemispheres of the brain, where the emissary/vizier usurps his wise and benevolent Master and rules the region for his own gain … until it collapses in ruin (2009, p. 14).

It is the impossibility of this controlling homunculus operating wholly successfully that causes the individual anxiety and difficulties of various kinds, as I will describe, and which is also behind the puffed-up grandiosity of the person attempting to convince themselves and others that they cannot be defeated.

I should add that the opposite of this attempted control of the other, is an acceptance and respect for the other as a separate individual in their own right – witness the picture (above) of the secure pair taking pleasure in the other and in the dialogue between them; and this does not necessarily mean being so respectful that the other cannot be challenged.

Clinical vignettes

In the following vignettes I will emphasize the underlying narcissistic elements and hope to show how they are interwoven with the individual's early relational experience, and specifically the traumatic aspects, which form our relational complexes (West 2016). It has been my experience that the traumatic complexes have to be addressed and worked through in order to release the personality to develop to its fuller potential, and that this also entails working through the

---

[1] I am capitalizing the word Self when it applies in Jung's sense of the word.

more primitive narcissistic defences. Each thumbnail sketch distils the characteristics of at least four or more people of various sexes.

Jed – the fight response and the narcissistic personality organization

'Jed' had a depressed mother, like the young boy described above, but, in addition, his father was rigid, controlling, and critical. Jed desperately needed to avoid and evacuate suffering as he had had too much of it, and insufficient help processing what he had experienced. He had learned to bury his vulnerable, affectionate nature, and took his father's rigid controlling nature as a role model, identifying with the aggressor.

As an adult he sought out relationships where he was in a position of power. He could not commit to relationships as he could not bear to be subject to someone else's moods or demands (as he had been to his parents'). Nor could he let relationships develop beyond a certain point, in case he might get in touch with his own dependence and vulnerability – he often made a virtue out of his self-reliance, saying that he depended on no-one. He would be rejecting and critical in a way that could be sadistic at times, until his partner could bear it no longer and would leave him.

Yet Jed manifested a compelling form of self-expressive, solar power and he could be decisive, effective, and engaging – he could make things happen. However, the shadow cast by his solar power in this defensive form is a solar blindness, where his own perspective blinded him to the other. Jed's energy could then be coercive and, when someone did something that distressed him, he could, like the Red Queen in *Alice Through the Looking Glass*, declare, 'Off with their head!'; and he would then find himself alone and isolated.

Yet, this primitive 'murderous' response is exactly what is necessary for the child to remove themself from unbearable dysregulation and annihilation by the parent – they must, in some way, 'escape'.

Despite his power and control, Jed felt himself to be the victim. He was continually 'wired' and anxious, partly because he feared counterattack because his confrontative manner often induced attack; partly because he could not maintain the powerful persona that he wanted, but felt worried about looking stupid, being criticized, being vulnerable, and about not being in control or seeming inadequate; and partly because he reacted to everything, and thus felt exposed and never at peace or at rest.

Jed had been controlled by his parents' moods and, in particular by his father's power and threats; he controlled others the same way himself, including me in the analysis sometimes; and was himself concerned about the threat of others' power. Jed's narcissistic personality organization is the pure form of narcissistic defence.

To introduce the political dimension, we all know certain politicians who have this personality organization, who can be compelling and decisive, yet who are blind to and blaming of the other – if they experience distress, the other is to blame. In addition, they cannot bear being subject to others, for example, immigrants or refugees. I will look at how this can develop and be transformed below.

I will more briefly describe how the flight, freeze, collapse and vigilant responses might manifest in schizoid, borderline, hysteric and obsessional organizations, and stress that we each have all of these potential responses within us.

Steve – the flight response and the schizoid personality organization

'Steve' avoids conflict; he has buried his fight response and his narcissistically controlling tendencies, and has become a people pleaser. Yet, in his own way, he is controlling as he is difficult to please and reacts with disappointment when the other doesn't, in turn, provide the perfect, idealized, non-conflictual environment that he provides for them, and in which he feels he might finally be able to be himself. Steve has taken the lunar route (see below) of accommodating to the other, yet he controls through disapproval and what is proper and socially acceptable, and is himself controlled in the same way, as he was in childhood by his strict and proper parents.

Lily – hypervigilance and the obsessional personality organization

'Lily' had been given too much responsibility too young, with little or no support or encouragement, being expected to behave like a 'grown up' at five years old. She was obsessionally vigilant about what would happen, and worried about what to do. She sought frequent reassurance that she was alright, that things would be alright, and for help with the impossible task of controlling and ensuring that everything would go as she hoped; a task which eventually led to depression and obsessional symptoms. Lily also took the lunar route of caring for others; she was controlled by anxiety, and I found myself at first drawn into reassuring her as I found it difficult to bear her not being able to bear her anxiety.

Magda – the collapse response and the hysteric personality organization

'Magda's' father had been brutal, controlling and violent, and her mother did not protect her against him. Magda was hypervigilant to what I might be feeling toward her, terrified that I might become similarly intolerant, angry, fed-up or rejecting. Magda had not been allowed to be herself but had to submit to her father's will in every way. In this collapsed state she abandoned her baby self on my analytic doorstep. Whilst Magda had been controlled by the power of her father's feelings throughout her childhood, I became similarly controlled by the power of her reactions if she felt narcissistically wounded by me; her solar self-expression was fraught with both control and the deepest anxiety.

Bryony – the freeze response and the borderline personality organization

Bryony's mother had been unremittingly depressed from early on, with her father absent, probably having affairs. Every expression of her baby self caused her mother anxiety and distress. Bryony was in a freeze state, in thrall to bad experience, anticipating and pre-empting it, reacting to everything as a worst-case scenario. She was deeply depressed and regressed, having little self-agency / solar self-expression, which was inhibited by a deep sense of shame. In a vicious circle, this lack of self-expression induced further shame, which could be crippling.

Bryony had been controlled by her mother's misery and I found that I became controlled by her misery too; it becoming my 'job' to make her feel better, apparently without her having to do anything herself. It was necessary to address the idealized wish that I would thus make up for what she hadn't had in childhood – a pattern of relating and attachment that kept her in a passive, regressed position, looking to the other for rescue.

Secure attachment and the mirror trap

In different ways, all of the people I have described were trapped in what I call a 'mirror trap'. A securely attached child – one who is secure in the knowledge that if they need help the attachment figure will come – is free to move away from mother, engaging what the neuroscientist Jaak Panksepp (1998) called their SEEKING system, to explore their environment and engage in other relationships. They are able to make good use of the 'solar' expression of their self. As adults, they are able to invest in their activities and relationships, and get satisfaction from this self-expression and the positive feedback that will likely follow – they have developed a positive sense of self-agency (Knox 2010).

The individuals I have described however are trapped; with either their relational or self-expressive capabilities inhibited (or both), they look to the other, and particularly the analyst, to provide support for their controlling, narcissistically compromised homunculus-ego.

And often this is a two-way trap, as the analyst feels trapped into having to, or trying to, supply the approval, love, intimacy, or reassurance that they did not get in infancy, lest they expose the individual to their early traumas of criticism, neglect, brutality, or anxiety, and thereby retraumatize them. And, of course, the archetypal example of the mirror trap is Narcissus himself, enthralled and entrapped by his own reflection in the pool.

Working through both the narcissistic wounding due to early relational trauma, and the narcissistic control of the analyst, allow release from the mirror trap, and represent a significant dynamic in the process of analysis.

The Rosarium of the Philosophers

In order to explore this more fully, I will now turn to the *Rosarium* which, I suggest, offers not only a potential resolution of these narcissistic difficulties but an illuminating description of the journey of development toward a fulfilled way of life, a full expression of the Self, of individuation.

The Rosarium is well-known through Jung's masterwork, 'The Psychology of the Transference', in Volume 16 of his *Collected Works*. It consists, however, of 20 woodcuts in all, although, for reasons I will not explore here, Jung only described the first 10, with the addition of one imported from the later section [I recommend Gus Cwik's (2006) discussion of Jung's omission in his own exploration of the full 20 woodcuts; and I will quote, below, from Nathan Schwartz-Salant (1998), who has also discussed the full series].

Figure 4: from Fabricius (1976, p. 230)

I will say very little about the first four woodcuts and will refer you instead to Jung himself (1946/54). The first woodcut (image 1; Figure 4) introduces us to the Mercurial Fountain, the *vas Hermeticum*, where the transformation will take place. From the Mercurial fountain – where Mercury is the 'living innate universal Spirit' (Jung 1955-56, para. 478) – comes the *acetum fontis*, the acid which will dissolve the current structures; the *lac virginis*, the virgin's milk, which will support the couple through their journey of transformation; and the *aqua vitae*, the waters of life.

The next three woodcuts (2-4; Figure 4) introduce us to the two protagonists in the process – *sol* and *luna*, sun and moon, the king and queen – in various states of openness and readiness as they descend into the *vas*, where the chemical reaction is to take place; or, in analytic terms, the analyst and analysand in the analytic vessel; (I must emphatically stress that people of whatever sex have both potentials within them).

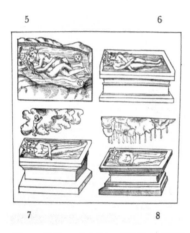

Figure 5: from Fabricius (1976, p. 230)

The lunar, relational cycle

Woodcuts 5 to 10 (Figures 5 & 6) describe the lunar, that is, relational cycle. Jung (1946/54) describes how the alchemical process goes through the stages of the *nigredo:* confusion, and *putrefaction*: death of the old; where the two individuals become mixed up with one another and their relationship becomes a third thing, a hermaphroditic *coniunctio* with its own characteristics. This is followed by the stage of *albedo* / whitening and purification, a relational process where the homunculus returns from heaven, purified (Woodcut 9).

What has occurred in this process, is that the analyst, typically, hopefully, has been able to accept and accommodate that which the patient has not been able to bear, whether that is a particular affect, characteristic, or part of the patient's Self, often felt to be 'bad'; for example, their aggression, self-hatred, or experience of failure; or perhaps the part lying in their shadow underdeveloped: their vulnerability, love, or effectiveness and power.

This relatedness offers what Ed Tronick et al. (1998) have called a 'dyadically expanded state of consciousness', where, because the analyst is able to accept this part of the patient in a soul-ful union, alongside of and in tune with the other, that part of the patient, in fact of both of them, is transformed.

Note that it is actually the male homunculus that ascends into heaven in this cycle. In alchemical terms the male represents the solar principle, and I suggest that this signifies that it is a part of the Self that is being integrated. Through repetition of this cycle (entailing varying degrees of difficulty), there can be an increasing integration of previously dissociated, disowned or undeveloped parts of the personality. Seeing that new aspects of the individual can emerge throughout one's lifetime, this process is lifelong. Jung (1955-56) said that this process of integration of the different parts of the Self, which he called the *unio mentalis*, was the first part of the process of individuation[2].

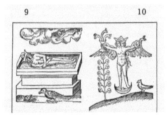

Figure 6: from Fabricius (1976, p. 230)

The outcome of this stage of the process (Woodcut 10; Figure 6) – the resplendent hermaphrodite known as the White Empress or the White Stone – brings a new stability to the individual. The stability, the (Philosopher's) 'stone', arises from the individual having accepted and integrated the parts that were previously dissociated, so that when, for example, their vulnerability is triggered they can 'stay with themselves' rather than dissociating.

This lunar stage is essentially relational in nature, and results from the empathy with, and acceptance and accommodation of, the other, in what has stereotypically / archetypically been thought to be the

---

2 Jung's conceptualization of the container and contained corresponds to the solar, self-expressive aspect of the individual being contained by the lunar, related-receptive other (whilst a solar aspect of the lunar 'container' may at the same time be contained by the primarily solar 'contained') (Jung 1925, para. 331c); whilst Bion's (1970) conceptualization of the container-contained offers an account of the transformation of the child's / patient's primitive beta elements by the parent's / analyst's alpha functioning, similar to the transformation of the patient's unacceptable parts as I have described in the lunar cycle (although I do not think that Bion's formulation quite captures Jung's understanding of the depth of engagement and involvement of both participants in the analytic process).

feminine role, hence the White *Empress*; with white being associated with the lunar / silvering phase. In order to allow this relational *coniunctio* to occur, the patient has also had to accommodate the analyst to some degree, although hopefully not too many of the analyst's projections into them.

I suggested earlier that one of the primary characteristics of narcissism was the aversion to suffering, allied to an aversion to relationship. The accommodating, analytic relationship demonstrates to the patient that the painful affect and disavowed parts of the self can be borne and integrated: that we don't have to be perfect, that we can bear loss, suffering and failure, and that, with the analyst's help and empathy, the individual's particular suffering and distress can be borne. As a result, the way the person sees themselves – their ego-identifications – can become broadened substantially, for example, to include and accommodate experiences of failure, defeat or intimacy.

In the woodcut (10; Figure 6), the *Rebis*, as it is also called (from the Latin *res bina*, meaning two things – the hermaphrodite), is winged, symbolizing its spiritual nature, which reflects the transitory *dis*-identifications from the early, narrowly-identified ego that have taken place, so that we can no longer see ourselves as, for example, invulnerable or solely heroic. Disidentification from the ego and submission to the Self are two of the key characteristics of spiritual experience, as I will describe (see also West 2017).

In my examples, this phase allowed Jed and Steve to accept certain vulnerable aspects of themselves, Bryony and Magda to recognize their aggression, and all of them to bear and process more of their distress. Jed and Steve, and Bryony and Magda, had previously projected their vulnerability and aggression (respectively), which bound them to their vulnerable or aggressive objects.

Shadow sides of the lunar cycle

However, the shadow side of this lunar cycle is that the other, the analyst, could be simply adopting a masochistic position of acceptance and submission, whereby the patient ejects their unbearable affects – in a way that can be sadistic at times – and is not prepared to do work on them themselves. Whilst the analyst's task *is* to contain and transform this expelled affect, which can also be understood as a communication (a living expression of the person's formative experience), they cannot continue to do this unilaterally. The resolution of this shadow aspect is described in the second, solar phase.

A second shadow outcome is where, like Bryony or Magda, the patient projects all of their vital, solar self, into the analyst. This may entail an exaggerated sense of dependence on, or an over-valuing of, the analyst, perhaps of an erotic nature, sometimes demanding that the analyst responds; for example: "If you don't tell me that you find me attractive how can I feel good about myself?!"; or an angry punishing of the analyst for, "Not making me feel good ... which I am paying you to do!" Both are examples of the mirror trap.

As Jung stated about working through the transference:

> the goal is to detach consciousness from the object so that the individual no longer places the guarantee of his happiness, or his life even, in factors outside himself, whether they be persons, ideas, or circumstances, but comes to realize that everything depends on whether he holds the treasure or not.
>
> (Jung 1935, Tavistock Lecture 5, para. 377)

This 'treasure' is being in touch with and expressing the Self.

The solar, self-expressive cycle

So now we come to the solar cycle, which shows how the solar energies, and our narcissism, can continue to be transformed. If the lunar cycle helped transform and integrate the painful, unacceptable affects and parts of the self, the solar cycle shows the kind of relationship we need to form with the solar energy, with the *aqua vitae*, the waters of life, through the process of yellowing and then reddening, to form the solar 'gold'.

And, specifically, I am referring to the continuing transformation of the controlling homunculus-ego, which would like to claim the power of the Self as its own, so as to maintain control and to be able to achieve a position of invulnerability and omnipotence.

Figure 7: from Fabricius (1976, p. 230)

In the first woodcut of the solar cycle (11 – Fermentation; Figure 7) we again have a *coniunctio* of the king and queen, but this time there is no penetration – note the position of the hand. The queen is now on top and she is not simply going to be the receptive 'other'.

In analytic terms, the analyst insists that the patient takes responsibility for what they have experienced and had previously been projecting and evacuating into the analyst, and respects the analyst as an individual in their own right. This is part of the process of working through the early trauma, where the patient can no longer justify, for example, being angry and controlling of the analyst when they are hurt 'because *they* were controlled and shouted at' in childhood. In other words, this is partly about drawing and maintaining boundaries (which, unfortunately, the patient had not been able to do).

And as I just quoted, it also symbolizes that the answer is not to be found wholly in the other. This is the *Nekkia*, the night sea journey (notice they are in water), where we must set forth from the known sources and ways of relating into the unknown, with only our souls to guide us.

In this phase I challenged Jed when he belittled me and others, and could encourage Bryony to rely on herself and recognize her own strengths, although she strongly resisted grieving for and separating from the idealized, all-accepting, all-giving mother that she wanted me to be (see Jung 1911-12).

'Illumination'

In the following woodcut (12; Figure 7), we have the sun/sol in the *vas* of transformation in its winged, spiritual form. The solar principle is contained within the *vas*, underlining the withdrawal of projections.

In the intense heat there is a 'blackening', which reminds us that this is a second stage of nigredo, associated with the *sol niger*[3], the sun that does not irradiate but contains its energies. This means, partly, needing to suffer the experiences that have previously been evacuated – it is about 'suffering oneself' – for example, feeling the pain, powerlessness and sadness that previously fuelled rage, punishment and blame. Stanton Marlon (2005) describes a similar openness to suffering in his book *The Black Sun,* although my understanding is somewhat different from his in that I take the blackening to be due to the intensity following the constraint in the *vas* and lack of radiation / evacuation, which causes the individual to have to 'nobly suffer themselves'; [his understanding of the philosopher's stone (2006) is also different to mine].

This represents a further level of reunion with the disavowed, dissociated parts, and an acceptance and reunification with the core self. It thereby signifies an intense, getting-and-staying-in-touch with the Self, which brings 'illumination', the name for the woodcut.

---

3 Jung says that a 'sol niger, a black sun, ... coincides with the *nigredo* and *putrefactio,* the state of death' (1955-56, para. 113).

Inflation and psychosis

However, this can be a powerful and potentially deadly process. There are two specific dangers here: inflation and psychosis. Inflation occurs when the ego annexes this new-found power of the Self to itself, attempting to omnipotently control once more. And psychotic states occur if the ego, in an attempt to protect itself, is taken over and overwhelmed by these archetypal forces – the killing effect of the *aqua vitae*.

These 'waters of life' can only be drunk through a suitable (human) vessel, and the quest for the Holy Grail can be thought of as the formation of just such a vessel. I suggest that the *Rosarium* is describing exactly how this can be achieved.

Figure 8: from Fabricius (1976, p. 232)

Fabricius (1976, p. 232), shows a variant of the woodcut (Figure 8) in a parallel series, which shows more clearly what is going on here: the solar king is being sacrificed and thus transformed by the lunar queen. Her previous example of self-sacrifice in the lunar cycle may facilitate his sacrifice of his self-centredness. As Schwartz-Salant says of this woodcut, 'This act of sacrifice is the epitome of a voluntary death of narcissism in favour of creativity' (1998, p. 202). Subjectively, this sacrifice is often accompanied and characterized by an experience of death, as the old ego-identifications are given up or lost, which can be alarming to say the least. In almost all religions and initiation ceremonies, this is symbolzed by the individual giving up their old life. Through this subjective experience of 'ego death', the individual is put more in touch with the Self, as Jung puts it: '... the experience of the Self is always a defeat for the ego' (1955-56, para. 778).

This is inevitably a momentous experience and a represents a profound shift. I suggest it represents precisely a disidentification from the controlling, homunculus-ego and a reliance on, and submission to, the Self. It is precisely the development of the ego that facilitates this shift; for example, the discipline, containment of affect and integration of disavowed parts, which represents a shift from an 'early' to a developed ego position, the latter being in a subordinate position to the Self.

In my clinical example, Jed struggled with this phase of the cycle, as he found it extremely difficult to relinquish ego-control, particularly the wish to know 'what to do', although he could begin to appreciate how his reliance on his controlling, (homunculus) ego contributed to his anxiety and continued sense of failure; and Bryony struggled to rely on herself, which entailed giving me up as the idealized parent who would make things better for her.

This shift to reliance on the Self can be a gradual process or a sudden one – a 'leap of faith', although the latter may not be once and for all. And regarding sacrifice and psychosis, Jung wrote:

> Only the man who can consciously assent to the inner voice becomes a personality; but if he succumbs to it he will be swept away by the blind flux of psychic events and destroyed. That is the great and liberating thing about any genuine personality: he voluntarily sacrifices himself to his vocation, and consciously translates into his own individual reality what would only lead to ruin if it were lived unconsciously by the group.
>
> (Jung 1934b, para. 308)

Figure 9: from Fabricius (1976, p. 230)

In the following woodcut (13 – Nourishment; Figure 9), the king and the queen now form a winged, hermaphrodite; there is 'nourishment' because it is the contact with the Self that truly nourishes – the treasure, discussed above. And 'spiritual' because there has been a disidentification from the homunculus-ego, which wants earthly power and control, and a shift in the centre of gravity toward the Self, which knows of more universal connections.

If narcissism alienates us from others due to our rejection of a world that causes pain and 'doesn't suit us', the new invigorating contact with the Self connects us to all humanity, to the universe, once again. It also, thereby, connects us to our social milieu. This is what Jung calls the third stage of individuation, the vision of *unus mundus* (1955-56, para. 759 ff.).

Incarnation

In woodcut 14 (Figure 9), the hermaphroditic couple have lost their wings and the woodcut is entitled 'fixation'. This is the beginning of the incarnation process proper, where the individual is 'fixed' in the world and can no longer avoid suffering through disidentification, through 'spiritual bypass'. This and the next two woodcuts (15 & 16) involve the further stage of individuation (Jung's second stage of individuation), the reunification of the more integrated ego, the *unio mentalis*, with the body (1955-56, para. 738 ff. & Stein 2019).

And this time, it is the anima who ascends into heaven – her form of submission must undergo transformation too. It is no longer a potentially masochistic suffering she undergoes, which may have had self-serving purposes, such as avoidance, security and attachment, but rather only a purposeful one.

Note that there is a larger and a smaller process going on at the same time: in the relational, lunar phase, elements of solar expression (the male homunculus) are integrated; in the solar phase of engagement with the Self, the way the lunar relatedness occurs is developed / transformed (the female homunculus), addressing the shadow aspects of that relatedness.

In woodcuts 15 & 16 ('Multiplication' & 'Reviving'; Figure 9), the benefits are being shared with others too, there is a 'multiplication', the name for the woodcut. The transformation that is occurring could be described as the individual no longer acting *for* themselves but rather acting *from* the Self. The solar self-expression is not simply an evacuation of what the individual cannot bear or does not like.

Porges (2018) describes how the response of the sympathetic nervous system when not in its defensive fight-flight form, can be creative, productive, effective, and about play – it is enlivening and 'reviving', the name for woodcut 16. There is a creative interplay between self and other. (Similarly, the parasympathetic nervous system's response, when not under threat, facilitates restfulness, peace and intimacy).

The solar blindness has gone, and this also reflects a different attitude to, and relationship with, the collective, as the Self is intimately connected with others and the community. It often reflects an awareness of social issues, where painful experience has been accepted and contained, but is nevertheless challenged. A good example of this is Mahatma Gandhi's peaceful 'salt march', which played a large part in the end of British rule in India; and I will discuss Nelson Mandela shortly.

In the analytic situation, this represents the resolution of the analyst's potential masochism; they have accepted, contained and understood the patient's evacuation into them and, from this position, calling on their own solar self-expression, now outline, interpret and challenge the behaviour, holding to their own selfhood.

Figure 10: from Fabricius (1976, p. 230)

In woodcut 17 (Figure 10), after the return of the homunculus from heaven, we have the formation of the Red Stone or the Red Empress, 'the Heavenly Marriage' (Fabricius 1976, p. 233); and note the bird pecking its breast to feed its young in the background of the picture – a symbol of self-sacrifice – yet whilst the powerful, solar lion is rampant beside it.

The philosopher's stone has been further developed: the stone, the stability (now represented as a rock upon which the *Rebis* stands), is provided by the contact with the Self, by which the individual is nourished, from which they nourish others, and to which the individual stays true, as well as staying with reality (suffering). The *Rebis* has bat wings, signifying its integration of the night-time, lunar, emotional-relational principles. Yet this is not the end of the process.

Rubedo – red death & putrefaction

In woodcut 18 (Figure 10), the sun is being swallowed by the 'green lion' – the solar power is absorbed and digested in our animal nature; this is the incarnation of the spirit into the animal world, the reddening, the *rubedo*. There is a conjunctio of the sublime, spiritual, solar power with the chthonic, earthly animal nature. The animal nature is also thereby transformed by the transformed solar power, which has been both contained, harnessed and humanized; (note the expression on the sun's face as it is devoured – the sun, which naturally radiates, ejects and evacuates suffering, is itself suffering; and the green lion is lean and capable of suffering, rather than rampant as in the previous woodcut. There is a dual conjunction of power and suffering on the spiritual and earthly levels).

To give one example, as Aristotle says of anger:

Anyone can become angry, that is easy; but to be angry with the right person, and to the right degree, and at the right time, and for the right purpose, and in the right way, that is not within everybody's power, that is not easy.

(Aristotle 320 B.C., Ch. 9, 1109a., 26-29)

In analysis, the analyst has learnt to recognize, contain, and constructively utilize their own primitive, narcissistic, murderous-evacuative responses to distress and to being controlled; perhaps becoming more able to address the murderousness to which they are subject or perhaps furthering the process of separation.

Sublimation of soul and spirit

In the following woodcut (19; Figure 10), Mary, the ultimate feminine principle, has been received into heaven; the ego has found its position in relation to the Self – it is tended and recognized by two larger beings, who offer their blessing. The individual has discovered, as McLean says, that 'the source of illumination lies outside of one's being' (1980, p. 129; quoted in Schwartz-Salant 1998, p. 210). As the *Koran* says, 'O soul at peace, return to your Lord, well-pleased and well-pleasing' ('The Dawn' *Surah Fajr*, 27, 28).

The final woodcut (20; Figure 10) depicts the ultimate transformation of suffering: Christ, who 'died for the sins of the world', that is, who was able to accept all 'badness' into himself, is reborn. This is the final transformation of narcissism – the individual has been able to accept the suffering, rejection and annihilation of their self(-expression), yet remain open and relate to the others, despite the pain that they cause(d); to continue to see them, rather than succumbing to solar blindness.

Yet the person is also able to express their Self, reborn after death, though this time from a universal, social perspective. Similarly, Christ rises transformed from the sarcophagus / *vas*, an expression of the unified lunar and solar principles, but as man, not God: he has been incarnated in an embodied-relational-social-spiritual form. (And just as the king and queen are symbols that are not limited to gender, so Christ is a symbol that is not limited to Christianity).

On the political level, I suggest that Nelson Mandela perfectly embodies this transformed position depicted by the final woodcut: having started his political life in armed struggle, he was able to accept his considerable suffering – his 27 years in prison – and, transforming his fight response into acceptance and effective self-expression, became the voice of his people; forming relationships with his guards and treating his former enemies as individuals in their own right. He thereby came to express what was right in the right way, and be effective through the power of his shining, determined, yet soulful example.

Conclusion

Thus, I believe that the *Rosarium* describes how the basic 'narcissistic' disposition, with which we all start life, can be transformed, if the individual has a calling to do so. Those same faculties of infant-like sensitivity about the self, and superego-vigilance toward the other, can, through the expansion of what we can bear and know, come to form the aspect of the Self by which we are guided.

For this to occur, we need to be prepared to disidentify from the narrow, controlling, early ego, to develop broader and more fluid ego-identifications, and surrender to the Self; to take responsibility for ourselves, and for our infant-like sensitivity, being prepared to suffer at times and accept the world as it is, not passively, but actively engaging with it in an embodied, relational, social, and spiritual way. And just as the process of recognizing new aspects of the Self and broadening our ego-identifications is a never-ending, life-long process, so developing the relationship with the Self and engaging therefrom with the world as it presents itself afresh is also a life-long, never-completed process.

References

Aristotle (350 B.C.). *Nicomachean Ethics*.
Beebe, B., Cohen, P., & Lachmann, F. (2016). *The Mother-Infant Interaction Picture Book – Origins of Attachment*. New York: W.W. Norton & Company.

Beebe, B., & Lachmann, F. (2002). *Infant Research and Adult Treatment: Co-constructing Interactions*. Hillsdale, NJ: Analytic Press.
— (2013). *The Origins of Attachment: Infant Research and Adult Treatment*. Abingdon: Taylor & Francis.
Benjamin, J. (2018). *Beyond Doer and Done to – Recognition Theory, Intersubjectivity and the Third*. Hove & New York: Routledge.
Bion, W.R. (1970). *Attention and Interpretation*. Oxford: Routledge.
Boston Change Process Study Group (BCPSG) (2007). 'The foundational level of psychodynamic meaning: implicit process in relation to conflict, defense, and the dynamic unconscious'. *International Journal of Psycho-Analysis*, 88, 843-60.
Bowlby, J. (1969). *Attachment and Loss, Volume I: Attachment*. Harmondsworth: Penguin Books.
Bromberg, P. (2011). *The Shadow of the Tsunami: and the Growth of the Relational Mind*. Abingdon: Taylor & Francis.
Cwik, G. (2006). 'Rosarium revisited'. In *Alchemy, Spring 74*; New Orleans: Spring Journal.
Fabricius, J. (1976). *Alchemy: The Mediaeval Alchemists and their Royal Art*. London: Aquarian Press.
Fordham, M. (1969). *Children as Individuals: An Analytical Psychologist's Study of Child Development*. London: Hodder & Stoughton.
Jung, C.G. (1911-12). *Symbols of Transformation*. CW 5.
— (1925). 'Marriage as a psychological relationship. In: CW 17.
— (1934a). 'A review of the complex theory'. In *The Structure and Dynamics of the Psyche*, CW 8.
— (1934b). 'The development of personality'. In CW 17.
— (1935). 'The Tavistock Lectures'. In *The Symbolic Life*, CW 18.
— (1946/54). 'The psychology of the transference'. In CW 16.
— (1955-56). *Mysterium Coniunctionis*. CW 14.
Knox, J. (2010). *Self-agency in Psychotherapy: Attachment, Autonomy, and Intimacy*. New York: W.W. Norton & Company, Inc.
Marlon, S. (2005). *The Black Sun*. College Station: Texas A & M University Press.
— (2006). 'From the Black Sun to the Philosophers' Stone'. In: *Alchemy, Spring 74*; New Orleans: Spring Journal.
McGilchrist, I. (2009). *The Master and his Emissary – The Divided Brain and the Making of the Western World*. New Haven & London: Yale University Press.
McLean, A. (1980). *The Rosary of the Philosophers*. Edinburgh: Magnum Opus Hermetic Sourceworks.
Panksepp, J. (1998). *Affective Neuroscience: The Foundations of Human and Animal Emotions*. New York: Oxford University Press.
Porges, S.W. (2011). *The Polyvagal Theory: Neurophysiological Foundations of Emotions, Attachment, Communication, and Self-regulation*. New York: W.W. Norton & Company.
— (2018). 'Polyvagal theory: a primer' pgs. 50-72; In S. Porges & D. Dana (Eds.); *Clinical Application of the Polyvagal Theory – The Emergence of Polyvagal Informed Therapies*. New York: W.W. Norton & Company.
Schwartz-Salant, N. (1998). *The Mystery of Human Relationship – Alchemy and the Transformation of the Self*. Hove & New York: Routledge.

Stein, M. (2019). 'Psychological individuation and spiritual enlightenment: some comparisons and points of contact'. *Journal of Analytical Psychology,* 64, 1, 6-22.

Tronick, E.Z. & Gianino, A. (1986). Interactive mismatch and repair: challenges to the coping infant. *Zero to Three, Bulletin of the National Center for Clinical Infant Programs,* 5, 1-6. Reprinted in *The Neurobehavioural and Social-Emotional Development of Infants and Children,* Tronick, E.Z. (2007). New York & London: Norton, 2007.

Tronick, E.Z., Bruschweiler-Stern N., Harrison A.M., Lyons-Ruth, K., Morgan A.C., & Nahum J.P. (1998). 'Dyadically expanded states of consciousness'. *Infant Mental Health Journal,* 19, 290-99.

West, M. (2007). *Feeling, Being and the Sense of Self – a new perspective on identity, affect and narcissistic disorders.* London & New York: Karnac.

— (2008). 'The narrow use of the term ego in analytical psychology: the 'not-I' is also who I am'. *The Journal of Analytical Psychology,* 53, 367-88.

— (2016). *Into the Darkest Places – Early Relational Trauma and Borderline States of Mind.* London & New York: Karnac.

— (2017). 'To the beginning and back again: trauma, splits and confluences'. In *Re-Encountering Jung – Analytical Psychology and Contemporary Psychoanalysis,* ed. Robin S. Brown. Hove & New York: Routledge.

Friday, 30 August 2019

Panel
Encountering the Other: Jungian Analysts and Traditional Healers in South Africa

Part I: The History

Peter Ammann
(SGAP) Aarau, Switzerland

Encountering the Other, encountering the Other in Africa! Let's start with our forefather. In her biography of Jung, Barbara Hannah reports that once he told her an active imagination according to which:

> his fantasy led him into a remote valley, evidently inhabited by primitive people. A tall and rather impressive medicine man figure was silently beside him, watching his every step and movement. Jung came on some writing carved on a rock, which he wanted to read, but found that it was in a language quite unknown to him. Since it was also rather illegible, he took a chisel and hammer and began carefully deepening the letters in the stone. The medicine man came close, watching him even more intently, until he suddenly complained that a splinter of stone had got into his eye. He commanded Jung to take it out, but the latter, seeing his opportunity, refused to do so until the medicine man had read and translated the inscription for him! The man was unwilling to do so, but Jung held onto him and waited... until at last he read the text of the whole inscription.

(Hannah 1991, p. 161)

Here is no time to analyse this story in detail. However, it gives us the frame for all the problems of our topic. Jung, the Western psychologist, finds himself alongside a representative of those 'other' people once upon a time called 'primitive'. He is even a counterpart of the Western doctor, an indigenous healer. Could it be that he is not as 'primitive' as it seems, but perhaps in possession of some 'other' knowledge, some indigenous wisdom? Jung's active imagination is unquestionably a story of encountering the other, the medicine man. But there is the other side of the coin: Jung is bluntly blackmailing the indigenous man: 'Yes, I'll take the splinter out of your eye, but on condition only that you tell me the meaning of the inscription.' Knowledge, science has become the end that justifies the means!

Is this attitude not exactly what Mountain Lake so sharply criticized when Jung met him during his visit to the Pueblo Indians in 1925? 'See,' Mountain Lake said, 'how cruel the whites look ... The whites always want something; they are always uneasy and restless' (1963, p. 276). Jung himself is a representative of these white men. Yet, to be fair, the same Jung was also conscious of the white man's sin: 'What we from our point of view call colonization, missions to the heathen, spread of civilization, etc., has another face – the face of a bird of prey seeking with cruel intentness for distant quarry – a face worthy of a race of pirates and highwaymen' (ibid., p. 277).

In his active imagination – which probably dates from about 1914 – Jung met an indigenous man. Several years later, he visited indigenous people in the outer reality, 1920 in North Africa, 1925 in New Mexico, Kenya and Uganda. Jung's aim during his trip to Kenya and Uganda is well summarized in a newspaper article of the *East African Standarten* (2005):

> A party of scientists have come to Kenya to strengthen new theories on psychology... By living there, the scientists hope to win the confidence of the natives and get behind their mind. It is hoped that when the natives find out that the white men are in sympathy with their customs and ceremonials, the natives will gradually produce material for which the scientists are searching

(Burleson 2005, pp. 141-42)

These lines very much recall the White Man in Jung's active imagination who invades and exploits the natives for the sake of his scientific ambitions, the White Man using, in fact abusing, the Indigenous Man for his own sake.... The White Man as an explorer, conqueror, even colonizer?

Yet, once again, there is another side of the coin: Blake W. Burleson, in his book *Jung in Africa* (2005), bears out that Jung throughout his entire safari was what in modern social anthropology is called a *participant observer*. This approach implies that one gives in to an alien reality and allows oneself to change in the course of the *experience*. A very Jungian approach! And it was indeed what Jung did. He allowed himself to be deeply affected and changed by the African experience. But it was definitely not an 'encounter with the other' on an equal level or a mutual exchange. I argue this altogether was hardly possible given the historic and cultural situation of the time.

The situation was considerably different 60 years later when Vera Bührmann, the Grand Old Lady of Jungian psychology in South Africa, did her pioneering research in a South African indigenous community. Though being part of the white dominant minority in South Africa she nevertheless lived in the midst of the black population and the language barrier was much smaller. Astrid Berg (2008) said of her mentor: '...Dr Bührmann may have been one of the first researchers from the West to truly respect the people she was researching.... She therefore did not try to impose her own terminologies on the indigenous language'. She and the black traditional healers entered into a real dialogue which resulted in the publication of her groundbreaking book *Living in Two Worlds – Communication between a white healer and her black counterparts* (1984). Bührmann, by her work, formed the foundation for understanding traditional healing from a Western perspective. But we must admit that the counterpart did not really happen.

And it did not happen either when, in 2007 at the IAAP Congress in Cape Town, I had the privilege to organize workshops in the course of which Jungian psychotherapists and African traditional healers could encounter each other (2008). One of the black healers called me after the Congress and said: 'You Jungians, you all are so interested in our work, but we black healers, we should also show some interest in your kind of work, shouldn't we?' The turning point came through a series of happy encounters and coincidences. First: when I met Nomfundo Mlisa, South African clinical psychologist trained according to Western standards, at the same time fully-fledged African traditional healer and, last but not least, deeply interested in Jungian psychology. Second: when Renee Ramsden and later Fred Borchardt, together with some of their colleagues of SAAJA, showed their genuine interest in an ongoing dialogue between Jungian analysts and traditional healers. Thanks to this conjunction – and two most generous donors, one anonymous and the other Nancy Furlotti – we could hold two 'small but beautiful' conferences in Hogsback 2016, and in Monkey Valley, Cape Town 2018, bringing together Jungian analysts and African traditional healers in order to establish an ongoing encounter between these two ways of healing. My South African colleagues will tell you more about it. Thank you.

References

Ammann, P. (2008). DVD: *Healing in Two Worlds – Jungian Psychotherapists Encounter African Traditional Healers, Panel-Workshop at IAAP Congress Cape Town 2007.*
Bührmann, V. (1984). *Living in Two Worlds – Communications Between a White Healer and her Black Counterparts.* Cape Town & Pretoria: Human & Rousseau.
Burleson, B.W. (2005). *Jung in Africa.* New York: Continuum.
Hannah, B. (1991). *Jung, his life and work.* Boston: Shambhala.
Jung, C.G. (1963). *Memories, Dreams, Reflections.* London: Flamingo, Fontana Paperbacks.

Part 2: The Context

Fred Borchardt
(SAAJA) Cape Town, South Africa

I want to say something about the context of our project. Traditional health practitioners in Africa were practising long before that continent was named 'Africa' by outsiders such as the Romans. This was long before European forces annexed large portions of the newly named continent on behalf of their kings and queens and then made subjects out of the newly named 'Africans' who had always lived there.

A good summary of the complications brought about by colonial history is provided by a widely reported event which happened in Cape Town on the 9th of March 2015, about 18 months before the first meeting between Jungian analysts and traditional health practitioners took place. On that day a man named Chumani Maxwele emptied a bucket of human faeces over a bronze statue of Cecil John Rhodes on the main campus of the University of Cape Town, while shouting: 'Where are *our* heroes and ancestors?' (*Timeline of the Rhodes Must Fall Movement*, 2017). This event led to the social activism movement #*RhodesMustFall*, which demanded the removal of the statue of the historical global financier and benefactor-founder of the university. As the movement gained momentum, it mutated into different sub-movements linked by general aims to address social injustices and racial discrimination in post-apartheid South African university settings. A focus of the protests were the thought systems imposed by colonialists on the populations they controlled, and the way in which this repressed indigenous thought systems.

Eighteen months later, in October 2016, by the time our small group of Jungians and traditional health practitioners had our first meeting, the statue had long been removed and the student revolt had been channelled into sporadic protests throughout the country and even abroad. While the different university campuses around the country still carried the visible scars of the protests, something else also still lingered: the political discourse in academic circles was now firmly focused on the question of the de-colonialization of the thought systems imposed by Western powers. Traditional health practitioners' systems were central to this discourse. The imperative to make this part of the dialogue of our project was pointed out at the formal opening of the first symposium by Mr. B. Gallant, the Dean of Student Affairs from the University of Fort Hare.

The first context for our project was therefore to come to terms with the global project of colonialization and how that impacted upon indigenous healing systems.

Over the years since 1652, the succession of European powers which politically controlled South Africa, systematically introduced European systems of medicine to the region. As a consequence, '... the introduction of Western medicine and culture gave rise to "cultural-ideological clash" which had hitherto created an unequal power-relation that practically undermined and stigmatized the traditional health care system in Africa because of the over-riding power of Western medicine' (Abdullahi 2011, p. 116). At the very least, the indigenous systems were politically marginalized by not being allowed to systematically organize themselves and grow. In extreme cases, there were attempts to ban or control aspects of traditional healing through legislation (Abdullahi 2011; Ross 2010).

Of course, the colonial control of the practice of traditional health practitioners failed. Today, eight out of every 10 black South Africans are believed to rely on traditional medicine on its own, or in combination with western medicine (Ross 2010; Berg 2003).

This, then, was the broad historical context for our project; global colonialization and the politics of power in the healing practices in South Africa. We were essentially attending to the question posed by Chumani Maxwele and many others.

Luckily for us, we had more than a bucket full of excrement in our hands. We had a spade, a tool for digging and for building. Our spade was the analytical psychology of Carl Jung, a theory very well-suited for this task. Astrid Berg sums it up well:

> Among the depth psychologies of the West, analytical psychology has a contribution to make to cross-cultural understanding. The notion of a collective unconscious and the concept of the archetypes form a basis upon which we can enter a dialogue with another culture
>
> (Berg 2003, p. 204)

My colleagues in this presentation are telling you more on how we used this spade.

On a personal level, it was obviously quite a challenging experience for a white settler from colonialist heritage to be part of a dialogue about the damage and repression of indigenous knowledge systems by colonialism. And then, on top of that, I am a Jungian analyst as well, and this was 2016, a year when there was already much talk in Jungian circles about apologies to people from African descent for the way in which they were described in Jungian literature. On both the cultural and professional fronts I felt a strong pull within me to be apologetic.

The process of our dialogue shaped a few questions for me in response to this dilemma. I understand that there are many other questions and answers about this issue, but these were my questions:

Firstly, would an apology have been enough? Although a formal apology can obviously bridge gaps and heal wounds, there are implicit shadows in such a gesture as well. It could, for instance, be an attempt to rid oneself of the discomfort of internal guilt. It could conceivably be an attempt of the defence mechanism of magical undoing of the past. Even worse, this gesture could potentially make it easier to convince oneself that a spoken apology on its own constitutes an adequate resolution of the past. To my mind the situation called for more than an apology. What was needed was sitting in the tension and discomfort of guilt, while listening and understanding.

Secondly, could being apologetic obscure similarities? An apology could be polarizing, as it presupposes and exaggerates different, opposing categories. Our dialogue was an exploration of spiritual roots, and we soon came to realise that we are all in the same boat here, we are all part of the same category. Our respective cultures are all involved in recovering the connection we lost with our spiritual, ancestral roots, through modernism and consumerism and materialism and so forth. We are fighting the same battle on the same side.

Thirdly, could being apologetic have been counterproductive? Where the previous questions addressed the past of both colonialism and Jungian writings, this question is specifically directed to the latter. In our dialogue there was already general agreement that Jungian analysis is one of the best tools for approaching cross-cultural understanding. Could any discourse into the historical development of that tool alter this fact in any significant way? What was needed was simply getting on with using the best tool that we have for the job. Which is what we did.

References

Abdullahi, A.A. (2011). 'Trends and challenges of traditional medicine in Africa'. In *African Journal of Traditional, Complimentary, and Alternative Medicines*, 8, 115-23.

Berg, A. (2003). 'Ancestor reverence and mental health in South Africa'. *Journal of Transcultural Psychiatry*, 40, 2, 194-207.

Mokgobi, M.G. (2014). 'Understanding traditional African healing'. *African Journal of Physical Health, Education, Recreation and Dance*. Sept, 20, 24-34.

Ross, E. (2010). 'African spirituality, ethics and traditional healing – implications for indigenous South African social work education and practice'. *SA Journal of Bioethics and Law*, 3, 1 44-51.

Timeline of the Rhodes Must Fall Movement (2017). Retrieved from thepoorprint.com/2017/04/28/rhodes-must-fall-a-timeline/

Part 3: The Traditional Health Practitioner's Stance and the World View

Nomfundo Lily-Rose Mlisa
East London, South Africa

Greetings from South African traditional health practitioners to all IAAP officials, colleagues, and respected ancestors around the world, gathered here. Traditional health practitioners are intrigued by the opportunity to be part of this academic dialogue. Indeed, we have to critically review the encounters 'within us; between us and *"us* and others in the *new* world"' as we traversed the delayed professional journey towards a common ground amongst psychotherapists. For the sake of our clients, we have to forge collective healing modalities for integrative health interventions. The reflections from our group participants at our workshop in Monkey Valley, in South Africa reflect the impact already made by these dialogues. Some of us already call it, 'a huge thing! Amazing encounter!' (Nompumelelo Kubeka, Vella Maseko and Buntu George). I call it a 'pardoned history' as traditional health practitioners begin to forget marginalization and the derogative names thrown at them by Western-trained professionals. Thank you to Jungians for the invitation, sponsorship and warm welcome to allow our engagement in such dialogues. In South Africa this engagement is called a baby – 'rainbow therapy'. Like any baby we are sceptical about challenges in the milestones of 'her' growth and are ready for any challenges as we are nurturing her. Our ultimate goal is to have a collective, healthy, professional engagement with all psychotherapists, irrespective of their school of thought, and with Jungians and traditional health practitioners being the key role-models in integrative therapeutic interventions.

The connection is a delayed process, as Torrey (1972) long ago made the demand for the integration of traditional healing and psychiatry. The World Health Organisation (1978-1995) stressed the importance of the recognition of traditional medicine and the inclusion of traditional health practitioners in the primary healthcare system. Without hesitation I thank our ancestor, Carl Jung, for providing traditional health practitioners with a Western relevant theory that explains our deep hurt during our spiritual journey. Indeed, as a 'wounded healer', I was able to identify the importance of being wounded first, to be able to understand the wounds of the other. There is a saying, 'Until you know who you are, you may never know how to become' (unknown). In analytical psychology students are taught that, 'knowing yourself first and self-introspection are the best teachers to enable one to understand others as well'. In our encounters in South Africa we learnt a lot about ourselves, as the videos depict [see the links to the videos in the abstracts].

We concentrate first on encounters 'within us'. From lessons learnt from previous diverse encounters and dialogues between traditional health practitioners and Jungian analysts, in our discursive dialogues in 2016, 2017 and 2018. There it became clear that our process of self-introspection was supported by the Johari Window process, a communication model created by Luft (1916-2014) and Ingham (1916-1995). An individual is like a four-pane window. There are things we know about ourselves as well as those unknown to us and others. So within an individual is an 'other' me. Likewise, within and between professions and other professions outside our scope of practices, thus calling for a continued process of introspection and learning between us and others.

What accompanies such a process is a non-judgemental attitude. Our previous encounters in South Africa opened our 'blind spots, hidden and unknown areas'. This was a rich and fertile interrelationship path which was not easy and still continues as we gradually open the 'panes of the window' in a calculated and risk-free space and pace. Continued introspection reflects Jung's life journey and his individuation process. We are aware that it is a long journey, and as Fred (Borchardt) said in 2018, 'We're only halfway round the circle'; we are aware of challenges and coping strategies needed in moving towards the ultimate growth and professional maturation we are eager to have.

The same developmental milestones that any baby undergoes, the rainbow healing therapy baby will follow suit. Central to this development is 'love', as Renee clearly quotes from Carl Jung in her opening in the workshop in Monkey Valley: 'Eros is a cosmic creator spirit.... For we are in the deepest sense the victims and instruments of cosmogonic 'love'.' Consequently, some of our group members also commented as follows:

Ester Haumann: 'I was left with a sense of greater connectedness and openness that gave me hope not just for us, but the greater hope for the country.'

Alan Fourie: 'It was good to become grounded again in clinical psychology ... the sense of connection, and openness, and hope.... Not only about the merging of the psychology and indigenous models, just for these possibilities to happen in South Africa, this kind of dialogue.'

Luc Ramsden: 'This helped inform me about the kinds of stories that need to be told ... I think you're all here for a reason, I can't imagine a better group, combination of people, and ideas and worldviews.... I have full confidence that you guys will carry this through, and realize your goals.'

Buntu George: 'It is a very strange combination that I saw today. I never thought that a psychologist can allow herself to be a traditional healer at the same time ... I can't wait to see this baby growing, and becoming national, and for the whole world to see, and how the whole world will receive this baby...'

These reflections are framed not only by the individual experiences of the diverse psychotherapeutic experiences and models in the group, but also by the deep, diverse historical basis – from the apartheid system to the current 'rainbow nation'. Masoga (2001) indicates that ancestors are dynamic. They have always been there, will always be there and everywhere. Hence, I am sure that my soul met all of you here even before I see you now. Jung met our ancestors, and therefore his language resonates with our African world views. Our training is based on dreams and without dreams there is no training for the initiates. In my book (Mlisa & Nel 2010), I debate and give full perspective to the value of dreams; folks/ancestors in our training and divination, who, according to Jung, connect with us through the collective unconscious. My papers on *umbilini* (Mlisa & Nel 2013; 2014), describe the role and value of intuition in divination. Dream analysis is central to divination. I was informed by a dream that my visa application for this conference was successful. My standing here today and connection with this world was revealed long before in my childhood dreams.

In conclusion, from my encounters, experiences and observations, I am of the view that the three levels are interrelated and will always be. Because within us, between us and with others diverse philosophical dialogues are always at play and thus there will always be 'others' no matter how we open our 'window panes'. What is critical is to have 'the love' our ancestor Jung refers to. The process of the encounters demands unconditional acceptance of each other and the passion to learn to 'love' each other with the realization that the universe includes a humankind that has no social, sectorial boundaries, colours or culture (van Binsbergen 1999 & 2003). Jungians and traditional health practitioners are the initiators, mentors and facilitators of such a possibility, together we can do it as we are closer to the universe and understand how it works. *Camagu!*

References

Masoga, M.A. (2001). 'Dimensions of oracle-speech in the Near-Eastern Mediterranean, and African contexts: A contribution towards African orality'. Unpublished Ph.D. thesis. Bloemfontein: University of the Free State.

Mlisa, L.N. & Nel, P. (2010). *Ukuthwasa The Training of Xhosa Women as traditional Healers: Ukuthwasa Initiation of Amagqirha and Identity Construction.* Saarbrucken: LAP LAMBERT Academic Publishing GmbH @ Co.KG.

— (2013). 'Types of Umbilini (intuition) in the "ukunyanga" (Xhosa Divination) tradition'. *Journal of Psychology In Africa*, 23, 4, 609-14.

— (2014). 'Umbilical experiential knowledge and indigenous healing praxis in Ukunyanga tradition'. *African Journal for Physical, Health Education, Recreation and Dance*, 21, 3-2, 913-29.

Mndende, N., (ed). (2004). *Searching For a Common Ground: A Critical Analysis Between Iphehlo and a Western Medical School: Perspectives and Methodologies Towards Nation Building*. Eastern Cape: Idutywa.

Torrey, E. F. (1972). *Witchdoctors and Psychiatrists: The Common Roots of Psychotherapy and Its Future*. New York: Harper & Row.

Traditional Health Practitioners Act (The). (2004). Act no. 35 of 2004. *Government Gazette* 476(27275).

Traditional Health Practitioners Bill (The). (2003). Notice 979 of 2003. *Government Gazette* 979(24704), 11 April 2003.

van Binsbergen, W.M.J. (1999). 'Cultures do not exist'. Exploding self-evidences in the investigation of interculturality. *Quest: An African Journal of Philosophy*, 13, 1-2, 37-114.

— (2003). *Intercultural Encounters: African and Anthropological Lessons Towards a Philosophy of Interculturality*. Munster: Lit Verlag;

World Health Organization (1978). *The Promotion and Development of Traditional Medicine*. Report of WHO meeting in Geneva, 28 November-2 December 1977. apps.who.int/iris/handle/10665/40995

World Health Organization (1989). *Report of a WHO Informal Consultation on Traditional Medicine and AIDS: In-Vitro Screening for Anti-HIV Activity*. Geneva, 6-8 February 1989. apps.who.int/iris/handle/10665/59664

World Health Organization (1995). *Traditional Practitioners as Primary Health Care Workers*. apps.who.int/medicinedocs/en/d/Jh2941e/

Part 4: Conclusion

Renee Ramsden
(SAAJA) Cape Town South Africa

David Barton (2016), in his article 'C.G. Jung and the indigenous psyche: two encounters', states:

> A true, open dialogue requires many things, including an equal share of power and willingness to exchange ideas without immediately dismissing them. Almost all indigenous knowledge is built upon an ontology that is foreign to the modern psychologist. Entering into a dialogue means entering into the temporary suspension of belief, which is increasingly difficult for those trained in specific modalities, each with their own foundational assumptions. Never mind that our psychological assumptions are the product of a particular cultural experience, growing out of the European Enlightenment and the rationalism of the nineteenth-century Europe and America, or that our models are based primarily on the experience of a narrow class and ethnicity. Overcoming such barriers is exceedingly difficult.
>
> (Barton 2016, p. 81)

On the morning that I returned from handing in my visa application to the Austrian embassy, I heard a discussion on the radio about an environmentalist company making 'seed bombs', with which they are intending to address reforesting of certain areas around the world. The speaker informed us that these 'seed bombs' are an old technology, dating back 1,000 years. On Google I found that 'seed bombs' are an ancient Japanese practice called Tsuchi Dango, meaning 'Earth Dumpling' (because they are made from earth). They were reintroduced in 1938 by the Japanese microbiologist/farmer and philosopher, Masanobu Fukuoka (1913-2008), author of *The One Straw Revolution* (1978).

So, what has this to do with our story? When Peter, Nomfundo and I started talking about how to approach this project of creating a forum for dialogue between Jungian analysts and traditional healers, we conceived this as a small beginning, a small group of people from both disciplines who could get to know, and thus to trust each other. We believed that only through trust can fruitful discussion emerge. In our first conference we achieved a beginning of this, but on reflection, we realized that we needed to abandon any attempt at academic discourse, and opted for a narrative approach with our second conference. This proved to be highly successful, in that each person had an equal chance to tell their story in an allotted time, be heard, and be dialogued with. Perhaps this is the 'seed bomb' that can assist with decolonization, the baby that can make new pathways towards mutual respect between our healing traditions.

Our Western culture is more and more aware of its one-sidedness, and the damage that this has done on so many levels, from colonizing 'indigenous' cultures, to destroying the environment. For me, Jungian psychology does bring a remedy, through turning to the ancient in us, the archetype embedded in the rhizome, the forgotten Spirit of the Deep, and our ancestors. Jung, through his encounter with this spirit, was led to alchemy, which has its roots in Hermeticism, and ancient shamanic practices (Eliade 1962). It is perhaps in this rhizome that we can find our common ground with traditional health practitioners, the shamans of today. Furthermore, scholars such as Dumisane Thabede (2008) claim that African culture has its roots in ancient Egypt and Hermeticism.

Both cultures need healing: Western culture from its overdeveloped rationalism, and African culture from the wounding of colonial practices. In South Africa this took the form of Apartheid, which legally defined cultures other than European, as inferior. I quote from Nomfundo Mlisa's thesis:

> Historically, ukuthwasa had always been seen as pagan and heathen and as such, the missionaries, colonization and the apartheid system tried hard to destroy African divination systems like ukuthwasa... Yet the survival of the divination systems and the current interest shown by the very cultures that once demoralized it proves the validity, authenticity and realistic nature of the natural existence of ukuthwasa. Instead of dying, it is mushrooming on the doorsteps of the so-called strong religions: Christianity, Islam and Buddhism, as well as the education system, which served as the handmaiden of religion.
>
> (Mlisa 2009, p. 8)

In our dialogue, we heard of the painful realities brought about by the apartheid system – the alienation of people from their natural religion, an attack on the soul of the African culture, born from arrogance and ignorance, which in itself was a mask for woundedness.

One of our members, sharing the pain of having to turn back from Christianity to traditional healing, told us:

> At that time I had an idea that I'm thwasa, because this big Afrikaner man, during the process told me, "… you are a sangoma, I've seen my employees on my farm, they do also these things that you are doing". For me, that's another painful fact, that because of socialization, I was so disconnected from myself, that I could not

see myself. I had to be seen by other people, by the descendants of the colonizers, and I had adopted the culture of the colonizer, and disowned myself completely. And this is the view that I had of myself: that I was crazy, I was sick, I did not want to become a sangoma, because this is evil. So I was shocked, and perhaps that is why, all my mentors, at the beginning, had to be people of other races.

Barton wonders why there has not been a sustained, in-depth dialogue between the Jungian community and indigenous people, and says that 'one part of the answer lies in the difficulty of such a project, given the shadow of colonization, the issues of distrust, guilt, anger, and betrayal that make dialogue difficult.'

Feelings of shame, guilt and grief were shared in this forum, as well as healing laughter. Through our narrative approach, we had the opportunity to share the stories of our lives, and sketch our journey towards becoming healers. What was striking was the similarities. The healing effect of finding common ground through respectful receiving of each other, was eloquently expressed by our interpreter, Buntu George:

> I didn't think clinical psychologists would ever ... think of ancestors, there is some people can't think of ancestors, you know. But ... as uneducated as some of us, traditionally as we are, we could sit at one table, and share each and every experience. And the little story I have, or you have, and each of us have, maybe I think my story is nothing for somebody else, it's my personal story, but from listening to the different stories we shared here, I picked up something from each and every individual story that can help me build my own life, moving forward.

What is this for SAAJA (Southern African Association of Jungian Analysts)? Our modest hope is to build on Vera's work, to break down barriers, to show remorse for ancestral hurt and to offer a healing path through a new pattern of dialogue.

References

Barton, G. (2016). 'Jung and the indigenous psyche: two encounters'. *International Journal of Jungian studies*, 8, 2, 75-84. dx.doi.org/10.1080/19409052.2016.1140066

Eliade, M. (1962). *The Forge and the Crucible*. Chicago & London: The University of Chicago Press.

Fukuoka, M. (1978). *The One Straw Revolution*. New York: New York Review Books Classics.

Mlisa, L.N. (2009). *Ukuthwasa Initiation of Amagqirha: Identity Construction and the Training of Xhosa Women as Traditional Healers*. Doctoral thesis. Bloemfontein: University of Free State.

Thabede, D. (2008). 'The African worldview as the basis of practice in the helping professions'. *Social Work/Maatskaplikewerk*, 44, 3, 233-45. socialwork.journals.ac.za

From horror to ethical responsibility: Carl Gustav Jung and Stephen King encounter the dark half within us, between us and in the world

Chiara Tozzi
(AIPA) *Rome, Italy*

The fear of horror

When going to the cinema with friends, some of whom are my colleagues, I have often heard people ask that one of the criteria for choosing the movie, besides being relevant and of artistic quality, is that it not be a horror movie. Some of the trainee analysts expressed the same concern with respect to possible 'horror' contents in movie clips that I intended to project during my seminars on active imagination at AIPA (Associazione Italiana Psicologia Analitica). In another example, again during the course on active imagination, I asked a trainee analyst to read out loud the contents of the disturbing images that appeared to Jung in 1913, and once they had finished reading, the trainee exclaimed, with unamused surprise: 'This is pure horror!'

There is a contrast between the type of request and reaction mentioned above and the experiences of many of my patients, who, although they have lived through great psychic distress, often fed by daydreams or visions of horrendous and unsettling images, they affirm that they love horror movies and are not particularly frightened by them. Actually, they are fascinated.

The aim of this paper is to explore the discrepancy between the testimonials and issues just indicated above, the relationship between C. G. Jung and Stephen King, and horror.

Something familiar: C. G. Jung and Stephen King

For reasons of apparent chance (although today I would prefer to talk about it in terms of synchronicity), I started loving C. G. Jung's and Stephen King's works at more or less the same time, that is, at the end of the '70s when I found myself reading for the first time and almost contemporaneously, Jung's *Memories, Dreams, Reflections* (1961) and King's *The Shining* (1977).

I was attracted and fascinated by the unravelling of Jung's memory, although marked by disturbing and unsettling recollections, in the same way that I was to King's novel. In both cases I felt like I was *dropping* (I did not choose this term by chance) into something that was suggestive, in some ways fearful, but *real*; not something real based on the thinking function but more on the feeling function. The subjects that Jung and King faced seemed definitely similar to the subjects found in fables such as *Bluebeard, Hansel and Gretel* and others, which my grandmother used to read to me with affectionate pathos when I was young. This likeness was similar to what Nancy Swift Furlotti referred to when she read *Memories, Dreams, Reflections* for the first time, saying that it 'made me feel like I had finally come home' (Tozzi 2019, p. 163). Jung spoke about his difficult, and in many ways horrific experiences of facing the unconscious, or the 'other' within himself. King gave voice to the unconscious and to the other within himself by creating stories that are like magnificent metaphors of the same experiences through which Jung lived. From then on, my studies on Jung's works and on King's narratives proceeded parallel to each other, and are reflected in my work as an analyst, Jungian teacher and writer.

My interest in, and passion for, horror seems particularly syntonic with references made by my patients, some of which I have reported, yet dystonic with what some of my Jungian colleagues and trainee analysts expressed. One of the main questions raised by this discrepancy is: why do some people like reading novels or watching movies that deal with horror? According to Panksepp and Biven (2012), the answer is quite simple: at the higher levels of mental activity, typical of tertiary processes (for example, autonoetic consciousness), our primary process systems can be manipulated *when we are in situations that are in fact safe*. We can, for example, enjoy a storm while most animals shake in fear. Without these higher-level reflective processes, as human beings we would only hesitantly, 'voluntarily' expose ourselves to *horrific* perceptions that could set off negative reactions in us, such as fear.

Then why is it that for some people, including a few of my colleagues and trainee analysts who have undergone extensive analytical training, this sense of security that we get when we examine the reality of it all, just isn't enough to *make them feel safe*? And why do some patients, who are more fragile and have partially compromised psychic defence mechanisms, find it possible to experience this sense of security? I continue to explore and elaborate this particular dilemma with the trainee analysts in my active imagination courses, and the conclusions we reach are always interesting and fascinating, both to me and to them. I will try to demonstrate some of the results of these explorations, by comparing the cases of two *special patients*: C. G. Jung and Stephen King. I will show you how they faced, and were able to make use of, horror by using a form of active imagination, intentionally in Jung's case, and spontaneously in King's.

The horror experience during C. G. Jung's and Stephen King's childhoods

Before Jung reached the age of four, waves from a waterfall in his town dragged a corpse close to his family's house. Young Carl Gustav saw blood and water flow into the stream, and this left a very strong impression on him. Subsequently, in 1883 the overflow of the river Wiese, where 14 people drowned to death, left some cadavers buried under the sand. Jung could not resist and went over to the site where he saw the dead body of a middle-aged man, wearing a black frock coat, and an arm bent over that covered his eyes; and in seeing this, Jung felt the same fascination as when he had once watched a pig being killed (Jung 1961).

Stephen King had just turned four when, one afternoon, he went outside to play with a friend. He returned home shortly after, speechless and white as a ghost, according to what his mother told him afterwards. He didn't speak for the entire day. Later, his mother found out that little Stephen's friend had been hit by a train while the two were playing together on the train tracks. King has no recollection of the event, but as psychiatrist and writer Janet Jeppson helped him recognize during a presentation, from that moment on he always wrote about that story (King 1981).

As I have examined and described elsewhere,[1] after the sight of the bloody waves and water and of the cadaver of the drowned man, Jung was also able to elaborate the horrific images by 'rewriting that story' through the active imagination represented in *The Red Book* (Jung 2009).

Active imagination, phase 1: C. G. Jung's theory of letting things happen and Stephen King's dowsing rod

Marie-Louise von Franz elucidated the active imagination process and defined it in *four phases* (von Franz, 1978). The first of these phases corresponds to a specific state of mind and psychic condition: that of emptying out, in which the ego accedes to stepping aside to leave space for the other. We must psychically be capable of letting things happen, allowing them to follow their natural flow, and for us this is a real art that hardly anyone knows (Jung 1957).

This capacity to let things happen metaphorically corresponds to the recollection of 'The Dowsing Rod' referred by Stephen King

---

1 *Facing the Waves*, Tozzi C., IAAP European Congress, Avignon 2018

(1981). When he was about 13 years old, between 1959 and 1960, in a particularly hot and dry summer, King, led by his Uncle Clayton, went looking for a new well with a dowsing rod. The story suggestively describes King's fascination when he, as sceptic as he was, got persuaded to experience the sensation of the special vibration of the dowser held in his hands, when placed over the spot where his uncle had perceived the presence of a water source. From this experience, King learned the following lesson:

> I will say that Uncle Clayt had lulled me into that same state that I have tried again and again to lull the readers of my stories into – that state of believability where the ossified shield of 'rationality' has been temporarily laid aside, the suspension of disbelief is at hand, and the sense of wonder is again within reach
>
> (King 1981, p. 93)

But it is not easy to just *let things happen* and it takes great courage. In fact, the ego accepts and welcomes the other part, all while holding onto the hope of not getting crushed. Jung accepted *letting things happen* in order to free himself from horrific visions, amongst which were the frightening flood, when water turned into blood and spread across all of Europe. And he described clearly the moment at which, on the night of 12th December 1913, while meditating *on the fears* that came from the invasion of these images that had continued to disturb him, he took the decisive step: 'I let myself drop. Suddenly it was as though the ground literally gave way at my feet and I plunged down into dark depth.... Before me was the entrance to a dark cave...' (Jung 1961, p. 123).

This type of experience comes up very often, if not constantly, in King's narratives. To name just a few: in *Rose Madder* (King 1995), a woman who is suffering domestic violence by her husband is able to get over her own fear by travelling through a painting of the myth of the Minotaur and the figure of the Erinyes; in the novel *11/22/63* (King 2011), the main character finds the courage to travel through time, which allows him to go back to right before the '60s to try to stop J. F. Kennedy's assassination and avoid all the political and social consequences that followed therefrom; and we all remember how in *The Shining* (King 1977), after great hesitation, little Danny succeeds in crossing the threshold of room 217 of the Overlook Hotel, where he was staying with his parents, and discovers the horror incarnated by the characters and events that drive his father crazy.

Since the dawn of time, the fear of 'opening that door', or crossing the threshold that separates the conscious from the unconscious, to face the anguish and horror of everything that belongs to the other, has animated and still animates cultural and religious manifestations of all humanity. In their works, Jung and King show us that not only is it possible to get over that threshold, but it is actually thanks to that passage that we can save our own lives.

Phases 2 and 3: accepting the irrational and incomprehensible and keeping track of the resulting contents – from the writing of *The Red Book* to *It*

The second phase of active imagination is the one that Jung describes as a chance to completely accept the irrational and the incomprehensible, seeing that both represent the process of becoming (Jung 1929/1957). This experience is then followed by phase three, that of recording the images that come from the unconscious through whatever expressive means that suit each individual.

The best representation of these two phases is definitely Jung's *The Red Book*, where he, after having chosen to drop into obscurity and having entered the dark cave that appeared before him, described the subsequent experiences as an *infernal journey into the future* (Jung 2009). The figures and characters that emerged, and that he accepted in the active imagination, are the very ones that have always constellated the horror of mythological tales, fables, novels and movies: cadavers, beetles, tangled snakes, streams of blood that spurt out, the Devil, murdered little girls whose livers have to be eaten, crows, magicians, mad people, young girls held prisoners in a castle, giants with axes, sea monsters, jinxed trees, Death.

As regards King, the work that in my opinion best represents these two phases of active imagination is the novel *It* (King 1986). Already the title alludes to this *other*, obscure and threatening entity that pops into the lives of a group of teenagers and the town in which they live.

It is a mercurial, shape-shifting creature, apparently elusive and powerful, and a perfect representation of evil. An evil that cyclically comes back (every 27 years) and that, mainly under the disguise of an innocent and joyful clown (a perfect representation of the trickster archetype), devours children – helpless beings who are more subject to fear. In this impressive novel of formation, with its highly symbolic content in the time frame that goes from childhood to adulthood, the group of protagonists discover that *It* appears *to each one of them in a different form*, resembling their own personal fears/nightmares. These fears are not only their fears, as they also represent *It*'s weaknesses. King's message, *mutatis mutandis*, is certainly akin to Jung's in *The Red Book*: you can free yourself from things that horrify you only by accepting that you are not afraid of fear itself, and by becoming familiar with your specific and individual representation of horror. Giving voice and space to the other within you, you can beat (at least episodically) not only the evil and horror that torment your individual psyche, *but also the evil that assails the collective psyche*. The courage that Jung found in facing the horrific images of his unconscious came from the recognition that those images did not involve only him, but many others as well. And by coming to face them, from that moment on, he ceased to belong to himself alone: 'From then on, my life belonged to the generality' (Jung 1961, p. 136). King offers us an analogous and significant intuition when the protagonists of the group in his novel discover that, by killing *It*, the town in which they live, by now contaminated with evil, is also destroyed.

Phase 4: ethical comparison

Jung's comparison with the images of the unconscious was neither intellectual nor aesthetic. In numerous contexts, Jung repeats that the goal of dialogue is the ethical confrontation of the ego if it is able to *really* face the unconscious at a symmetric level, and not as superior, as is usually the case. It is exactly as if a dialogue were taking place between two human beings with equal rights (Jung 1957/1958).

In King's case, his conclusions are significantly similar when he says that being able to create a story in which the characters come to life and *act on their own*, in a certain way independently from the will (and therefore the ego) of the writer, not only gives great pleasure but also solves a lot of the writer's problems (King 2000). Instead, because it is correlated to logic, the rational, conscious mind usually tends to look at the unconscious from above and with superiority, and considers it as something dark and irrational that comes from a lower level. And this is where we significantly go back to the theme of fear evoked by the horror of what comes from the *other*, which I mentioned at the beginning. For Jung the frightening dimension of certain objects and situations is relative to the devaluation or avoidance that the ego exerts on certain unknown, foreign objects and situations, in other words, *others*. By treating these objects and situations as signals, through the *reductive* method, these elements are framed and conceived only rationally, weakened to a mere symptom and momentarily put aside, but then to give rise to complexes. Instead, by treating, *encountering and getting to know* these objects or situations as *symbols*, through the *constructive* method, the conscious mind acquires the possibility of not remaining in fear of all that is different, and the ego of not remaining in fear of any *other* part of the psyche (Jung 1934).

The message that comes from this interpretation is clear. The more we continue to explore and examine the psyche, especially through the thinking function, making us feel apparently safe thanks to the logical refuge provided by categories, interpretations, judgements and theories, the more we will be victims of fear for what is hosted in the unconscious, whether our own, that of our patients, or of the world in which we live. If, instead, we accept and face the unconscious, especially through the feeling function, it is possible to guarantee greater symmetry. In fact, Jung states that:

> intellectual understanding and aestheticism both produce the deceptive, treacherous sense of liberation and superiority which is liable to collapse if feeling intervenes. Feeling always binds one to reality and meaning of symbolic contents, and these in turn impose binding standards of ethical behaviour from which aestheticism and intellectualism are only too ready to emancipate themselves.
>
> (Jung 1946, para. 489)

Furthermore, Jung believes that 'when we feel it is in order to attach a proper value to something' (Jung 1928). In all of Jung's writings, and King's stories and novels, the engagement with images of the other part leads to a greater knowledge of oneself and consequently to greater reflection regarding the *value* of objects and choices that all individuals have to face throughout their lives. In Jung's opinion:

> It is equally a grave mistake to think that it is enough to gain some understanding of the images and that knowledge can here make a halt. Insight into them must be converted into an ethical obligation. Not to do so is to fall prey to the power principle, and this produces dangerous effects which are destructive not only to others but even to the knower. The images of the unconscious place a great responsibility upon a man. Failure to understand them, or a shirking of ethical responsibility, deprives him of his wholeness and imposes a painful fragmentariness on his life.
>
> (Jung 1961, p. 237)

King's view is the same: ethical comparison translates into a sort of duty: '...I think they also say that nobility must fully reside not in success, but in trying to do the right thing ... and that when we fail to do that, or wilfully turn away from the challenge, hell follows' (King 2010, Afterword).

In each chapter of *The Red Book*, Jung encounters events and characters through the *feeling function*: Jung's very ego, the soul, Philemon, Elijah and Solomon, the Devil and Satan, one of the Humbles, Ammonius, Death, Izdubar, the Cabiri, the Crow, the child who was not conceived, Hap, the Blue Shadow, the psychiatrist, the madman (Jung 2009). These symbolic images place him, each time, before what are sometimes dramatic and horrendous events and characters to whom he must give *value*, consequently taking a sometimes extreme, sacrificial and apparently irrational stance. Nonetheless, this leads Jung to discover that the end of all this confrontation is the individuation and expression of the Self, which is figuratively represented in the mandala, as the centre of one's psychic development (Jung 1961).

At the same time, in order to be able to save themselves or others, the characters of King's stories and novels are forced to face horrifying challenges that require courage and apparently irrational decision-making. Here are some examples:

Carrie (King 1974) is a young girl who is entirely at the disposal of her bigoted and obsessed-by-sin mother; she decides to defend herself from this abuse by using her telekinetic powers, which she is not able to master, thus ends up succumbing.

Danny (King 1977) is a five-year-old boy who assists the progressive degeneration of his family life due to the father's inability to face his unemployment and financial problems. Once established at the Overlook Hotel with the family, he is able to save himself from his father's destructive madness by escaping and telepathically asking for help from the hotel's cook, gifted like him of the *shining*, meaning extrasensory ability.

Dolores Clairborne (King 1993) is a cleaning lady accused of homicide by her employer; she tells us about the dramatic choice she had to make during the solar eclipse to save herself and her daughter from domestic abuse and violence.

Cujo (King 1981) is a sweet and loyal Saint Bernard that get rabies and starts to sow destruction and death, even in his owner's family, which he loves. King succeeds in telling the story from the dog's point of view, lost and incapable of controlling the rage that possesses him.

Now, try to superimpose, examine and closely compare the dilemmas of these characters, and the others previously mentioned, and compare them to those of our patients. Who, amongst us, has not had or does not have an adolescent like Carrie in therapy, someone who is disturbed by violent, aggressive, destructive or self-destructive behaviours and who lives in the shadow-cone of a separated father or mother, for whom they represent the only reason for living?

How many of our female patients come to us describing themselves as guilty, like Dolores Clairborne or Rose Madder, before they are actually able to realize and elaborate the domestic violence and abuse of which they are victims?

How many of our patients, of all ages, carry inside either the confusion of a traumatized child, like Danny in *The Shining*, obliged to live through the pathologies of their parents, or the sense of helplessness, due to the contagion of the prevailing collective anger, like the dog Cujo? And who amongst us, or our patients, has not been in a situation of having to face the cyclical recurrence of annihilating fear that is often ostensibly intolerable and indestructible, as in *It*? But ... have we been, or are we able to face these cases, and what these stories symbolize, with the same courage as Jung through his active imagination, or Stephen King through his narratives? To profoundly take in all the horror that these people and/or images epitomize symbolically?

The reassuring image of a strong ego, collective horrors and the responsibility of an individual, formative and clinical choice

At the beginning of this year, a conference on Analytical Psychology and Human Rights (Pasquarelli 2019) was held at the Associazione Italiana Psicologia Analitica (AIPA) in Rome. I proposed this event and, together with colleagues on the AIPA committee, we organized it. The themes discussed concerned justice, ethics, Jungian therapy and images. It was an opportunity to make good, helpful and exciting encounters. There were two questions that arose during the conference that are particularly relevant to what I have reported up until now. The first question regards a cry for help addressed to us, Jungian analysts, from lawyer Keith Hiatt,[2] who handles investigations on the violation of human rights at the UN. Hiatt explained to us how watching crime on video is not necessarily less cruel and devastating than watching it happen in real life, because the power of images continues to work and stays vivid in the memory and psyche of the spectator. The human toll on the investigators being continually exposed to these terrible violations of human rights cannot yet be predicted: *'It is up to you, psychotherapists, to evaluate this'*, concluded Hiatt.

In contrast, Giovanni Sorge presented the documentary movie that was awarded the 2018 Mercurius Prize,[3] called 'The Island of the Hungry Ghost', by Gabrielle Brady. The movie describes the steps taken by a psychotherapist who, through sandplay therapy, treats the traumas of asylum seekers held in a detention centre in Australia. After hearing the representative stories told by the asylum seekers of the repeated impact with horror, as well as her own powerlessness in being unable to help her patients escape from the inhumane conditions of the detention centre, the psychotherapist understands that she is not able to tolerate the horror of this kind of therapeutic experience and, therefore, decides to in turn 'emigrate' elsewhere.

In both cases, notwithstanding adequate training, the difficulty in

---

2 Lawyer Keith Hiatt is a manager in investigative information technology for the UN and research fellow for Handa Center for Human Rights and International Justice of Stanford University.
3 The International Mercurius Prize, with head office in Zurich and presided by Professor Murray Stein, was founded in 2017 with the goal of advocating the connection between the Jungian Psychology world and the audience, authors and other players of the cinematographic world. The Mercurius Prize is assigned to films, short films and documentaries that are particularly relevant to the psychology and sensitivity of human rights, and capable of promoting greater awareness and responsibility at an individual and collective level.

enduring this is relative to the true horror, that which surrounds us daily at a collective level.

This brings me back to the discrepancy that I mentioned at the beginning of this presentation: that is, why different people, colleagues amongst them, tend to avoid watching horror movies, even those of high quality, and why the almost qualified trainees in their last year of training find it difficult to face the images of Jung's disturbing visions of 1913, of which they were already fully aware. And the possibility, in contrast, that some patients think horror movies are interesting and comforting. The answer was suggested thanks to the work carried out together with trainees during the active imagination course: 'In all these years of training, we had *only* studied the visions of Jung that gave origin to The Red Book. Instead now, we are actually facing it.' This was the significant conclusion they reached. So, up until that moment, the meaning of Jung's troubled confrontation with the unconscious was examined only at a theoretical level, through the thinking function. And the thinking function had obviously avoided the intensity and the feeling of those images, as they were 'irrational and unlikely'. These were read and studied not in their symbolic dimension, but as sign and symptomatological manifestations. In other words, as something that 'is not true' and therefore not credible. Instead, as soon as we started to approach those contents through active imagination, the reality showed up in the conscious, causing fear, horror and repulsion. It would seem, therefore, that 'feeling safe', as described by Panksepp and Biven, is reinforced by the thinking function and by a unilateral incentive of the theoretical approach of study, consequently weakening, instead of reinforcing, the egos of trainee analysts and of our colleagues.

As regards the patients who can watch horror movies with interest, the explanation seems clear to me. Their psychic life is disturbed by the images of their inner horrors, which are often a result of real-life traumatic experiences and often extremely similar to those in horror movies and novels. The horror they lived through, in solitude, can be devastating because it is limitless, inexplicable and not credible. So, reading or watching horror stories can have a somewhat encouraging and containing effect, the same kind of effect that, as we know well, myths and fables produced and still produce.

King is right when he replies to the question he is asked frequently regarding why he tells such horrific stories when there is already so much horror in the world: 'We make up horrors to help us cope with the real ones' (King 1981). Those who have lived through such horror for autobiographical reasons, like in the patients' cases, find something familiar and thus fascinating in the horror stories narrated in novels and movies. Nancy Swift Furlotti told us, with extreme courage and generosity, how, for her, the *dark emanations from the psyche* can be found in her personal story; and how reading gloomy and horrific gothic fables and watching horror movies helped her because 'they seemed to speak to the same level of danger that I experienced in my life' (Tozzi 2019, Op. cit.).

Active imagination may provide a similar, if not better, type of psychotherapeutic support. And yet, still to this day, it is considered with scepticism and concern that this type of exercise can be dangerous, especially for fear that the patients' egos (as well as those of the trainee analysts, evidently) may not be strong enough. It would be like telling people not to read fables to children because it may be dangerous, seeing that their ego is not strong enough yet.

According to Hillman (1983), that strong ego is the imaginal figure that doesn't lose control, that doesn't give over to what comes in. According to Hillman, it is this strong ego that has been studied by psychologists for years, forcing the images of the unconscious to enter only through slits, holes, and broken windows, in short, through symptoms. Because, as Jung stated in 1958 regarding the insistence of seeking refuge in theories, 'the unconscious always finds the chink in the wall of one's own theory or built-up system' (McGuire & Hull 1977). And, consequently, Hillman (1983) asserts that if we start building forts, the psyche will only be able to reach us in the form of an invader. I therefore ask myself: why be surprised if the collective psyche reveals a similar tendency to seek refuge, as happens today, in forms of authoritarianism, nationalism and strong or dictatorial figures? What and how much do we, Jungian psychologists, do to counter this tendency?

The horror constellated by the images of our times forces us to take on the responsibility for a deep confrontation with horrific images; not only our own, those of our patients and our trainees, but also with those of the world around us and of those who ask us for help and support in order to face treating the traumatized, collective psyche and the violated rights of human beings. With his works and journey, Jung showed us that we have no other choice but to accept exposing ourselves to facing the horrors of the unconscious images by means of active imagination.

In fact, active imagination, together with sandplay therapy, represents the only truly unique and peculiar methodology of Jungian psychotherapy; and, for this reason, it should be the basis of analytical psychology. Why is it, instead, often subordinated to the study and teaching of other therapeutic models? Why is it considered and evaluated almost as an accessory in training?

This is why I am extremely grateful to all my IAAP and AIPA colleagues who embrace and encourage the research, spreading and teaching of active imagination. I am just as grateful to all the trainees with whom I have worked in Italy, Hungary and Serbia, for the trust, courage and acquiescence with which they agreed to try different workshops in active imagination with me. I also feel, in the same way, gratitude towards my patients, with whom I work mainly with an *attitude* (Adler 1966) of active imagination. My trainees, patients and I all know well how shocking and sometimes painful this type of approach is, as well as how much commitment it requires.

Truly facing images means really putting oneself at stake. It means accepting a risk. Taking on a responsibility. Identifying oneself, even at the cost of ending up isolated, different and adverse.

From the prison of horror to the freedom of the individuation process

Our time, characterized by all the contradictions of postmodernity, presents a presumed and apparently boundless freedom, which is in conflict with the effective increase in psychological restrictions, closures, divisions and reclusions.

Pursuing an individuation process, in a time like this one, seems paradoxical. Manifesting the right to your own specificity and divergence of your own way of being, compared to the collective way, be it cultural, political, religious or emotional, is dangerous. It frightens people. And being dominated by fear is like living in a prison, serving the horror of a sentence of which it is difficult to see the end date.

What can we do? In *The Red Book*, Jung says that 'Our freedom does not lie outside us but within us. One can be bound outside, and yet one will still feel free since one has burst inner bonds. One can certainly gain outer freedom through powerful actions, but one creates inner freedom only through the symbol' (Jung 2009, p. 392).

I started this paper by addressing the symbolic meaning of the escape from horror. C.G. Jung and Stephen King show us there is an opposite kind of behaviour to escaping: that of facing the horror and from that forming the possibility of a *transformation*, which ensures us a total and real freedom.

Andy Dufresne is the protagonist of Stephen King's story *Rita Hayworth and the Shawshank Redemption* (King 1982), from which director F. Darabont made the movie *The Shawshank Redemption*. With the protagonist's journey, Stephen King delivers a touching representation of the individuation of his freedom, despite living in chains, through various choices that seem to truly represent, in a symbolic way, the ethical achievement of an active imagination.

In the most touching sequence in the movie, despite being wrongfully imprisoned, and despite having experienced the horror of a prison where the law is applied with violence and no respect for human rights, prisoner Andy Dufresne decides to take on the ethical responsibility of rebelling against the prohibition imposed by the director of the prison, listening to and making all prisoners listen to a piece by Mozart. For a few long-lasting moments the light, reassuring sound of the duet 'Sull'aria' from 'The Marriage of Figaro' touches the prisoners' bodies and souls like a sign of possible transformation and redemption.

www.youtube.com/watch?v=Bjqmg_7J53s

Andy Dufresne knows he will pay for his choice by being locked in an inhumane solitary isolation. But since he is now capable of facing horror through the feeling function, after leaving that cell he will be able to affirm – similarly to Jung (Jung 2009) – that the beauty of music is that nobody can take it away from you; a prison is a place where music makes sense as it helps us remember that not all places in this world are made of stone, and that there is something inside you that no one will be able to touch nor take away from you, if you don't allow them to.

References

Adler G. (1966). *Studies in Analytical Psychology*, London: Hodder & Stoughton.
Hillman, J. (1983). (with Pozzo, L.) *Inter Views, Conversation with Laura Pozzo on Psychotherapy, Biography, Love, Soul, Dreams, Work, Imagination and the State of the Culture*. New York: Harper & Row.
Jung, C.G. (1961). *Memory, Dreams, Reflections*, New York: Vintage Books.
– (1929/1957) 'Commentary on *The Secret of the Golden Flower*'. *CW* 13.
– (2009) *The Red Book, Liber Novus*, (Ed. S. Shamdasani). New York: Philemon Foundation & W.W. Norton & Co.
– (1934). 'General considerations on the theory of complexes', *CW* 8.
– (1946). 'Specific problems of psychotherapy. The psychology of transference. Purification'. *CW* 16.
– (1928). 'A psychological theory of Types'. Appendix 3. *CW* 6.
– (1957/1958). 'The transcendent function'. *CW* 8.
King, S. (1974). *Carrie*. New York: Doubleday and Company.
– (1977). *The Shining*. London: New English Library.
– (1981). *Danse Macabre*. New York: Gallery Books.
– (1981). *Cujo*. New York: New American Library.
– (1982). Rita Hayworth and Shawshank Redemption. In *Different Seasons*. New York: The Viking Press.
– (1993). *Dolores Claiborne*. New York: The Viking Press.
– (1995). *Rose Madder*. New York: The Viking Press.
– (2011). *11/22/63*. New York: Scribner.
– (1986). *It*. New York: Scribner.
– (2000). *On Writing*. New York: Pocket Books.
– (2010). *Full Dark, No Star*. New York: Scribner.

McGuire, W., Hull, R.F.C., eds. (1958). *C.G. Jung Speaking. Interviews and Encounters*. 'From Esther Harding's Notebook'. New York, Quadrant City: Macmillan.

Panksepp, J., & Biven. L. (2012). *The Archaeology of Mind*, New York: W.W. Norton & Co.

Pasquarelli, E. (2019). 'Psicologia Analitica e Diritti Umani', AIPA, Rome 19/01/2019, in *Studi Junghiani*, 25, 1, 107-130 (ISSN 1828-5147, ISSNe 1971-8411).

Tozzi, C. (2019). 'The dark emanations from the psyche. Interview with Nancy Swift Furlotti', *Studi Junghiani*, 25, 1, 107-130 (ISSN 1828-5147, ISSNe 1971-8411).

von Franz, M.L. (1978) 'L'immaginazione attiva', in *Rivista di Psicologia Analitica*, n. 17, Roma: Astrolabio.

Farewell Address

Marianne Müller
President IAAP

Dear Colleagues,

I look back at my three years as president, but at the same time also at 15 years of being active within the IAAP. This is a long time, and yet, for me the last three years have been unthinkable without all the years before. It was only through the various functions within the IAAP that I acquired a true understanding of the complexity and extensive range of activities of the organisation. Likewise, over time I understood even better how significant the IAAP is for Analytical Psychology, with all its tasks, duties and responsibilities. It has been my endeavour to accomplish these to the best of my ability. During the last three years we succeeded in introducing some innovations in the IAAP and in initiating various projects. We have also developed further many existing projects and left behind some that were outdated.

All this has only been possible together with a well-functioning team. It includes the Executive Committee as well as the other permanent committees within the IAAP: The Ethics Committee, the Programme Committee and Organising Committee for the Congress, the Training Committee and all those members who contributed within the context of training or a Working Party. I would like to sincerely thank my colleagues for their support and their effective and inspiring cooperation. It will not be possible to mention them all by name. However, I want to state that what has always been most important to me are the people from all over the world with whom I have had the privilege to work and to get to know them.

I feel very honoured that I was given the opportunity to take on all the tasks within the IAAP and finally the presidency. Here I could make good use of my experience of life thus far, but I have also had the chance to familiarise myself with much that was new. I am of the same age as the IAAP, having been born in 1955. Hence, I am fully aware that the IAAP looks back at a long history, which others have shaped and for which they accepted responsibility. Some years ago, we relocated the archive of the IAAP. In this context, but also in connection with the preparations for the most recent revision of the Constitution, which I had the honour and pleasure to chair, I became even more aware of the various stages of this development. The IAAP was founded by representatives of three societies and around twenty analysts. Today, and this is including the results of the decisions by the Delegates at the Meeting of Delegates on Wednesday, we have 72

Group Members and 153 Individual Members, of whom the majority will join the existing Groups. Altogether, today we are about 3480 Jungian Analysts worldwide.

The world of 1955 was indeed quite different. Today we face new challenges – I will return to this later. And yet, the basic concept and the underlying values of the IAAP have not changed very much, as the Constitution demonstrates. I am thinking of the idea of a federal structure which, while granting much autonomy to the individual groups, demands a democratic structure as a central requirement. Likewise, the aims of the IAAP remained unchanged: These are the promotion of Analytical Psychology, the maintenance of high standards of training and practice, and the organisation of congresses.

It is with gratitude that I think of my predecessors; they provided the essential ingredients so that today the IAAP is in many ways in a good and solid position. Many conceptions became integral and proven parts of its structure. These are, for example, the organisation of the Executive Committee, which is divided into individually elected Officers and the representatives of Group Members; the clearly stated limits of the terms of Officers, the introduction of standing Committees, but also the sharing out of responsibilities of the Executive Committee to Sub-Committees and Working Parties. Newly introduced in recent years was the function of the Finance Officer, which during the present and previous Administrations was performed by the President-elect. The implementation of this important task undoubtedly contributed to a better control over the IAAP finances and it constitutes an excellent preparation for the presidency.

Over the past three years, further modifications were added, such as the Diversity Working Party, the expanded structuring of the Education Committee, IAAP funded research projects and surveys as well as the organisation and implementation of joint Conferences IAAP/University.

It is the central task of the IAAP, apart from cultivation and promotion of Analytical Psychology, to provide worldwide cohesion and exchange among analysts. A professional association, and particularly an international one, has a duty of integration and inclusion of all its members. This is especially true for the IAAP. This has always been a particular concern of mine.

Analytical Psychology today faces major challenges worldwide. Among them are the aging of the member societies in many countries of Europe and North America, structural changes of legislation, and the conception of training. On the other side, however, and this is very gratifying, there is great interest in Analytical Psychology and its expansion in the so-called 'new countries', such as those in Eastern Europe, Latin America and Asia. Here new groups are forming and an ever-growing number of them offer their own training. It falls to the

IAAP to accompany both, old and new groups, to support them and to promote contacts between them. During the Congress we could once again clearly experience the importance of this mutual exchange.

It is true that the IAAP advocated training in these 'new countries' and reacted with offers to their needs and requests for teaching. This has developed into a great commitment within the IAAP – one of the forward-looking projects involving Developing Groups and the Router Programme. This was only possible, however, through the support by members from the already existing IAAP Group Members, mostly the Group Members who have had a long tradition and experience in training. During my many years within the IAAP, I could gain a comprehensive insight into this project and I am convinced of its great significance for Analytical Psychology and for the IAAP. We have invested much energy, time and money, and every IAAP member contributed, so that we could, and still can implement it. This is a forward-looking project, but already now we see the returns. This is apparent in the large number of trained analysts and new groups all over the world, some of whom are already offering their own training. Nevertheless, it has also been a concern for this Administration to manage judiciously and carefully the great demand for training in the context of the Router Programme. Likewise, we endeavoured to implement improvements, adjustments and renewals. It is not our ambition to train as many analysts as possible, but to configure training as responsibly and carefully as possible.

In a similar vein, the IAAP is often directly involved in the formation of new Group Members. The transition from Individual to Group Membership can be, as we have seen, a difficult process: it raises many questions and gives rise to uncertainties. It has, therefore, become increasingly important to support groups in this formation process. As President and Chair of the Consultation and Mediation Service, I tried to accompany groups during this phase. It demonstrated to me once again how in many cases the process of group formation can be complex and demanding. Old, lingering conflicts might be reactivated, or the cooperation within a democratic framework must first be practiced. Likewise, existing groups are subject to permanent change and they must face their internal conflicts. The IAAP offers its useful services of mediation here too, if this is requested, and the IAAP is invited for this purpose. Over the past three years, we have received rather frequent demands for this service, to which we have been happy to respond.

I want to refrain from listing in detail all the business of the IAAP here again as this has already been covered during the Meeting of Delegates. Rather, it is important for me to place the activities and innovations of this Administration into a wider context.

We have started a new project with the series 'Joint Conferences

IAAP/University'. The underlying idea for the project, its meaning, purpose and objective, is to make Analytical Psychology visible at the universities, to be in an exchange with the academic world and scholarship and to make students aware of Analytical Psychology. We want to promote Analytical Psychology as a scholarly subject, entirely in the spirit of C.G. Jung. We are sure that without this reference to the wider academic scholarship, Analytical Psychology will hardly have a future. Two of these conferences have already taken place. The first one was at the University of Vilnius in collaboration with the local professor and Jungian Analyst, Gražina Gudaite, and a second one at the University of Basel in cooperation with Professor Christian Roesler of the University of Basel, and Professor Harald Atmanspacher of the University of Zurich. Further conferences are envisaged and are already at a concrete stage of planning. Is it not interesting and highly gratifying that especially in the newer groups in Latin America, Eastern Europe, and also in Asia, several of our colleagues are already working at universities and are building these bridges?

Within the IAAP we have initiated, implemented and financed two research projects. During this Congress we will present both of them to you. One was a large-scale survey among IAAP members, which Pilar Amezaga carried out in Montevideo together with a team of social scientists. Almost 50% of our members participated. This is an exceptionally high rate of participation. Once again, a heartfelt Thank You to all the contributors. The survey provides us with valuable insights into the activities and the training within our international societies and gives us indications for future actions. The results of the survey can be viewed on the IAAP website.

A further research project was developed by Gražina Gudaite and her team in Vilnius. The topic was 'Understanding Core Competencies in Jungian Psychoanalysis: Narratives of Becoming an Analyst in the Post-Soviet Region'. Analysts and trainees were asked what, in their opinion, are the most important competencies of an analyst. This is a research project from our Education Committee. It relates to the situation of Analytical Psychology in Eastern Europe, but it is of equal significance for the whole of the Association.

The Executive Committee decided to produce and post a printed version of the triennial Newsletter and the Members' list to each member of IAAP. In today's digital world the purpose of such publications must continually be re-considered and we hope that our decision to go ahead with the printed versions of the two publications will contribute to a sense of identity and shared perception of community. I would like to thank Emilija Kiehl again for her enormous and most careful work on editing the Newsletter and the electronic News Sheet.

During this Administration the IAAP has been approached with questions regarding several social and political issues. The demand has been for the IAAP to engage and take on responsibility for handling these issues. Personally, I think that Analytical Psychology is indeed downright obliged to engage in general questions concerning our time. We must consider and analyse socio-political phenomena and social problems or their effects on the individual from a psychological perspective. Analytical Psychology is particularly called upon to do so as it has recourse to resources of insights, which go way beyond mere science and also surpass simple social sciences, but touch upon fundamental questions of religion and philosophy, as Navid Kermani demonstrated in his paper. However, of equal importance as theory and analysis are concrete projects which offer practical psychological support as a response to shortcomings of our time, to catastrophes and to people's needs. I think that we must also face our responsibility regarding these questions. We can contribute considerably to finding answers or solutions to these issues. And we know from Jung: Individuation does not exclude the world but includes it.

However, what does this mean for the IAAP if the demand is made to take action, to take a stand, and if this is associated with very concrete requests? During this Administration we have had reasons to deal with this situation intensively. The first major issue was about the question why we have so few analysts of colour in our association and whether this is linked to the writings of C.G. Jung.

After thorough discussion in the Executive Committee, after consulting our members, and after holding a symposium during which the various points of view around the topic were discussed, it was evident to us that the reasoning and opinions regarding this subject are widely divergent within the IAAP. The Executive Committee therefore decided that the IAAP cannot publish a statement on behalf of our membership as the worldwide community of analytical psychologists received and debated the subject in such a controversial manner. For one, such a proposal would hardly find a majority with the Delegates. Secondly, the IAAP as an international society, cannot adopt the concerns of an interest group and make it their own as this could jeopardize the cohesion of the whole community and, finally, result in its weakening. As I said at the beginning, it is a central task of a professional organisations such as ours to care for the inner cohesion. This seems to me particularly important in our time when so much in our world is at risk of falling apart. Therefore, the IAAP shall and will provide a roof and an internal forum for discussion within the Jungian community to all groups and to all its members.

This, however, does not at all mean that topical disputes should not be possible. On the contrary, they do need to take place if Analytical Psychology wants to remain renewed and alive. It was our concern for the symposium, which was held in Prague in November 2017, to have a broad-based discussion on the topic. Controversial opinions could be expressed and a process of rapprochement and mutual understanding was at least partially possible. I think that, if and when necessary, the IAAP could in this way provide a frame for any future controversial, but constructive confrontations with difficult issues. With regard to the protection of minorities, it will be the task of the newly instated Diversity Working Party to pick up upcoming questions within the IAAP and to facilitate further discussions. The IAAP very much welcomes and depends on conversations and discussions being held in individual groups and regions, where it is easier to establish the immediate connection with the local situations, their historical contexts and cultural customs and traditions. Our colleagues from South Africa have shown this so clearly and impressively in their presentation this morning.

The other major issue, which was brought to the IAAP for consideration, is climate change. Undoubtedly, this is a central topic of our time. It merits and, yes, it demands our attention. However, the question arises again whether it can be the duty of an international professional organisation to take, so to speak, the responsibility for the CO_2 emission of its members. Is it really a moral duty of the IAAP to tell its members and participants at congresses that they have to pay for their 'ecological footprint' and how much? We started to talk about this during the Meeting of Delegates. Here we are dealing with the fundamental question: what should the IAAP engage in directly and explicitly, including the provision of funds. The discussion of this subject will continue within the IAAP and the Executive Committee. We will see in the near future to what extent governments and perhaps airlines will raise levies. This will also affect the IAAP. After all, it is not just about the CO_2 load resulting from flying, but also from other areas of daily living, such as heating, driving a car, food, consumption generally, and much more. Personally, I hope that everybody will take responsibility for their actions individually, but also that state regulations will take effect. I am afraid the IAAP would otherwise have to spend much money and energy on this topic and the real 'business', i.e. Analytical Psychology, would miss out. I hope that for a long time to come, we will hold international conferences, during which we can meet in person for mutual exchange, such as here in Vienna. A community lives on personal conversations and contacts across the most varied borders and, in this sense, on the encounter with the other. To enable this is one of the tasks of the IAAP.

Before coming to conclusion, I would like to thank once again all those many colleagues, who over the past three years helped to shape the IAAP. They all greatly contributed to our community. At this point, I would like most sincerely to thank the local Organising Committee for the Congress here in Vienna, especially Asa Lilijenroth-Denk and Petra Denk, but also the whole Austrian Society for Analytical Psychology with their president Eleonore Armster. You invited us to Vienna, and 1200 participants came. We have never been so many.

I also must and want to mention Selma and Daniel Gubser, our secretary and our accountant in Switzerland. Both of them have also supported us greatly during this Administration. Selma has taken on more and more tasks and she has been extremely conscientious, competent and swift in everything. She has contributed a lot to the preparation of this congress, and we are very grateful to her for that. Martin Amsler, the long-standing treasurer and solicitor of the IAAP is about to retire. We would like to thank him warmly for his competent and helpful support over many years.

Likewise, I would once more like to thank the Executive Committee for their excellent cooperation. For me it was a special experience to witness over the course of the past three years how the EC has grown into a team, capable of leading difficult discussions constructively and of tolerating divergence with the aim of finally arriving at a solution. Much trust and friendship has grown among members of the Executive Committee and I am delighted about this.

A big Thank You goes out to my fellow Officers, with whom I worked closely over the past three years: Martin Schmidt was an articulate, humorous, hard-working and conscientious Honorary Secretary. George Hogenson, as Chair of the Programme Committee, put all his energy into the implementation of this wonderful programme. Misser Berg demonstrated once again her extraordinary organisational skills and she was during many areas a great support to me. I had regular exchanges with Toshio Kawai. Together we discussed many questions of principle, but also very concrete issues – in Swiss German, in fact. His impulses and suggestions have always been helpful and further-reaching.

I would also like to thank my husband, Hans Witschi Müller, who not only tolerated my frequent absences, albeit with a sigh, but who also assisted, supported and encouraged me in all my activities.

I wish the IAAP all the best for the future, many active members, good cohesion and a lively exchange about topical questions of Analytical Psychology.

I now hand over the presidency to Toshio Kawai with positive feelings. Toshio is perfectly prepared for his new task. He knows the most diverse areas of our IAAP and hence he guarantees continuity. At the same time, based on his life experience in the ancient and rich culture of Japan, but also in the scientific field, he will provide the IAAP with new ideas and emphases.

I thank you all,
Marianne Müller

Thank you, Marianne

Dear Marianne,

On behalf of the Executive Committee of the IAAP and also on behalf of all members of the IAAP, I would like to dedicate to you some words of our heartfelt gratitude and highest esteem.

You officially joined the IAAP activity in 2004, served six years as a member of the Executive Committee, then three years as Vice President, another three years as President-elect and finally three years as President. In total, fifteen years of commitment! I know that you did not necessarily want to go further in each step, but people asked you to again and again – after all, the IAAP certainly needed you!

I cannot mention here all the work that you have accomplished in the IAAP, but I would like to mention some of the particular significance. With your previous experience as a lawyer, you contributed greatly to the revision of the Constitution of the IAAP. Without your support, it would have been difficult, if not impossible for the IAAP to revise the Constitution. This was by all means an enormous and important contribution from you. Thank you very much!

In this regard, I would also like to mention briefly our recent change of the treasurer. Without your connection in Switzerland it would have been impossible to find the highly competent lawyer that we now have.

You were the Regional Organiser for Central Europe from 2013 to 2016 and had worked a lot for the router program in various other regions. I was often surprised to see how conflicts and problems in certain places were very often solved or decreased, once you were involved in those places. It looked like magic. But this is due to your extraordinary capacity to mediate and to create, so to speak, a good group process. Your ability and contribution in this field are truly admirable.

We noticed this capacity in the Executive Committee and in various other meetings. You have a unique balance between openness and leadership. You can be very open to diverse opinions and discussions without losing a clear line. Therefore, following this openness, we could trust you and could find creative solutions.

Finally, I would like to point out this Vienna Congress as your masterpiece. I know that you have put all your energy into making this Congress successful. Finding the keynote speaker, inviting an extra speaker for a plenary, organising an evening concert, creating the logo for the Congress, I cannot list all here. Many colleagues, the

Austrian society, and the agency Austropa helped and worked for this Congress. But I can still say that you made this Congress such a beautiful and successful one. Thank you!

I met you, Marianne, for the first time at the IAAP Executive Committee meeting in the deep snow of Einsiedeln in Switzerland, in 2005, when I was a member of the Barcelona Congress program committee. I can still remember the strong congeniality I felt when I first met you. Since then, we have worked together on various occasions. But especially in the recent three years, as President and President-elect, we have worked really closely together. We travelled together to meetings and conferences, we had a weekly Skype session in Swiss German. I have learned a lot from you, have shared a lot with you, but I have also very much appreciated and enjoyed working with you.

My personal thanks to you, Marianne.

I cannot help but add that I appreciate your high sense of aesthetics. That is why I have prepared a present for you – something with Japanese aesthetics (which I would like to give you later).

The amount of work and the hours Marianne dedicated to the work for the IAAP are enormous. Just by looking at all the of emails you wrote or were copied in I could see how many hours you spent thinking and working on so many matters. Although your work has been brilliant, I have to point out that this must have been possible only with various sacrifices on your part. I would like to mention here just three. Firstly, I know that you had your own project but could not realize it because of your appointment as President-elect and then President of the IAAP. Fortunately, although not so fortunately for the IAAP, you are still younger than the average age of the IAAP analysts so, I hope that now, after your presidency, you will have time to complete it.

Secondly, this work has only been possible with scarifying much of your personal and family life. Very often you had to go away from home. I have visited your nice place in Bern, Switzerland, twice and I like your husband, Hans, very much. I hope that you will now have more time for your personal and family life.

Last but not but least, is the sacrifice of your personal feelings. When I first met you, you came across as a very open and friendly person, which proved to be true. But as I've got to know you better, I noticed that you have very strong, passionate and deep personal feelings, which are usually hidden. Being a President, one often has to sacrifice one's personal feelings. But you are now free, even though not totally. So, this is a farewell for us and for you as President, but we are looking forward to seeing you again as a dearest friend.

Thank you, Marianne!

Toshio Kawai, President Elect

Breakout presentations in the e-book version, edited by Jacqueline Egli

Pre-Congress Workshop

Active Imagination in Movement – Encountering the Other: Within Us, Between Us, and In the World
T. Stromsted, A. Adorisio & M. Méndez

Introduction
Tina Stromsted

Presentations & Experiential sessions

Active Imagination and Inner Conflict: A Jungian Approach to Bodily Experiences
Antonella Adorisio

The Living Body in Analysis
Joan Chodorow

Bright Darkness: Facing 'the Other' Within
Tina Stromsted

Danced Myths of the Body: Within Us, Between Us and in the World
Margarita Mendez

Conclusion
Tina Stromsted with Antonella Adorisio, Margarita Mendez, David Gerbi and workshop participants

Supervision Masterclass I

Let's Play! Encountering the Other in Hakoniwa Group Sandplay – A potential model for analytic candidate training groups
Sachiko Taki-Reece, Ellen Searle LeBel, Mark Troedson

Exploring potentials for candidates in analytical training with the Hakoniwa Group Sandplay
Sachiko Taki-Reece and Mark Troedson

Monday, 26 August 2019 Breakout Sessions

Is the Self other to the self? Why does the numinosum feel like another? The relevance of Matte Blanco to our understanding of the unconscious
Lionel Corbett

Focusing on the Self in mapping of the psyche: The Inner Other, fears and possibilities
E. Slesareva & V. Kalinenko

BREAKOUT PRESENTATIONS IN THE E-BOOK VERSION

The Clinical Impact of Urban Terror on the Self
Leslie Stein

Terrorism Psychosis: when unconscious thought processes modulate the perception of the Other
Rosario Puglisi

The Soul's Trip: The Journey that is not... a Journey
Ronald Schenk

Our Most Precious Inheritance: C.G. Jung's attitude towards the Other
Andrés Ocazionez

Visit from the Minotaur: How far can we go within tolerable limits?
Gunilla Midbøe

Experiencing the ecological self: how to awaken from the illusion of separateness
Harri Virtanen

Nature as Other: Separation and Reconnection in an Ever-Changing World
Stephen Foster

Without Words Or Thought: Psyche As Only Incarnate, or On Working Analytically With Embodied Awareness
Harry Wells Fogarty

Introducing Dance of Three in a Hospital Setting: Restoring the Soul in Psychosomatic Medicine
Masako Machizawa

Exploring Teacher archetypal image in the Chinese collective psyche and its influence in the analytical relationship
Shiuya Sara Liuh

Cultural Otherness: Implications for the Analytic Attitude
Tom Kelly & Jan Wiener

The Story of Cain: The Myth We Would Like to Forget
Beth Darlington

Encountering the Other through Serbian Mythology: A Jungian Perspective
Svetlana Zdravković

Exploring the effects of competing complexes on a not fully developed or weakened ego
Peter W. Demuth

The Encounter with Otherness in Adoptive and Donor Conceived Families
Penelope Boisset

Silent interweaving: synchronicity between individual unconscious, group unconscious and social macro-group unconscious
Mauro Bonetti & Ambra Cusin

Encounters With the Other in Group Dreaming
Judith Hecker

The Other, Emergence, Group Supervision
P. Ancona, L. Di Stefano & C. Vezzoli

The Night Sea Journey: Towards the definition of cultural regression
Małgorzata Kalinowska

Repression of animus of women in a collectivist culture
Anahit Khananyan

Brunilde on the cliff edge: The Other and Sandplay
Massimiliano Scarpelli

Early Maternal Deprivation and the Psychoidal Capacity to Heal: The Case of May
Laura J. Chapman

A dream as a space for an encounter with the other
Snežana Manojlović & Bojana Stamenković

The inner couple in shadow, or the agony of the outer couple?
Mario E. Saiz

Erotic City Come Alive: Prince, Performance, and the Transcendent Function
Constance Evans Romero

Hail, Aphrodite! Re-sacralization of the Goddess of Love and Sex in David Ives' *Venus in Fur*
Judith R. Cooper

To hear what cannot yet be seen: Music in analysis as an acoustic mirror for the emergent unbearable other
Joel Kroeker

Music, Mandala and Embodiment: Epistemological Crisis East and West
Donald Grasing

Jungian Perspective of the Disintegrated Mind: Encountering Psychosis
Hideki Ota & Tadashi Maeda

Complexes and the body/brain: Testing Jung's and Freud's ideas of autonomous complexes inside us, using functional magnetic brain imaging
Michael Escamilla

The Voice of the Other in Jung's North American Cross Cultural Encounters
Willow Young

The diversifying soul through the encountering with Other
Tsuyoshi Inomata

Contorted Images
Sharn Waldron

Mad Men and the Otherness of Death In Postwar America
Priscilla Rodgers

Heteroerotics – Opus contra Naturam
Sylvester Wojtkowski

The Stranger Patient: The Healer and Key to Development
Avi Baumann

The Agony of Integration and the Blessings of Finitude
Ann Belford Ulanov

Los Hijos de La Chingada: A Cultural Trauma Complex
Jorge de la O

A glimpse into unaccompanied minors and their resilience and vulnerability factors: collective and individual experiences
Mariapaola Lanti & Sara Piscicelli

I and other, and I, the other: The use of images for education on individuation
Anna M. Gassol

The Phenomena of Modern Sexuality: Symbol of Transformation vs Political Manipulation
Natalia Pavlikova & Yulia Kazakevich

Monday's Poster Sessions

My Mother Has a Penis. When imagination and reality cross their ways
Elisabetta Bertolotti

The Other within us: Analysis of a patient with life threatening disease. A clinical case presentation
Giedre Bulotiene

Shù Shēng (Tree-Origin): Transformation Through the Roots of the Banya Tree in Taiwanese Mythology
Viola Hsueh-Chun Chen

The interpretation of the Chinese Myth *The Herding Boy and the Weaving Maiden*
Mei-Fang Huang

Tuesday, 27 August 2019 Breakout Sessions

Reflections on Exclusion and Inclusion of Ethnically and Economically Diverse Populations in the Experience of the C.G. Jung Institute of San Francisco: Organizational Change and 'the Other'
Alan G. Vaughan et al , Lynn Alicia Franco , Gordon Murray, Karen Naifeh & Anna M. Spielvogel

Encountering the other within us through illness: a modern encounter between Analytical Psychology and Medicine
Francesca Picone

Embodying the invisible Other: The experience of illness and medical cultural complexes
Antonella Adorisio

The Otherness of Art
Sarah Jackson

Woman's Path – Human Way. Tales of Tenar, based on U.K. Le Guin's *Earthsea*
Aleksandra Szczepaniak

Beyond the polarised female in a male analysand from Northern Europe
Kaj Noschis

Synchronicity in Dreams and Individuation in Groups
Marion Rauscher Gallbach

Synchronistic Events in Analysis: The Specificity of Analytical Psychology when Encountering the Other
Riccardo Daniele Pecora

Ageing, Sexuality and Dementia: Reflecting on the loss of intimacy in the couple relationship
Susan Carol Albert

Some reflections on archetypal sexuality, imaginatio, the subtle body and the psychoid
Dorte Odde

Owning 'The Other' Within: An Asian Transcultural Dilemma
Aditee Ghate

Two Sides of a Coin: A look at Otherness through the Prism of Personal Experience
Tatiana Rudakova

Personal and collective shadow: The changing of archetypal foundations and patterns of communication with the Other in Movies and Psychoanalysis
Volker Münch

The Totally Other. The problem of opposites in Analytical Psychology and its practical implications
Ralf T. Vogel

"And he shall rest peacefully upon his lying place, and let us say: Amen." – Letting go of the post-traumatic dead
Gadi Maoz

The Psychological Meaning of Disaster
Chan-Seung Chung

Complexity according to Edgar Morin and Individuation according to C.G. Jung: A work, a task, a practice
Claire Raguet

Feeling connected to the world and to others. Is it still possible when technology steals our souls?
Sophie Braun

Meeting An-Other in the Orthodox Icons: Parallel views on the Attachment Complex and more
Lavinia Tânculescu

Loss, Search and Discovery in Recovering from Addiction
Mary Addenbrooke

The Abject to the Sublime: Encountering Otherness in the Art of Francis Bacon
Mark Winborn

The Abject, Resurrected Corpses and the Terrible Father: an interrogation into the Mother/Child Dyad
Joanna de Waal

The *other* in the analytic room and in the analyst's mind: integrating neuroscience and infant research contributions in the clinical work with 0 to 3 years old children
Chiara Rogora

The world of the trauma in the therapeutic relationship with a child
Marta Moneti

The 'other' in adolescence: how the integration between the real world 'other' and the 'other' internal world takes shape in the therapeutic relationship
Barbara Fionda

The 'Other' son: Difficult relations between parents and an adopted son turned adolescent
Sara Boschetti

Wounded Children Blinded by Pain
Eloí Terezinha Lauxen Peruzzolo

The 'Strange' within us, draw it – Basics on drawing/picture interpretation, trauma and dissociation
Maria-Luiza Keiko Aeschbach-Hatanaka

Following the Gypsy: When the Other is the Self
Marlene A. Schiwy

Three Gentlemen of Vienna: The Late Work of Beethoven, Schubert and Mahler – Conversations with the Inner-Other
Melinda Haas

Cultural trauma as the 'other within' and/or the 'other without': Further findings from the evaluation of the IAAP Router training programme
John Merchant

Breakout presentations in the e-book version

When Jungian Theory Itself is Other to One's Soul: Gender-Fluid Models of Individuation from Ancient Egyptian Myth
Karen A. Smyers

Experiencing ME and OTHER through scenes of fights in Sandplay Therapy
Maria Kendler

Music as a symbol in the understanding and working with the gaps within us at the level of archetypal defences – illustrated by the musical *The Phantom of the Opera*
Christel Bormann

Music Performance and Dream Analysis
Masamichi Adachi

Sibling Relations: Significant Encounters with Others and the 'Other' within Oneself
Lisbeth von Benedek

The Psychology of the Sibling Archetype
Gustavo Barcellos

Two research studies with vulnerable children and adolescents with behavioral problems
Reinalda Melo da Matta, Denise Ramos & Viviane Rojas

The Hestia-Hermes archetype and the spirit of the place: Looking for orientation in the Brexit turmoil
Cécile Buckenmeyer

The Analyst's Rorschach: Assessing the 'Other' in Countertransference Vulnerability
William Alexy

The Use of Intuitive Collage to Encounter the Other in the Transference Work
Andréa Fiuza Hunt

Transcendent and Transcendental Functions: A Personal and a Mathematical Equation
Peter Holland

The Analytic Attitude: Ethical Prohibition and Ethical Action
Mark Winborn

Tuesday's Poster Sessions
Michael Monhart

Thursday, 29 August 2019 Breakout Sessions

"See me so that I may understand you" – the inhibition of reflective functioning in a traumatized society: A view from South Africa
Astrid Berg

Being white, being Jungian: implications of Jung's encounter with the 'non-European' other
Jane Johnson

From the Freudian Feeling of Worrying Strangeness to the Jungian Feeling of Being a Stranger
Marcel Gaumond

The child: a terrifying other?
Eve Pilyser

The meeting of the Other: In us, between us and in the world – Harlequin and Persona
Carleen Binet, Luis Caldera & Elaïné Franzini Soria

Implications of the worldwide appeal of Japanese Anime: Softening the ground for a relationship with the Other
John R. Ranyard

A Jungian Perspective on Cyberpunk, Geek Culture and Manga in Japan
Bartosz Samitowski

The Boy and the Medicine are One
Barry Williams

"Is there anything more fundamental than the realization: *This is what I am?*"
Kristina Schellinski

Views from the back of a Dragon: Discourse with the Ineffable Unknown 'Other Within and Without'
Carolyn Jeffress Johnston

The Devil's golden hairs: encountering the dark side of the self
Carlo Melodia

Welcoming the Stranger – an *Opus contra Naturam*?
Arthur Niesser

Expelling the other, expelling the Self: Where to start from anew? Can Analytical Psychology contribute to supporting the need for a new humanism?
Paola Terrile

Narcissism – psychological oneness excluding love of the other
Susan E. Schwartz

Trans identification and the attempt to evade psychological distress
Robert Withers

Breakout presentations in the e-book version

The Patriarchy, Haute Couture and Gay Male Individuation: Archetypal Patterns in *The Dressmaker*
Robert Sheavly

Dangerous expeditions: Occult foundations of psychoanalysis
Elizabeth Colistra

Mary and Yemanjá: Two Faces, Same Archetype
Leda Maria Perillo Seixas

At War with the Natural World: Nature as Other
John Colverson

Encountering the Anthropocene: Development, Individuation and the Global Other
Andrew Fellows

The four basic functions – psychic organs of encounter with oneself, others and the Self
Monika Rafalski

The gaze of the Other. Voices from the Near East
Alessandra Perugini

The Promethean society and its enemies: *the other* as the awakener of the spirit in the shadow
Damián Ruiz López

Encountering the other In and Outside Analysis. Some Notes on a particular Therapeutic Factor
Patrizia Peresso

Let the Alienated Soul Imagine: Working with Dissociation Disorder Patients
Tsukasa Ikegami

Between self and persona: The disabled other within us
Nathalie Pilard

I Am Not I: The Self as Participation
Jason E. Smith

Both black and white, neither black nor white: a mixed-race person in analysis
Dale Mathers

Childhood dreams without Lysis – their final implication for the collective
Helga Thomas

The Bluebeard Affair: A debate between Freudian and Jungian analysts
Christian Gaillard et al.

  Minerva and Bluebeard's secret chamber, the taming of the animus
Carleen Binet

Bluebeard and Gilles de Rais: Instinctual sexuality, infantile sexuality and sexual death drive
Thomas Aichhorn

Resonance to the therapeutic process: *Bluebeard* from a Jungian point of view
Verena Kast

Women and Bluebeard: the issues involved in overcoming terror and melancholic confinement
Alain Gibeault

Bluebeard on the couch: Charles Perrault's words; Gustave Doré's images
Christian Gaillard

The Journey of the Immigrant Erich Neumann from *Me as the Other* to *The Other Within*
Tamar Kron & David Wieler

Encountering the Other in da Vinci's Salvator Mundi
John Gosling

Integrating the worlds of biology and psychology through Jung's Theory of Archetypes (TA)
Nami Lee

AI analysing C.G. Jung: Analyzing C.G. Jung's personality traits and changes through time from his works with artificial intelligence
Tine Papic

The Red Book on the clinical work of the Latin American Jungian analyst: qualitative and quantitative research
Durval Luiz de Faria & Denis Canal Mendes

Intergenerational transmission of trauma in refugee populations: Being the 'Other'
Ruth Williams

When the Other Takes Over: Helping Torture Survivors Overcome the Introjected Other of the Torturer
Barbara JoAnn Whitaker

Psychology's uroboric encounter with its own Other – in us, between us, and in the world
John Hoedl

Exploring the Paradigm Shift between Our Self as *Other*, and *Other* in Our World, with Psychic States of *Oneness*
Deborah Bryon

Ego-Self Axis and Facing the Other-within: Clinical Applications in Jungian Analysis Influenced by *The Secret of the Golden Flower*
Jerome Braun

Jungian understanding of 'the pairs of Dharma' in *The Platform Sutra of the Sixth Patriarch*
                                                Moon-Sung Rhee

Illness and/as the Encounter with the Other
                                                María Mora Viñas

Meetings at the Crossroads: Encounter of the Other Within and Without
                                                Frances M. Parks

When the Other is no longer other: do current developments in Gender Politics challenge the essentials of Analytical Psychology?
                                                John. F. Miller

The Redemption of the Irrational as a Pathway to Wholeness
                                                Laraine P. Kurisko

Thursday's Poster Sessions

Zombies: Archetypal Images and Narratives of the Other as Enemy
                                                Paul Northway

At-one-ment with Oneself and the World: The Ethical Imperative of the Analytic Attitude
                                                Alex Sierck

Complexes emerging from the mother-daughter relationship in contemporary China
                                                Lin Ye & Shu-Chiung Lin

Awake from Dream, Encountering the Other: An Interpretation of the *Yellow Millet Dream* (or: *Into the Porcelain Pillow*). A Chinese Tale from the Tang Dynasty
                                                Li Ying

Jung's Encounter with Chinese Culture
                                                Xiao You

Friday, 30 August 2019 Breakout Sessions

Encountering the Child: Within us, between us and in the world
                  Audrey Punnett, Margo Leahy, Liza Ravitz & Brian Feldman

    Defining Jungian Child Analysis: Jung and the Post-Jungians
                                                Margo Leahy

    Multidimensional Space in Jungian Child Analysis
                                                Liza Ravitz

    Thinking about Autistic States of Mind in Infancy and Childhood with Michael Fordham: The Importance of Infant Observation
                                                Brian Feldman

    Encountering the Child
                                                Audrey Punnett

The skin between collective and individual states of mind
Monica Luci

Encountering the Other in My Journey to Become a Jungian Analyst: What Litarafoo Can Teach Us
Sherri Mahdavi

The day the clock stopped. About otherness, a faceted countertransference and the birth of intimacy
Antonio deRienzo

On the depths of Kakure Kirishitan (Hidden Christians) in comparison with Fucan Fabian's life and thoughts
Yasuhiro Tanaka

An-other to 'ganz Andere': From Cell to Society
Josephine Evetts-Secker

A Prince / A Bug / A Poet / A Martyr: All About Transformation Processes
Joanne Wieland-Burston

Under His Eye: Oppression of the Feminine in Margaret Atwood's *The Handmaid's Tale*
Kathryn Madden

The Venda Sacred Trail: A Pilgrimage
Philippa Anne Colinese

Shadow Dances: Reclaiming 'The Other'
Tina Stromsted

The Encounter of Soul and Body by Means of Breath in Analytic Body Work
Lisa Malin

Cold Flame of the Salamander: Identity Transformations of an Artistically Gifted Patient
Natalia Serebrennikova

The *Other* Made Visible: Jungian Art Therapy, Early Medical Trauma and Spontaneous Agents of Change
Nora Swan-Foster

Epigenetics and the return to the great mother archetype
Regina Alvares Biscaro

Epigenetics and analytical psychology: transformation and the construction of the third thread in the encounter with the other
A.A.M. Caetano & T.C. Machado

Social Dreaming Matrix: A glimpse of the Infinite – A tale from the IAAP Congress in Vienna
Dominique Lepori

Author Index (e-book)

Adachi, Masamichi
Addenbrooke, Mary
Adorisio, Antonella
Aeschbach-Hatanaka, Maria-Luiza Keiko
Aichhorn, Thomas
Albert, Susan Carol
Alexy, William
Ammann, Peter
Ancona, P.
Barcellos, Gustavo
Baumann, Avi
Benedek, Lisbeth von
Berg, Astrid
Bertolotti, Elisabetta
Binet, Carleen
Biscaro, Regina Alvares
Boisset, Penelope
Bonetti, Mauro
Borchardt, Fred
Bormann, Christel
Boschetti, Sara
Braun, Jerome
Braun, Sophie
Bryon, Deborah
Buckenmeyer, Cécile
Bulotiene, Giedre
Caetano, A.A.M.
Caldera, Luis
Chapman, Laura J.
Chen, Viola Hsueh-Chun
Chodorow, Joan
Chung, Chan-Seung
Colinese, Philippa Anne
Colistra, Elizabeth
Colverson, John
Cooper, Judith R.
Corbett, Lionel
Cusin, Ambra
Darlington, Beth
Demuth, Peter W.
deRienzo, Antonio
Egli, Jacqueline
Escamilla, Michael
Eulert-Fuchs, Daniela
Evetts-Secker, Josephine
Falzeder, Ernst
Faria, Durval Luiz de
Feldman, Brian
Fellows, Andrew
Fionda, Barbara
Fogarty, Harry Wells
Foster, Stephen
Franco, Lynn Alicia
Gaillard, Christian
Gallbach, Marion Rauscher
Gassol, Anna M.
Gaumond, Marcel
Ghate, Aditee
Gibeault, Alain
Gosling, John
Grasing, Donald
Haas, Melinda
Hecker, Judith
Hoedl, John
Holland, Peter
Huang, Mei-Fang
Hunt, Andréa Fiuza
Ikegami, Tsukasa
Inomata, Tsuyoshi

Jackson, Sarah
Johnson, Jane
Johnston, Carolyn Jeffress
Kalinenko, V.
Kalinowska, Małgorzata
Kalsched, Donald E.
Kast, Verena
Kawai, Toshio
Kazakevich, Yulia
Kelly, Tom
Kendler, Maria
Kermani, Navid
Khananyan, Anahit
Kiehl, Emilija
Kroeker, Joel
Kron, Tamar
Kurisko, Laraine P.
Lanti, Mariapaola
Leahy, Margo
LeBel, Ellen Searle
Lee, Nami
Lepori, Dominique
Lin, Shu-Chiung
Liuh, Shiuya Sara
López, Damián Ruiz
Luci, Monica
Machado, T. C.
Machizawa, Masako
Madden, Kathryn
Maeda, Tadashi
Mahdavi, Sherri
Malin, Lisa
Manojlović, Snežana
Maoz, Gadi
Mathers, Dale
Matta, Reinalda Melo da
Melodia, Carlo
Mendes, Denis Canal
Mendez, Margarita
Merchant, John
Midbøe, Gunilla
Miller, John. F.
Mlisa, Nomfundo Lily-Rose
Moneti, Marta
Monhart, Michael

Müller, Marianne
Münch, Volker
Murray, Gordon
Naifeh, Karen
Niesser, Arthur
Northway, Paul
Noschis, Kaj
Ocazionez, Andrés
Odde, Dorte
O, Jorge de la
Ota, Hideki
Papic, Tine
Parks, Frances M.
Pavlikova, Natalia
Pecora, Riccardo Daniele
Peresso, Patrizia
Perugini, Alessandra
Peruzzolo, Eloí Terezinha Lauxen
Picone, Francesca
Pilard, Nathalie
Pilyser, Eve
Piscicelli, Sara
Puglisi, Rosario
Punnett, Audrey
Rafalski, Monika
Raguet, Claire
Ramos, Denise
Ramsden, Renee
Ranyard, John R.
Rasche, Jörg
Ravitz, Liza
Rhee, Moon-Sung
Rodgers, Priscilla
Roesler, Christian
Rogora, Chiara
Rojas, Viviane
Romero, Constance Evans
Rudakova, Tatiana
Saiz, Mario E.
Samitowski, Bartosz
Scarpelli, Massimiliano
Schellinski, Kristina
Schenk, Ronald
Schiwy, Marlene A.
Schwartz, Susan E.

Seixas, Leda Maria Perillo
Serebrennikova, Natalia
Sheavly, Robert
Sierck, Alex
Slesareva, E.
Smith, Jason E.
Smyers, Karen A.
Soria, Elaïné Franzini
Spielvogel, Anna M.
Stamenković, Bojana
Stefano, L. Di
Stein, Leslie
Stromsted, Tina
Swan-Foster, Nora
Szczepaniak, Aleksandra
Taki-Reece, Sachiko
Tanaka, Yasuhiro
Tânculescu, Lavinia
Terrile, Paola
Thomas, Helga
Tozzi, Chiara
Troedson, Mark
Tyminski, Robert
Ulanov, Ann Belford

Vaughan, Alan G.
Vedfelt, Ole
Vezzoli, C.
Viñas, María Mora
Virtanen, Harri
Vogel, Ralf T.
Waal, Joanna de
Waldron, Sharn
West, Marcus
Whitaker, Barbara JoAnn
Wieland-Burston, Joanne
Wieler, David
Wiener, Jan
Williams, Barry
Williams, Ruth
Winborn, Mark
Withers, Robert
Wojtkowski, Sylvester
Ye, Lin
Ying, Li
Young, Willow
You, Xiao
Zdravković, Svetlana

IAAP CONGRESS PROCEEDINGS

MONTREAL 2010
Facing Multiplicity: Psyche, Nature, Culture
Proceedings of the 18th International Congress for Analytical Psychology
edited by Pramila Bennett
illustrated, 240 pages in print + 1789 pages on CD, ISBN 978-3-85630-744-8

CAPE TOWN 2007
Journeys, Encounters: Clinical, Communal, Cultural
Proceedings of the 17th International Congress for Analytical Psychology
edited by Pramila Bennett
illustrated, 288 pages in print + 1142 pages on CD, ISBN 978-3-85630-728-8

BARCELONA 2004
Edges of Experience: Memory and Emergence
Proceedings of the 16th International Congress for Analytical Psychology
edited by Lyn Cowan
illustrated, 240 printed pages, 1380 pages on CD, ISBN 978-3-85630-700-4

CAMBRIDGE 2001
Proceedings of the 15th International Congress for Analytical Psychology
768 pages, paperback, ISBN 978-3-85630-609-0

FLORENCE 1998: DESTRUCTION AND CREATION
Proceedings of the 14th International Congress for Analytical Psychology,
edited by Mary Ann Mattoon, 620 pages, illustrated
hardbound: ISBN 978-3-85630-584-0 / paperback: ISBN 978-3-85630-583-3

ZURICH 1995: OPEN QUESTIONS IN ANALYTICAL PSYCHOLOGY
Proceedings of the 13th International Congress for Analytical Psychology
edited by Mary Ann Mattoon
752 pages, illustrated, hardbound: ISBN 978-3-85630-555-0
paperback: ISBN 978-3-85630-556-7

CHICAGO 1992
The Transcendent Function: Individual and Collective Aspects
edited by Mary Ann Mattoon
hardbound: ISBN 978-3-85630-537-6 / paperback: ISBN 978-3-85630-538-3

PARIS 1989
Personal and Archetypal Dynamics in the Analytical Relationship.
edited by Mary Ann Mattoon
hardbound: ISBN 978-3-85630-529-1 / paperback: ISBN 978-3-85630-524-6

BERLIN 1986
The Archetype of Shadow in a Split World
edited by Mary Ann Mattoon
The 10th International Congress of Analytical Psychology was held in Berlin, September 2 – 9, 1986. 456 pages, numerous illustrations and diagrams
hardbound: ISBN 978-3-85630-514-7 / paperback: ISBN 978-3-85630-506-2

JERUSALEM 1983
Symbolic and Clinical Approaches in Theory and Practice
edited by Luigi Zoja and Robert Hinshaw
This handsome volume, drawn from the 9th International Congress of Analytical Psychology in Jerusalem, contains contributions reflecting on the meaning and significance of contemporary analytical work from 25 prominent Jungian analysts from around the world.
375 pages, hardbound, illustrated, ISBN 978-3-85630-504-8

IAAP CONGRESS PROCEEDINGS

Kyoto 2016
Anima Mundi in Transition: Cultural, Clinical & Professional Challenges

Proceedings of the Twentieth Congress of the International Association for Analytical Psychology

Edited by Emilija Kiehl & Margaret Klenck

The Congress in Kyoto, Japan was the beginning of a new era in the life of the IAAP: for the first time in its history, this creative and stimulating triennial gathering of Jungian analysts from all over the world took place in Asia. And with it, scientific and cultural dialogue between Jungians from 'West' and 'East' enters a new dimension. As is evident in these pages, there are ever more mutually enriching developments emerging: both in theory and in clinical work, from culturally – and often, politically – different points of view.

214 pages in printed book + 1500 pages on CD, ISBN 978-3-85630-772-1

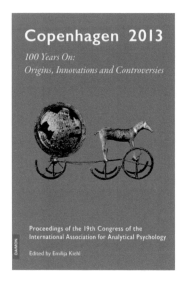

Copenhagen 2013
100 Years On: Origins, Innovations and Controversies

Proceedings of the 19th Congress of the International Association for Analytical Psychology

Edited by Emilija Kiehl

Copenhagen 2013 – 100 years on: Origins, Innovations and Controversies was the theme, honoring the psychological transformations experienced by C.G. Jung beginning in 1913, while also reflecting upon the evolving world and Jungian Community a century later. This volume consists of all of the plenary presentations in printed form and they are joined with the daily break-out sessions and posters on the CD that is an integral part of these Proceedings (inside back cover).

214 pages in printed book + 1320 pages on CD, ISBN 978-3-85630-755-4

English Titles from Daimon

- Ruth Ammann - *The Enchantment of Gardens*
- Susan R. Bach - *Life Paints its Own Span*
- Renate Daniel - *Taking the Fear Out of the Night: Coping with Nightmares*
  - *The Self: Quest for Meaning in a Changing World*
- Diana Baynes Jansen - *Jung's Apprentice: A Biography of Helton Godwin Baynes*
- John Beebe (Ed.) - *Terror, Violence and the Impulse to Destroy*
- E.A. Bennet - *Meetings with Jung*
- W.H. Bleek / L.C. Lloyd (Ed.) - *Specimens of Bushman Folklore*
- Tess Castleman - *Threads, Knots, Tapestries*
  - *Sacred Dream Circles*
- Renate Daniel - *Taking the Fear out of the Night*
  - *The Self: Quest for Meaning in a Changing World*
- Eranos Yearbook 69 - *Eranos Reborn*
- Eranos Yearbook 70 - *Love on a Fragile Thread*
- Eranos Yearbook 71 - *Beyond Masters*
- Eranos Yearbook 72 - *Soul between Enchantment and Disenchantment*
- Eranos Yearbook 73 - *The World and its Shadow*
- Michael Escamilla - *Bleuler, Jung, and the Schizophrenias*
- Heinrich Karl Fierz - *Jungian Psychiatry*
- John Fraim - *Battle of Symbols*
- Liliane Frey-Rohn - *Friedrich Nietzsche, A Psychological Approach*
- Marion Gallbach - *Learning from Dreams*
- Ralph Goldstein (Ed.) - *Images, Meanings & Connections: Essays in Memory of Susan Bach*
- Yael Haft - *Hands: Archetypal Chirology*
- Fred Gustafson - *The Black Madonna of Einsiedeln*
- Daniel Hell - *Soul-Hunger: The Feeling Human Being and the Life-Sciences*
- Siegmund Hurwitz - *Lilith, the first Eve*
- Aniela Jaffé - *The Myth of Meaning*
  - *Was C.G. Jung a Mystic?*
  - *From the Life and Work of C.G. Jung*
  - *Death Dreams and Ghosts*
- C.G. Jung - *The Solar Myths and Opicinus de Canistris*
- Verena Kast - *A Time to Mourn*
  - *Sisyphus*
- Hayao Kawai - *Dreams, Myths and Fairy Tales in Japan*
- James Kirsch - *The Reluctant Prophet*
- Eva Langley-Dános - *Prison on Wheels: Ravensbrück to Burgau*
- Rivkah Schärf Kluger - *The Gilgamesh Epic*
- Yehezkel Kluger & Naomi Kluger-Nash - *RUTH in the Light of Mythology, Legend and Kabbalah*
- Paul Kugler (Ed.) - *Jungian Perspectives on Clinical Supervision*
- Paul Kugler - *The Alchemy of Discourse*
- Rafael López-Pedraza - *Cultural Anxiety*
  - *Hermes and his Children*
- Alan McGlashan - *The Savage and Beautiful Country*
  - *Gravity & Levity*
- Gregory McNamee (Ed.) - *The Girl Who Made Stars: Bushman Folklore*
  - *The North Wind and the Sun & Other Fables of Aesop*
- Gitta Mallasz / Hanna Dallos - *Talking with Angels*
- C.A. Meier - *Healing Dream and Ritual*
  - *A Testament to the Wilderness*
  - *Personality: The Individuation Process*
- Haruki Murakami - *Haruki Murakami Goes to Meet Hayao Kawai*

English Titles from Daimon

Eva Pattis Zoja (Ed.) - *Sandplay Therapy*
Laurens van der Post - *The Rock Rabbit and the Rainbow*
Jane Reid - *Jung, My Mother and I: The Analytic Diaries of Catharine Rush Cabot*
R.M. Rilke - *Duino Elegies*
A. Schweizer / R. Schweizer-Vüllers - *Stone by Stone: Reflections on Jung*
- *Wisdom has Built her House*
Miguel Serrano - *C.G. Jung and Hermann Hesse*
Helene Shulman - *Living at the Edge of Chaos*
D. Slattery / G. Slater (Eds.) - *Varieties of Mythic Experience*
David Tacey - *Edge of the Sacred: Jung, Psyche, Earth*
Susan Tiberghien - *Looking for Gold*
Ann Ulanov - *Spiritual Aspects of Clinical Work*
- *The Female Ancestors of Christ*
- *Healing Imagination*
- *Picturing God*
- *Receiving Woman*
- *Spirit in Jung*
- *The Wisdom of the Psyche*
- *The Wizards' Gate, Picturing Consciousness*
- *The Psychoid, Soul and Psyche*
- *Knots and their Untying*
Ann & Barry Ulanov - *Cinderella and her Sisters*
Eva Wertenschlag-Birkhäuser - *Windows on Eternity: The Paintings of Peter Birkhäuser*
Harry Wilmer - *How Dreams Help*
- *Quest for Silence*
Luigi Zoja - *Drugs, Addiction and Initiation*
Luigi Zoja & Donald Williams - *Jungian Reflections on September 11*
Jungian Congress Papers - *Jerusalem 1983: Symbolic & Clinical Approaches*
- *Berlin 1986: Archetype of Shadow in a Split World*
- *Paris 1989: Dynamics in Relationship*
- *Chicago 1992: The Transcendent Function*
- *Zürich 1995: Open Questions*
- *Florence 1998: Destruction and Creation*
- *Cambridge 2001*
- *Barcelona 2004: Edges of Experience*
- *Cape Town 2007: Journeys, Encounters*
- *Montreal 2010: Facing Multiplicity*
- *Copenhagen 2013: 100 Years on*
- *Kyoto 2016: Anima Mundi in Transition*
- *Vienna 2019: Encountering the Other*

Our books are available from your bookstore or from our distributors:

Baker & Taylor
30 Amberwood Parkway
Ashland OH 44805, USA
Phone: 419-281-5100
Fax: 419-281-0200
www.btpubservices.com

Gazelle Book Services Ltd.
White Cross Mills, High Town
Lancaster LA1 4XS, UK
Tel: +44 1524 528500
Email: sales@gazellebookservices.co.uk
www.gazellebookservices.co.uk

Daimon Verlag - Hauptstrasse 85 - CH-8840 Einsiedeln - Switzerland
Phone: (41)(55) 412 2266
Email: info@daimon.ch
Visit our website: **www.daimon.ch** or write for our complete catalog